Anton Boisen

Anton Boisen

Madness, Mysticism, and the Origins of Clinical Pastoral Education

Sean J. LaBat

LEXINGTON BOOKS/FORTRESS ACADEMIC
Lanham • Boulder • New York • London

Published by Lexington Books/Fortress Academic
Lexington Books is an imprint of The Rowman & Littlefield Publishing Group, Inc.
4501 Forbes Boulevard, Suite 200, Lanham, Maryland 20706
www.rowman.com

6 Tinworth Street, London SE11 5AL, United Kingdom

Copyright © 2021 The Rowman & Littlefield Publishing Group, Inc.

All rights reserved. No part of this book may be reproduced in any form or by any electronic or mechanical means, including information storage and retrieval systems, without written permission from the publisher, except by a reviewer who may quote passages in a review.

British Library Cataloguing in Publication Information Available

Library of Congress Cataloging-in-Publication Data Available

Library of Congress Control Number: 2020948055
ISBN 9781978711556 (cloth) | ISBN 9781978711570 (pbk)

Contents

Acknowledgments	vii
Introduction	1
1 Visit to a Little-Known Country	11
2 Searching for Meaning in the Madness	39
3 How Boisen Interpreted His Experience and Illness	67
4 My Friends Are Coming to Help Me	83
5 Boisen's Productive "Retirement"	113
6 The Scientific Seer	145
Bibliography	171
Credits	177
Index	179
About the Author	181

Acknowledgments

There are many I would like to thank for their help and support in researching and writing this book, this is not an exhaustive list. First, my editors at Rowman and Littlefield, who believed in this project and made it possible: Neil Elliot, Gayla Freeman, and Courtney Morales. Robert Charles Powell for reading this manuscript and offering his advice and suggestions—this text and I are better for them. Thanks to all of the archives, presses, and organizations that gave permission for use of their texts and archival material. I would like to acknowledge Ms. Yasmine Abou El-Kheir at Lapp Learning Commons at Chicago Theological Seminary in regard to the Anton T. Boisen Papers and for her assistance.

I would like to thank my colleagues at Central Virginia VAMC, and especially Oscar D. Stone, for their help and support. Through this work, I hope to emulate my parents, Joseph and Karen, before me who serve the commonwealth. I especially dedicate this book to my grandfather Hugh Lilevjen and my wife Mary C. Riley. Also to all who have visited little-known countries of their own and returned to tell of it.

Thank you
Sean J. LaBat
Richmond, Virginia

Introduction

The Elgin State Hospital cemetery lies halfway between the "back hospital" and the Farm Colony. It is reached by a gravel track around the water tower, past rusting piles of old-issue hospital beds, and two raw gravel pits. On the low hillside a bulldozer labored without pause; over the ridge a pile of burning refuse billowed dark smoke. The burying ground itself is neat, almost inconspicuous. There is a low, pleasant carpet of native grass. There is a fence, a hedgerow to the north, a gentle slope and rows of plain grave markers. The filled space occupies only a bit more than half of the enclosed plot. This is unspectacular waste ground and the hospital seems to use it as repository for that which has lived out its usefulness.

The scene was not spectacular, today. The weather was modestly autumnal, and the sky just ordinarily overcast. Except for the cluster of awkward mourners—forty or fifty persons including Chaplain Charles Sullivan, Professor Victor Obenhaus (who, respectively, read the requested service and the obituary), a few patients, a handful of friends, a few hospital staff, a little group of ex-students—it was an unremarkable state hospital burial.

There were no tears.

There was little conversation, little drama.

But, because he lived and suffered and imposed his always-distant urgency on others, some of the living seem less likely to be scattered as burned-out ashes "back of the hospital," over the fallow waste ground.[1]

Anton Boisen died a forgotten man. Ten years after Boisen's death, Historian and Psychiatrist Robert Powell puzzled at Boisen's awkward nonremembrance at a session hosted by the Association for Clinical Pastoral Education

(ACPE), the premier organization dedicated to the clinical training of theologians, pastors, and institutional chaplains:

> It was the 50th anniversary celebration in 1975 that the custom began of handing down "Pappy's" [a Boisen nickname] cane to the Association's incoming president. At that very time it had struck me as odd, for, as I had noted in my keynote address earlier that day, Boisen's name appeared nowhere on the program.[2]

Boisen's successors engaged in the ritual of handing down a 'holy relic' of a founder they could not bring themselves to name. Why? Seward Hiltner, one of Boisen's most prominent, and sympathetic, students offered, "he has drawn upon many branches of knowledge—psychology, psychiatry, sociology, history, as well as theology—with the result that a publisher or a librarian may say: But where does he belong?"[3] The day after Boisen's death, Hiltner hurried to his typewriter and tapped out twelve pages dedicated to his former teacher's "heritage." Hiltner revisited the wide and deep interests and learning that fertilized Boisen's work and yet made him annoyingly difficult to classify by a single, discrete, specialization. He also delved the thornier issue of "Boisen's own serious mental illness, erupting in his mid-forties, the significance of which he came to interpret religiously and theologically, and which clarified for him the critical mysticism that was also part of his view."[4] Boisen's intense interest in mental illness and mystical experience, inspiration, and psychopathology was driven by his own intense personal experiences—something he made scant effort to conceal in his copious writings.

Hiltner hinted that Boisen stood at the crossroads of several critical issues. What relationship is there, if any, between mental illness and mystical experience, and how did these two critical factors shape one person's life and work? How could Boisen, someone who experienced, arguably, mystical visions, and suffered, undeniably, serious psychoses, operate effectively as creator of a new way of learning in his creation of clinical pastoral education. How could he develop the new profession of institutional chaplain—as distinct from church pastor? Boisen's signature, driving, vilusion, experienced in a state of psychosis, was of breaking "an opening in the wall which separated medicine and religion," a delusion/vision that occurred amid growing enmity between "science" and "religion" that ramped into the Scopes Trial extravaganza of summer 1925. As the court tried a high school teacher named John T. Scopes in Dayton, Tennessee, for violating state law forbidding the teaching of evolution, Boisen's first class of clinical students, whom he called "theologs," commenced their work and study at Worcester State Hospital in Massachusetts.[5] Boisen saw his educational, clinical, and pastoral work as a scientific as well as a pastoral endeavor and as an effort to bring the apparently irreconcilable domains of religion and science together in amicable dialogue.

Boisen was a riddle and puzzle to his friends and his detractors. He stood at the crossroads of several scholarly fields that are separate by specialization: science and religion being the most prominent. His vivid personal experiences fused with his professional work and intersect between the inspired and the psychotic. He was alienated from, and a dissenter within, the profession and discipline he started. Boisen was adamantly committed to patient and person-centered care. He sharply critiqued his profession of clinical pastoral education as it shifted from patient care to student-centered therapeutics. He challenged his students, clinical pastoral education, and the state mental hospitals where he lived and did the majority of his work to prioritize patient care even as their priorities drifted elsewhere.

Along with Seward Hiltner, Paul Pruyser and Henri Nouwen were among Boisen's most nuanced and observant acquaintances and critics. Nouwen recalled a dialogue with Pruyser:

> I mentioned that I was fascinated by the work he had accomplished in spite of being a schizophrenic, and Dr. P[ruyser]. pointed out that Boisen, if he'd heard that, would have been very quick to correct me, and to say that it was not in spite of being a schizophrenic, but because of his being schizophrenic, his viewing the entire schizophrenic breakdown in many people as a constructive process. It was a very hopeful attitude, against the mainstream of American psychiatric thought at that time and very similar to some things developed here at Menninger. A very positive attitude, it was a problem-solving experience.[6]

Nouwen and Pruyser's dialogue reaches the central issue of Boisen's life and significance: the intersection of mysticism and mental illness, inspiration and insanity. Was Boisen "ill" or "inspired"; can he, can others be, both at the same time. Boisen was consciously aware of himself as a successor to William James' tradition of pragmatic assessment of religious, mystical, and psychological experience. The Harvard psychologist, philosopher, and medical doctor was not so much interested in religion in its formal institutional and dogmatic forms as "the feelings, acts, and experiences of individual men in their solitude, so far as they apprehend themselves to stand in relation to whatever they may consider the divine."[7] James, as Ann Taves explains, tried to bridge the gulf between two realms: "Indeed, his aim as a psychologist was to explain religious experience in psychological terms, while at the same time leaving open the possibility that it pointed to something more."[8] Boisen's analysis often began with "the prophet appearing as a mere lonely madman" as against experiences he viewed and experienced as unhelpful in words not dissimilar to James': "excitement takes pathological forms whenever other interests are too few and the intellect too narrow."[9]

Understanding Boisen means taking his experiences seriously. The title of this book intentionally, perhaps provocatively, uses the word "mysticism" as a means of referring to Boisen not so much as a *believer in* (even though he certainly was that) but rather as an *experiencer of* religious and spiritual states and phenomena that may not be perceived by others as normal or objectively observable. Boisen at times saw visions, dreamed dreams, heard voices, described experiences—"automatisms" as he often called them—that were not objectively observable by others. I assert these states should not be automatically dismissed as illness, while not denying that he required treatment and even hospitalization during the midst of many of them.

Boisen's corpus of works, including his 1936 *Exploration of the Inner World*, his most complete and fully developed explication on the interplay of illness and inspiration specifically refers to "mysticism" as an area of interest and study.[10] A "mystic," for Boisen, is someone who succeeds in transforming, taming, the crisis of inexplicable experience, "automatisms," into new realizations or experiences that could be transformative for self and possibly yield new insights for others. In the vein of Jamesian pragmatism, Boisen hinted that the difference between a mystic and a mere madman was that a mystic is someone who offered experience and insight that healed self and also could be verified as useful to larger society. Verified by what Boisen referred to as the "fellowship of the best," an individual's larger community that could aid in separating experiential wheat from chaff. Boisen considered his bouts of mental illness (including some of his psychotic states) as experiential problem solving, as a spiritual means of struggling with crisis that, eventually, yielded new insights and healing for himself—which he hoped could provide insight for others as well. He wanted to gain greater understanding through his experiences and provide tools to aid others who had experiences similar to him.

Ann Taves' study of religion picks up in the tradition of William James and Boisen; she considers varied experiences that may, or may not, have spiritual, religious, inspirational, possibly psychotic, charge. Taves alludes, "we should disaggregate the concept of 'religious experience' and study the wide range of experiences to which religious significance has been attributed. . . . things deemed religious in turn allows us to make a distinction between *simple ascriptions*, in which an individual thing is set apart as special, and *complex ascriptions*, in which simple ascriptions are incorporated into more complex formations, such as those that scholars and others designate as 'spiritualities' or 'religions.'"[11] Religious and spiritual experiences may be closely related to psychology. Taves warns against equating these experiences solely with emotion: "although experience can usually be construed as having an emotional valence, it is not always its most salient feature. Defining experience in terms of emotion deflects attention from a range of unusual experiences that are granted special significance, such as lucid dreams, auditory and visual hallucinations, sensed presences, possession trance, and out-of-body experiences."[12]

Anton Boisen, candidly, recorded experiences—hallucinations at the very least—that he may not have always called "special" and he may not have quite gone so far as to ascribe religious significance to them, but they were deeply significant to his life and work. While some of Boisen's experience may equate with Taves' "special things," many of his experiences were, by his own explicit claim, psychotic. The exact nature of Boisen's periodic bouts of serious mental illness remains debated. Some claim he suffered from schizophrenia, or some species of schizoaffective disorder, and some claim bipolar disorder with psychotic features. Some stick with a term more or less contemporary to Boisen: "dementia praecox," which was, even then, passing out of fashion. Boisen's psychological diagnosis remains a moving target due to his many observers, his long life, and the historically and socially conditioned nature of wellness, illness, and how mental illness should be described and categorized. The hallucinatory and delusional (but not without insight and inspiration) nature of Boisen's psychotic episodes is undeniable.

Boisen's life and work introduce us to how we treat the mentally ill and how we interact with mental illness. Heather Vacek draws attention to cultural, specifically American Protestant, stigmatization of mental illness and the mentally ill, "pinn[ing] illness on individual and social failures. Persistent mental illness prompted suspicions of personal culpability."[13] His life, work, and memory played out in the shadow of stigma. However, Boisen did not write and work "at the risk of exposing his own illness."[14] He was quite explicit about it. The significance of Boisen's research and writing, according to Pruyser, lies in its against-the-grain hopefulness "that the mentally ill are not hopelessly fixed in their miserable condition. They can be helped when one realizes that in their symptoms, they are already trying to help themselves. Mental illness is somehow beyond good or evil; it is 'the price we pay for being human,' as Boisen often said."[15]

The period of the 1920s through the 1960s marks the apogee of the American state mental hospital and brings us to the cusp of "deinstitutionalization" and the rise of "community-centered" care of the mentally ill. Boisen's work also draws attention to patient-centered and person-centered health care. Boisen's early clinical, pastoral, and research work with the mentally ill focused on direct service to patients, which also coincided with a dire need of understaffed and overburdened state hospitals to obtain trained and caring staff. Boisen and his "theologs" were devoted to patient-centered care.

In 1930 he advertised his clinical program: "There is probably no one in the employ of the hospital upon whom the welfare of the patient is more dependent than the attendant or nurse who is with him on the ward all day long. But to secure such attendants is no easy matter. . . . He is generally a floater who has previously worked in some other hospital who stays about three and a half months and is then either discharged for inefficiency or brutality or drunkenness, or else he leaves without notice." Boisen, who spent a year and a half as an inpatient at Westboro State Hospital in Massachusetts, had firsthand experience with the neglect mixed with occasional "brutality" from untrained and unmotivated attendants. Boisen's, original, clinical students worked primarily as attendants who did their clinical studies in addition to their 'day job' with the hospital. Boisen provided an appealing group of motivated, low-cost employees, "a group of intelligent and willing college graduates who are keenly interested in the patients and their problems." Although the "employees" Boisen recruited for his hospitals were understood to be temporaries, their work for the hospital provided some of the funding required for their clinical education and provided at least a few more hands who truly cared about the population with which they worked.[16]

Boisen, arguably both mystic and madman, implemented a complex vision of creating a profession of institutional, especially mental health, chaplaincy distinct from the church pastorate. Boisen's "theologs" had the classroom and clinical training to provide spirituality care specifically geared toward a health-care environment and conversant with the doctors, nurses, psychologists, and social workers who were their professional colleagues. In so doing, he created a new form of theological education—not so much taught by books or in classrooms (even though Boisen did value a solid didactic foundation which he viewed as a necessary foundation for clinical training) but through the observed workings of the actual lives of people experiencing crisis in real time.

How does someone who could have been (and often has been) dismissed as, to borrow a phrase from James, "a mere lonely madman" change his profession and how people are trained for it? He did not do it all by himself, and there is serious doubt he ever would have been released from custodial care at Westboro Hospital were it not for patient and sympathetic friends and acquaintances who believed in him and what he was trying to do. Boisen's friends provided the professional, and personal, tools and support he would need to pursue and implement his vision while managing and containing his illnesses when they manifested.

In her work on American Protestant responses to mental illness, Vacek writes, "mental illness causes suffering. Stigma exacerbates suffering. Christians deem suffering problematic but sometimes fail to respond."[17] Whether or not by conscious design, Boisen's friends did respond and reflected an example of a reshaped practice toward mental illness, to which Vacek's work points. Boisen's friends had to be circumspect—some may accuse to the point of enabling—when his symptoms flared up due to the stigmatization of illness that at several times threatened to end his career and his work. Yet, they recognized his ill aspects for what they were, and in 1930 and 1935, they insisted that he receive hospitalization and escorted him to treatment. Boisen's friends, for the most part, did not abandon him nor give up on the visionary aspects of his work; nor did they give up on him personally.

Boisen's life, and his friends and colleagues' relation to him, reflects the difficult work, to which Vacek points "to respond in creative ways to overcome stigma and fear" that often surrounds mental illness and the mentally ill in how they welcomed and incorporated their undeniably odd, and sometimes ill, friend who also possessed (or was possessed by?) a vision that changed his corner of the world.[18]

Anton Boisen stood at the crossroads of several significant issues, the most significant of which is the relationship between mysticism and mental illness, illness and inspiration. Where does the one end and the other begin? Can someone be inspired and ill at the same time, and how were Boisen's friends, colleagues, and acquaintances challenged to interact with their mystical, and mad, friend, affirming the former yet not denying the latter. Boisen's life and work also point to the fraught relationship between the needs of patients and the needs of the medical institutions that are charged with providing for their care. In envisioning a new opening between medicine (and science in a larger sense) and religion, Boisen was driven with a vision that illuminated his, often shadowed, path and inspired others to take up the work. Trying to understand Boisen, as he would be understood, implies struggling with dualities that often appear irreconcilable: mysticism and psychosis, inspiration and illness, institution and the individual, science and religion.

NOTES

1. Thomas W. Klink, "Anton T. Boisen: 1876–1965: A Remembrance of the Committal of His Ashes, October 6, 1965," *The Journal of Pastoral Care* 19, no. 4 (1965): 230.

2. Robert Charles Powell, "Whatever Happened to 'CPE'—Clinical Pastoral Education?" (*Lecture, Ninth Plenary Meeting*, College of Pastoral Supervision and Psychotherapy, April 18, 1999), Last accessed July 26, 2019, www.pastoralreport.com/pastoralreportarticles/3778818.

3. Seward Hiltner, "Editorial: Boisen and Human Knowledge," *Pastoral Psychology* 2, no. 23 (1952).

4. Seward Hiltner, "The Heritage of Anton T. Boisen" (Unpublished Manuscript, October 2, 1965), Box 1, Folder 12, Anton T. Boisen Papers, Kansas Historical Society, Topeka, KS.

5. Anton T. Boisen, "An Experiment in Theological Education, 1926" (Unpublished Manuscript, 1926), Series 2, Box 1, Folder 16, Anton T. Boisen Papers, Chicago Theological Seminary. Boisen to Fred Eastman, January 20, 1926, Series 2, Box 3, Folder 27, Boisen Papers, Chicago Theological Seminary.

6. Henri Nouwen, "Paul Pruyser Interview," June 14, 1967, Box 290, File 333, Henri Nouwen Papers, John M. Kelly Library, University of St. Michael's College, Toronto, ON.

7. William James, *The Varieties of Religious Experience* (Cambridge, MA: Harvard University Press, 1985), 34.

8. Ann Taves, *Religious Experience Reconsidered: A Building-Block Approach to the Study of Religion and Other Special Things* (Princeton, NJ: Princeton University Press, 2009), 4–5.

9. James, *The Varieties of Religious Experience*, 270, 273.

10. Anton T. Boisen, *The Exploration of the Inner World: A Study of Mental Disorder and Religious Experience* (New York, NY: Willett, Clark and Company, 1936), 1, 306–8. Boisen specifically uses the term "mysticism" in the first page of his introduction to *Exploration of the Inner World*. Boisen, helpfully, explicates specifically on what he means by "Mysticism": "Religion shows two common tendencies. It may place the emphasis upon form, ceremony, custom, tradition; or it may stress experiences which are interpreted as manifestations of the super personal. The latter is what is meant in this book by the term 'mysticism.' A mystical experience is one which brings to the individual a sense of fellowship with God." Boisen continues: "sanctification" is "the transformation of character which is the goal of all religious or mystical experience. It is the old theological term which denotes the integration or unification of the personality which merely begins with the acceptance of the Christian ideal and the identification with the Christian fellowship." In the title to this work, he uses a synonymous term "religious experience"; the term "religious experience" also appears in the first page, as well as the title, of his autobiography. Anton T. Boisen, *Out of the Depths: An Autobiographical Study of Mental Disorder and Religious Experience* (New York, NY: Harper and Brothers, Publishers, 1960), 9. Boisen's lifelong interest in "mysticism" and "religious experience" points to experience of, perhaps struggle with, the inexplicable. While he suggests these experiences are often positive, he also implies the opposite in "sin," and "guilt," "out of harmony with the fellowship to which the individual aspires . . . a breach of trust as regards what he conceives to be his ultimate loyalty."

11. Taves, *Religious Experience Reconsidered*, 8–9.

12. Taves, *Religious Experience Reconsidered*, 11.

13. Heather H. Vacek, *Madness: American Protestant Responses to Mental Illness* (Waco, TX: Baylor University Press, 2015), 160.

14. Vacek, *Madness*, 169.

15. Paul W. Pruyser, "Anton T. Boisen and the Psychology of Religion," *The Journal of Pastoral Care* 21, no. 4 (1967): 212–13. While Boisen advocated an optimistic reappraisal of mental illnesses, it depended on his overarching interest in so-called "functional disorders." Pruyser critically points out that "he divided the mentally ill into two rigorously distinct groups: the organic and the functional disorders. The first group has 'some disease of the brain which has so affected their social

adjustments that they are said to have a 'psychosis.' He simply did not deal further with these patients in his writings."

16. Anton T. Boisen, "Theological Education Via the Clinic," *Religious Education* 25, no. 3 (1930): 237–38.

17. Vacek, *Madness*, 169.

18. Vacek, *Madness*, 180.

Chapter 1

Visit to a Little-Known Country

Not even Anton Boisen would deny that he suffered from, at least intermittent, severe bouts of mental illness during his eighty-eight-year-long life. What is remarkable about this was his relative openness about his deeply personal and deeply stigmatizing illness in a time of pervasive pessimism in the American medical and mental health community. Boisen's sojourn in "a little-known country," his euphemism for his experience of mental illness, drove his life quest to look for answers for himself and for humanity. Any effort to understand Boisen and his work must wrestle with his experience of mental illness as well as how others experienced him when he exhibited symptoms of mental illness.

Heather Vacek, in her exploration of American Protestant responses to mental illness, cites Boisen, and his case, as a rare example of compassion and engagement in the midst of stigma. She explains that "social stigma marks some as deviant and others as normal"; however, even if you are deemed "normal" you assume risk, "curtesy stigma," in being associated with the abnormal. The loyal spouse of the mental patient, the daughter of the excon, the parent of the cripple, the friend of the blind, the family of the hangman, all are obliged to share some of the discredit of the stigmatized person to whom they are related.[1]

The 1920s witnessed a medical context very different from what we take for granted today—which expects new medicines and technologies to address our ills. The deeply pessimistic medical community of that era, all the more so in regard to mental illness, further aggravated Boisen's stigmatized status. John H. Warner explains that the medical community at the beginning of the twentieth century was "profoundly despondent about the state and prospects of therapeutics." While scientific research could help explain, demonstrate, exemplify illness and disorder, it offered little hope for cure.[2] Only the occasional curative "breakthrough" fanned the embers of hope that sick people could become well through medical intervention.[3]

Among the factors that made Boisen an astounding figure was the fact that he was relatively open about his mental illness as well as his hope and conviction that sick people could become better even amid the stigma, shame, and therapeutic skepticism prevalent in his day. Soon after release from his first hospitalization at Westboro State Hospital, Boisen shopped his germinating idea for engagement with, and learning from, sick souls. Among "hoped for" results were: "1) The rehabilitation of a number of particular individuals. 2) Verification, modification and amplification of the conclusions already formed thru the consideration of an increased body of facts." For Boisen, direct engagement with the mentally ill worked hand in hand with research for "laying the foundation for a new message of salvation to the soul that is sick." Among qualifications that Boisen listed for potential employers, he added "Fifteen months as a patient in a hospital for the insane (1920–22). The fact that while there as a patient he was nearly all the time quite well."[4] Whereas, insanity was the illness whose name was not to be spoken, Boisen put it on his resume.[5]

Understanding Boisen's illness means wrestling with how mental illness has been understood over time. Over a century ago, German psychologist Emil Kraepelin created a taxonomy of mental illnesses that has strongly influenced how science understands and categorizes mental disorders to the present day. Kraepelin firmly distinguished "'dementia praecox' with, as he saw it, a poor prognosis, from manic-depressive illness (today called bipolar disorder) with a good, or at least better, prognosis for recovery. With respect to 'dementia praecox,' he supposed an organic defect as the basis of the illness, a kind of 'auto-intoxication,' leading to the destruction of the cortical neurons."[6] In 1920, Kraepelin's organicist views and firm boundaries represented the mainstream of American scientific thought on mental illness. However, even by that time Sigmund Freud's more fluid, psychodynamic, views were beginning to challenge, or at least coexist with, Kraepelinian orthodoxy. The assumptions of the 1920s regarding Boisen's treatment and prognosis down to the ongoing controversy regarding how best to describe Boisen's illness reflects the debate between Kraepelinians and Freudians and reflects the ongoing tenacity of Kraepelin's views and taxonomy.[7]

Historians have wrestled with how to describe the illness or illnesses that afflicted, but also, drove Boisen. Historian and psychiatrist Robert Powell passionately cites the fact of Boisen's apparent diagnosis: "what his doctors called 'dementia praecox, catatonic type,' a form of schizophrenia." In footnote he proceeds to explain that two manifestations of "catatonia," "stuporous," and "excited" can lead to confusion with "manic-depressive psychosis, manic phase." Powell, taking a Kraepelinian bent, points to observations from medical professionals and colleagues that point to Boisen having a disorder of thought rather than affect (thus pointing to schizophrenia over bipolar disorder) . . . although there undoubtedly were excessively affective components to Boisen's behavior during his disturbed episodes, one may feel some confidence in his self-diagnosis of 'dementia praecox, catatonia.'"[8]

Powell implicitly refutes Carol Norths' and William M. Clements' tentative argument. Applying criteria found in the *DSM-III*, North and Clements propose that Boisen's diagnosis may more closely relate to what would be called bipolar affective disorder in a present-day diagnostic context.[9]

Curtis Hart, influenced by Freud, proposes a more dynamic way of viewing Boisen's diagnosis, recognizing the possibility that Boisen's symptoms may have changed over time, and likewise, that diagnosis may drift relative to historical context. Yet, Hart repeats the Kraepelinian dogma that "dementia praecox" and "manic depressive illness" cannot coexist in the same patient. While "Boisen was not bipolar and schizophrenic at the same time but demonstrated aspects of both in his thought, affect, and behavior. These aspects of illness overlapped at some points and remained distinct at others."[10] Diagnostic categories have expanded and changed considerably between Boisen's first hospitalization in 1920 and the present time. In 1918, the *Statistical Manual for the Use of Institutions for the Insane*, a predecessor of the *DSM* series, offers a tentative description of "Dementia Praecox," including the "catatonic" type often ascribed to Boisen. The *Statistical Manual* relates that "the term 'schizophrenia' is now being used by many writers instead of dementia praecox." It also warns that "this group (dementia praecox) cannot be satisfactorily defined at the present time as there are still too many points at issue as to what constitute the essential clinical features of dementia praecox."[11] The *DSM-V*, however, seems to be tentatively creeping beyond the long-lived Kraepelinian Dichotomy that firmly separates schizophrenia from bipolar disorder. It admits the possibility of mental illnesses that manifest "Delusions with significant overlapping mood episodes," in other words a crossing of categories of thought and mood disorder.[12]

Diagnostic categories of mental illnesses can, and do, change over time and interact with the time in which a diagnosis is made as well as who is making the observation(s) and when the observation is made of the symptomatic person. Diagnostic categories are a moving target; Boisen, as a person with a diagnosis (or diagnoses), has been a moving target as well.

BOISEN'S EXPERIENCE AND INTERPRETATION OF HIS MENTAL ILLNESS

It is difficult to separate how Boisen experienced mental illness from how he experienced spirituality. For him the two interact as separate sides of the same coin. The starting point for Boisen is experience, and then the question moves on to how the experience informed the experiencer's life—did it work toward greater understanding and integration or did it militate toward growing delusion and disintegration? He writes that "certain forms of mental disorder and certain forms of religious experience are closely interrelated. Mental disorder is, I hold, the price humanity has to pay for having the power of choice and capacity for growth." Boisen's experience of mental illness was, however, undeniably frightening and painful for him, and at times for others as well. Recalling his first hospitalization in 1920, Boisen recalled delusions of global catastrophe, death and rebirth, and vivid personal transformations: "I had over and over again ideas of going through all stages of evolution from the single cell on. It was all very terrible." His experiences occurred in a context of institutional isolation, stigma, and even violence. Upon disobeying an attendant, he "was given a . . . severe beating. . . . One of the older attendants told me later that I was given what was known as 'the old bughouse knockout.'" Corresponding with Norman Nash, a seminary classmate, Boisen described life at Westboro State Hospital thus: "the hardest thing is to realize that those of us who are here are practically counted as among the dead. . . .it is a place of weeping and gnashing of teeth, where the light is gone and the loved ones cut away, . . .Over the door I would write, 'Lasciate ogni Speranza, voi ch'entrate.' [All hope abandon, ye who enter here.] . . . I am accomplishing nothing. I am rusting, and sometimes I get very impatient." Overall, Boisen recalls in his autobiography, "a long and wearisome and fragmentary account of a very unpleasant experience. I have given it with a definite purpose. It suggests what seems to me a very important principle: *The cure has lain in the faithful carrying through of the delusion itself.*"[13] For Boisen, the ordeal of his illness was a means to gain greater understanding both for himself and for humanity.

Acute aspects of Boisen's illnesses tended to manifest rapidly and tended to resolve relatively rapidly as well. Boisen appears to have had considerable capacity for focus and concentration. While Boisen's concentration contributed, later, to his professional drive and productivity and made him an effective interviewer, caregiver, and scholar, it also contributed to the onset of his illnesses in obsessive behavior and loss of perspective. The triggering factors in Boisen's significant episode in 1898, as well as his illnesses in 1920, 1930, and 1935—which required hospitalization—revolve primarily around his experience of sexuality, spirituality, and his search for meaningful life work.

Boisen was well aware of the significance of his experiences and his, often fraught, relationship, with sexuality and the intimate women in his life to the onset of his episodes of mental illness. During his first hospitalization at Westboro, Boisen requested, and received, a therapeutic and diagnostic interview with Elwood Worcester, an interview that would be crucial to Boisen's release from custodial care.¹⁴ In his letter to Worcester, Boisen noted issues that contributed to his onset. Boisen wrote of an unrequited intimate relationship that intertwined with his spirituality:

> My love for Miss B. (Alice Batchelder) has thru all these years been so interwoven with all that is best in my life and with my deepest religious faith that I could not forget, not without greatest loss. Nor do I think it necessary. There has been of course the element of desire. This is the thing which in the past has stood in the way. But the other and helpful elements have always been more important and stronger. I told her at the very first that it was her friendship I wanted.¹⁵

In his decades-long, platonic, and often distant relationship with Batchelder, there was an immediate connection between Boisen's, often difficult, relationship between sexuality and spirituality.¹⁶

Boisen attributes his first experience with mental illness (and of finding a resolution to that illness) with his experiences of Easter Day 1898. Writing to Fred Eastman, his lifelong friend, Boisen attributes this episode as "key to the whole thing . . . which brought relief and hope and life when all seemed darkness and despair."¹⁷ What brought "relief" to Boisen was the result of "throw[ing] myself on my knees with an agonized call for help," with the answer he perceived: "Don't be afraid to tell," motivating him to share his travails with sympathetic others. In this case Boisen shared his concerns with his mother and with a favorite professor at Indiana University, Dr. William Lowe Bryan—who would become his lifelong friend.¹⁸

Boisen, talented in languages, studied German, French, and Greek in college. Reading French novelist Emile Zola's work, Boisen became sexually aroused and "crossed the line I had determined not to cross. As a result, I felt stripped of self-respect and burdened with a heavy sense of failure and guilt. It was in this mood that I entered a new quarter of study." Boisen's erotic focus and obsession continued through the new term: "As I turned the leaves of my Greek dictionary, obscene words would leap out of its pages and hit me in the eye; and they would leap out of other dictionaries also. It was obvious that something was seriously wrong." Awaking on Easter morning "after a sleepless night," Boisen resolved to talk about the matter with his favorite professor. While Boisen could not "remember much of that talk . . . one thing stands out clear": a gracious, but less than entirely comfortable, Bryan "told me that it would always be necessary to fight for control of the instincts and that I must look to Christ for help, and to some good woman."¹⁹

While Boisen's experience of 1898 resolved in a reasonably equanimous way, it provided a template for Boisen's later triggers as well as a means for Boisen to come to terms with his convulsive experiences. The 1898 episode included a fraught combination of sex/sexuality, spirituality, and the impulse to "tell" both to gain greater self-understanding and to have a greater understanding of the larger human experience, with tools and training to help others.[20]

Boisen's breakdown, and hospitalization, in 1920 provided him a meticulously documented record of descent into illness and his effort to overcome. Boisen, then in his forties, had engaged in a number of brief careers with the YMCA, as a forester, and with several small churches. He was in the process of negotiating gaining accreditation with the Presbyterian Church for a new pastorate but "ran into unexpected difficulties. Churches were not too plentiful . . . Whenever I was being considered, the first question was likely to be, 'are you married?' and the second, 'Do you expect to be married?' Neither of these questions could be answered in the affirmative. I would then be told that I must be content with a 'modest' church. This meant . . . a salary so low as scarcely to permit marriage if things worked out as I still hoped they might." In an attempt to better his odds, Boisen worked on a new "Statement of Religious Experience and a Statement of Belief," since "It seemed to me that I was now entering a new period and was in a very real sense offering myself anew."[21]

Boisen threw himself into the task and "became intensely absorbed in it, so much so that I lay awake at night letting ideas take shape of themselves. . . . the absorption went beyond the ordinary. I was no longer interested in anything else, and I spent all the time possible in my room, writing." Following several days of intense concentration, and little sleep, "some strange ideas came surging into my mind, ideas of doom, ideas of my own unsuspected importance. With them began the frank psychosis."[22] In Boisen's published autobiography, and in his unpublished personal case study, he includes a complete copy of the statement during the writing of which his "psychosis" triggered. Boisen, helpfully, includes an in-text reference to even the exact point in this statement where he felt his "abnormal condition" begin. At that point, Boisen's writing launches into his first iteration of the "family-of-four" delusion that would become an ongoing hallmark of Boisen's illnesses in the years to come.[23]

The 1898 and 1920 episodes provide examples of Boisen's experience of onset of mental illness. Prominent features included sustained periods of deep, intense, exclusive concentration on a matter of concern that often lasted several days coupled with sleeplessness, which resulted in a loss of perspective and significant behavioral change: "these abnormal conditions do not come all at once. It is easy to recognize the symptoms. There is always the extreme absorption, the resulting sleeplessness, ending finally in a condition more or less hypnotic. At first in this condition there has been confusion and terror."[24] After decades of experience with helping Boisen with his troubles, in 1935, Fred Eastman counseled, "May I suggest that you do not write to those outside the Seminary family about the ideas which create the disturbances in these periods? While I am no psychiatrist, it seems to me the more you surrender to the domination of those ideas and commit yourself to writing about them, the stronger the hold they will gain upon your mind."[25] While Boisen was able to resolve his experience in 1898 by "telling" of his troubles, his later episodes required more intensive effort to turn his experience of illness into opportunities for personal resolution and refocus on service to others.

Boisen's upsets of 1930 and 1935 largely centered on two significant women in his life: Alice Batchelder and Helen Flanders Dunbar. The breakdown of November 1930 resulted from several factors. Boisen saw career success in the incorporation of the clinical pastoral care movement he spearheaded. His mother died in the summer of 1930. However, the proximate cause of his new fixation and upset revolved around an emotional triangle among himself, Batchelder, and Dunbar.[26]

Boisen's relationship with Batchelder, whom he credited as his "guiding hand," spanned thirty-three years from their first meeting in 1902 at Indiana University until Batchelder's death in 1935.[27] For Boisen, Batchelder was love at first sight: "I fell in love with her then and there. It was a one-sided affair . . . I told her of my love for her, asking at least for her friendship. She was very gentle in her answer, but it was not the one I longed for. She felt it best that our relationship should cease entirely."[28] While Boisen insisted that this relationship was "one-sided" and that Batchelder never returned his affection, their relationship, such as it was, persisted over several decades, Batchelder often showing concern, aid, guidance, at times even what could be viewed as a form of "love" albeit of an unconventional kind.

Batchelder's way of relating to Boisen equivocated over the decades. At times she rejected him outright in stinging terms and going for years without allowing him to visit her. In 1920, the year of Boisen's first hospitalization, she wrote: "I have no love to give you, and not even friendship unless it can be on a sane and normal basis." Batchelder urged Boisen to be "sane and normal" repeatedly during this letter. Batchelder, however, did give clues to why Boisen would value her "guiding hand" over the years. Batchelder, throughout her letters, returned consistently to Boisen's "work." She repeatedly and consistently urged him to keep his focus on finding and maintaining a life's path that would bring meaning to himself and others. She quoted Holy Writ to "'enable you to speak with authority and power.' [This] I cannot [do for you], or can anyone else."[29] Batchelder's temper started becoming palpable in her letters as Boisen became "too much absorbed [as Boisen's triangle with Batchelder and Dunbar became increasingly complicated] by the perplexing question of 'relationships.'" She urged in conclusion: "put the force of your concentration on the work which is your service to the world. . . . I would add 'forget thyself.'"[30]

We know little about Alice Batchelder and how she lived her life. What is known is that she was dedicated to her family and her work. Never married, to Boisen nor to anybody else, she was a dedicated employee at a Chicago bank and a devoted housekeeper and caretaker for her sister Anne and their friend Catherine Wilson, confined to a wheelchair throughout her life. In 1928, addressing Boisen as "My dear friend," she wrote apologetically:

> I really had not known that I was disappointing you in limiting our meetings . . . "holding down a job" and keeping house at the same time meant a sacrifice of amusements and social affairs. I leave the house at 7:30 each morning and do not get back until 6 o'clock at night—and before I leave there is breakfast to get and clear away, beds to make, and dusting and mopping to do. In the evening there is dinner, mending, some cooking, accounts, entertaining—and at 10 o'clock bedtime in order to be up at 6 and start over again. Saturday afternoons take care of the bigger household tasks like baking and cleaning and shopping. Sunday mornings are full with church, and it's a rare Sunday when we don't have guests all afternoon and evening. Thus it goes—and whatever else I do has to be occasional, so that it has come to be a matter of course that many of my friends I see but seldom.

Batchelder put duty first, in her case: household, church, and work. It is not surprising that she would counsel Boisen to do likewise.[31]

Boisen maintained a long-standing friendship, almost as an honorary family member, with the Batchelder family in the decades following Alice's death in 1935. He maintained a correspondence with Alice's brother Paul, starting in the 1930s, upon Alice's death, and ending with Boisen's own demise, in the 1960s. In 1937, Paul wrote, "While I believe that I did once meet [you] in New York, about 1909 or 1910, you have nevertheless remained a very enigmatic figure to me . . . writing to ask if I may have the privilege of an interview with you."[32] The relationship between the two men grew over the years. Paul discussing his career as a professor at the University of Texas, and they both talked about common interests regarding science, religion, spiritual experience, and above all Alice. Paul gave money to the "Alice L. Batchelder Memorial Fund" at Chicago Theological Seminary, where Boisen taught. Boisen expressed his gratitude for a picture of Alice that Paul gave him saying, "I shall keep it always among my most treasured possessions, along with the one she gave me in 1910."[33] Paul speculated that his sister may have been open to marriage at one point—an opportunity missed: "It was certainly a tragedy for you (and possibly Alice also) that you did not follow the lead which she gave you in 1911. However, with a normal married life you probably would have escaped your experiences with mental illness, and the world would have lost your unique contributions to science. Thus, it is impossible to say what was best from the standpoint of the world at large."[34] In Paul, Boisen gained a brother of sorts, even though he never gained the spouse he desired.

Helen Flanders Dunbar was a remarkable woman for any time, but especially for the times in which she lived. On the one hand, her biographer Robert Powell describes an "enigma," a term suitable for Boisen and Batchelder as well, that "even her closest colleagues asked and could not answer. No one knew. One of her associates over a period of two decades assured me that he never knew Dunbar in person, but only as a persona, as a mask growing more impenetrable over the years."[35] What is known is that her accomplishments were as extraordinary as Batchelder's were pedestrian. Upon her meeting with Boisen at the advanced age of twenty-two, she was concurrently completing her Bachelor of Divinity degree (a postundergraduate seminary degree, the predecessor of the modern Master of Divinity degree) at Union Seminary in New York and a Ph.D. dissertation in comparative literature ("Medieval Symbolism and Its Consummation in the Divine Comedy," a Boisen favorite) at Columbia University. Dunbar afterward enrolled in, and graduated from, Yale Medical School, specializing in obstetrics and psychiatry. Boisen and Dunbar shared a common passion for, and talent with, language. She was conversant in fifteen languages and dialects when they first met. As Boisen built his project for clinical education at Worcester State Hospital, he stopped at Union Seminary (Boisen's alma mater) to recruit students, Dunbar was Boisen's first, and only, recruit. Upon Boisen, Dunbar "made a deep impression."[36]

While Boisen wrote Batchelder regularly, with few responses, Dunbar showed Boisen the attention and esteem Batchelder withheld. Dunbar worked with Boisen for only one month in 1925, but she continued contact with Boisen and returned, in 1927, to work with him at Worcester during her time in medical school. Dunbar had studied medieval symbolism at Columbia and wanted to continue her study of symbols in "acutely disturbed patients and under what conditions it occurred. She made several visits to the hospital and she worked out a questionnaire on schizophrenic thinking which impressed me more than ever with her keen understanding. I became more and more impressed with her, especially after I had stopped writing to Alice and Alice did not reply to my letter."[37]

The year 1928 witnessed growing complication in Boisen's triangle with Batchelder and Dunbar. At the beginning of the year, Batchelder unexpectedly responded to a Christmas letter Boisen had sent her. Concurrently, Boisen commenced work on his "own case history" at Dunbar's suggestion. To complicate matters further, the two women in Boisen's life "consented to meet" on June 2, 1928, a meeting from which Dunbar backed out. As Boisen worked on his autobiography, "Helen suggested that we attempt to work out our philosophy of sex. In doing this severe conflicts arose. I had the feeling that I was getting too much interested in Helen, . . . prompting a near-psychotic affair. It followed several sleepless nights and a visit to my father's grave. . . . It came in the form of words which were almost audible, 'You do not love her.'"[38]

An academic fellowship took Dunbar to Switzerland and Austria for most of 1929, temporarily forestalling Boisen's growing turmoil. During that time, Boisen and Dunbar "exchange[d] letters about once a month." Boisen also taught at Chicago Theological Seminary during the Fall Semesters, resuming frequent—often daily—correspondence with Batchelder, "and I had reason to believe that she was not indifferent. On Thanksgiving Day of that year we knelt together before the altar in Hilton Chapel and entered into a covenant of friendship, one with the other. In that covenant we included Helen."[39]

Soon afterward Batchelder wrote:

You have been very much in my thoughts today, both because of the lovely and unusual roses which found awaiting me when I reached home, and because of the events of last night. I don't know why I should be any less direct and honest in speaking of something like that, than in uttering words of warning—so I will tell you what perhaps you could see for yourself, that I was profoundly moved by what took place. I was, and am, thankful for the prayer. I believe that brought us closer together than anything that has ever happened—that fact that we could in one spirit come to God together. And the little roses you gave me to wear—still fresh on the table—have been a message and a reminder of our covenant, and for the first time in all these twenty seven years I feel that I can with safety and with entire honesty sign myself—with real affection, Alice.

Shortly afterward, upon Boisen's return to Massachusetts, Batchelder continued in her letter: "Write Sunday evenings, <u>if</u> you want to and <u>when</u> you want to, but don't ever feel that it is a custom or a rite or anything that <u>must</u> be observed. . . . You are absolutely free in every way (emphasis original)."[40] Batchelder wrote Boisen in thanks for a pin he had found in Germany and gave to her: "You took me completely by surprise and I gave expression to my first quick feeling that you must not give me costly gifts. But I want you to know what I think of the pin itself—which is that I consider it one of the most exquisite things I have ever owned. . . . I look at it and say to myself, 'Is it really mine?' And it <u>is mine</u>, given and accepted as a memento of our covenant of friendship." A deeply gratified Boisen recalled "fulfilment of this dream of a lifetime. Alice was full of delightful surprises. She was all I had thought and more."[41]

Dunbar returned from Europe in the early months of 1930. This time she completed the promised visit between her and Batchelder. Boisen recollected, "Just what happened at that meeting I do not know. All I could get out of Alice was that she was now convinced that Helen was not a myth but a real woman and a very charming one. I have reason to believe that Alice herself reverted to her old position that she had never loved me and that she thought of me only as a friend." Dunbar studied with Carl Jung in Switzerland and brought her findings on European psychiatry to Boisen:

> she told me of an occasion at a Swiss carnival when a distinguished psychiatrist, whom we both honored [the identity of this "distinguished psychiatrist" is unclear], recognized her and offered to introduce her to the "art of love." She also discussed contraceptives and spoke of a particularly good one she had learned about. . . .On our arrival in New York we went to her apartment, where I was to help her with the translation of a book by Eugen Kahn which she had undertaken. . . .the fact remains that this was our nearest approach to physical intimacy. She recognized and accepted my loyalty to Alice.[42]

Boisen stewed over his conflict between the two women during summer and fall of 1930, explicitly contemplating marriage to Dunbar. He confided to Batchelder:

> Thru You there has come to me a new opportunity, new life and, in a very literal sense, a new birth. I feel myself bound forever unto You by the ties of tenderest love and gratitude, and so long was we both shall live I would be for You a true and loving friend. In that same covenant of friendship have included also another friend, one who in training and interest and fine understanding has seemed to me an instrument of the finest precision to aid in the accomplishment of the task which has come to me thru my love for You.[43]

Included in Boisen's unpublished case record was a response from Batchelder dated October 22, 1930, which makes no direct reference to the crux of Boisen's predicament: "I am certainly 'not much' these days as a correspondent. I am not finding any extra time at the Bank, and my few 'leisure evenings' are far from that. . . . I am very sure also that you and the work are to be congratulated in getting Helen as Medical Director. All in all, with the increased budget and the greater number of students and with Helen accepting that position. I should think prospects would look pretty bright to you. I send my best wishes for the work and you."[44]

The year 1930 brought Boisen a heady mix of conflicted love, sex, and previously unknown professional success as his project in clinical pastoral education spread beyond Worcester and as his students moved on to replicate new clinical centers throughout New England and the Mid-Atlantic:

> As in the previous episodes, the actual disturbance followed a period of intensified absorption and prayer. . . . I recall a period of uncontrollable sobbing. It seemed that something which ought to have been, was not to be. I had failed, and the world was in danger. In great distress of mind, I started forth in my car. First, I looked up Phil Guiles and turned over to him the responsibility for the project. Then . . . I drove to my sister's home. . . . From there I went to the home of a cousin in Exeter, New Hampshire, thence back to Boston. There I parked the car and took a train for New York. After a few hours there I returned to Boston and called on Dr. Cabot. Of that visit I recall that I identified with my father, inquiring about myself in the third person. Dr. Cabot was much alarmed and saw to it that I was at once hospitalized.[45]

Boisen's descent continued: "Something terrible was about to happen. This world of ours was to have become a brilliant star; but something had gone wrong, and it was now to become a Milky Way. I was, it seemed, or should have been, a very important person, and my failure was chiefly responsible for the impending catastrophe. The family-of-four idea was also present."[46]

Some of his colleagues, including Dr. Richard Cabot[47] and Austin Philip Guiles,[48] wanted Boisen removed, or at very least sidelined, from the growing clinical education project. Dunbar, however, stood resolutely by him—even though a romantic relationship was now out of the question.[49] As she contributed to his harm, she also effected his cure. Boisen biographer Robert Leas observes, "Dunbar came to visit. He had asked for her specifically. They were together some time. She left without saying a word. From that day on he was better."[50] Over the decades to follow, Dunbar and Boisen continued their correspondence and professional contacts—albeit at a distance, Boisen expressing regret for having "cracked up" and "wish[ing] to do whatever lies in my power to lessen the painful memories." Yet, in his elderly years "feel[ing] increasingly the need of good understanding with those who have meant so much to me as you have meant . . . your note encourages me to assume that I may still use the name you gave me years ago and sign this letter."[51]

The death of Boisen's mother, Louise Wylie Boisen, in June 1930, has been conjectured as the cause of Boisen's 1930 breakdown. While this may have caused additional stress for Boisen, it does not seem the proximate cause for his loss of balance. He wrote: "She lived for her children and made every sacrifice in order that they might have their chance to develop. . . . She was even too careful to leave us free to choose for ourselves."[52] In the aftermath of Boisen's 1920 hospitalization, his sister Marie, with whom he had a contested relationship, pressed him to move back to Bloomington to care for their aging mother.

Boisen retorted smartly to his sister's suggestion: "I am of course very sorry that you do not approve of my course in life. . . . With reference to Mother I have not failed to consider her. . . . The first duty a man owes to his parents is to establish himself and this means very often cutting loose from home." Boisen notes that Marie apparently did not object to his previous peripatetic professions prior to his breakdown: "I think you will probably recognize that I should not have been in any better position to have her with me if I had remained with the Forest Service. I should then also have been a wanderer and without any home."[53] Decades later, Boisen described his mother's final years: "She also was remarkably free from physical illness but was troubled with the loss of memory and sight and hearing and developed ideas that we were stealing from her. Her final years like those of her mother were very unhappy."[54]

Boisen did not have problems 'cutting the apron strings' from his mother, and her death did not trigger the fixation and loss of perspective that signaled the onset of his episodes of illness. His mother's death may have been a contributing factor in his growing upset. The proximate cause of Boisen's 1930 illness, however, was his fraught triangle with Batchelder and Dunbar, which tore his mind and soul: a triangle that mixed together his passions/pathologies in a single brew—spirituality, sex, work. This triangle came to a head in October and culminated in late November, with Boisen's breakdown and hospitalization—almost one year to the day of Boisen's Thanksgiving Day spiritual covenant with Batchelder.

Batchelder's 1935 terminal illness and death triggered Boisen's final instance of psychiatric hospitalization. In August, Boisen received a note in which Batchelder notified him she was to have an operation for cancer and that she was to receive "no callers, no flowers." Boisen's career had reached its apogee; he was working on the dedication of what was to become, arguably, his critically best-received book *Exploration of the Inner World*, a book he was dedicating to Batchelder. As the weight of the loss of the love of his life pressed upon him, Boisen's mental state slipped into "an abnormal condition" that he had witnessed previously: "I now became wholly absorbed in the task of writing. . . . How often I had disappointed her! What poor use I had made of our friendship, failing in these later years to reach the deeper levels of understanding! And now she was leaving! . . . Again, I had the idea that this earth should have become a brilliant star, but something had gone wrong and instead it would only become a Milky Way. I recall identifying myself with my father and feeling that he was getting old and would be unable to carry on much longer."[55]

By 1935, Boisen had become a professor at Chicago Theological Seminary, a published author, a clinical educator, and a chaplain at Elgin State Hospital northwest of Chicago. He had caring friends and colleagues nearby, including a former student and his current deputy at Elgin State Hospital: Donald Beatty. They "were quick to recognize the signs of trouble and that there was no disruption of the social situation. They guarded me carefully, and on November 11 they spirited me away to the Sheppard and Enoch Pratt Hospital in Baltimore so quietly that scarcely anyone in Elgin knew about it."[56]

THE FAMILY-OF-FOUR

Many elements of Boisen's life and experience are difficult to understand. Prominent among them was his passionate love for Alice Batchelder, a woman who often ignored and scorned him. A feature that puzzled even Boisen was the "family-of-four" vision/delusion that coincided with his more severe "abnormal" states. While Boisen's vilusions were unquestionably the product of psychosis, as he himself grants "the family-of-four was of course a crazy idea." Still, a key aspect of Boisen's life and work was to follow the example of "Dr. Adolph Meyer [who] said that he could listen with as much respect to the ideas of an excited schizophrenic as he could to those of an Oriental philosopher because he knew that those ideas had meaning, and his job as a psychiatrist was to discover the sense in the nonsense."[57]

While the "family-of-four" emerged on numerous occasions in Boisen's life, it initially emerged amid Boisen's fevered effort to rewrite his statement of belief and experience:

> (writing of Jesus of Nazareth's Crucifixion) . . .culminating in his death upon the cross, where he died, the just for the unjust, the perfect for the imperfect, the strong for the weak.
>
> And this process has been going on for nineteen centuries. The strong have been giving themselves for the weak and the perfect for the imperfect. A crossing process has thus resulted. The divine, in consequence, has been coming into the world disguised in ugliness, crippled by disease, shackled by sin, and impotent with weakness.
>
> I believe that the weak and the imperfect should no longer accept this sacrifice and that they should be willing to give their lives, the imperfect for the perfect and the weak for the strong, that the divine may be freed from its prison house of infirmity and be able to come into the world in beauty and in power and not in disguise, and that the reign of love may be able to replace that of brute force and ruthless competition, where survival goes to the strong and to

the merciless. . . . This would come through the refusal of the weak and the imperfect to accept their claim of pity and of need.⁵⁸

This excerpt captures the essence of Boisen's "family-of-four" vilusion of strong/weak, perfect/imperfect. As he concentrated intently upon writing his statement, it "came surging into my mind with tremendous power this idea about the voluntary sacrifice of the weak for the sake of the strong. Along with this came a curious scheme which I copied down mechanically and kept repeating over and over again, as if learning a lesson. . . . the impact was terrific, and I felt myself caught up, as it were, into another world."⁵⁹

Boisen puzzled over what, if any, meaning to attribute to his family-of-four: "It really seemed as though some deeper self were trying to impart some urgent message."⁶⁰ Sometimes the message related to concrete events and relationships in his life—such as his unrequited love/unconventional love affair with Alice Batchelder, a woman for whom he felt himself unworthy and he had felt condescended to his weakness over the decades. He speculated that a successful instance of him as the weak "no longer accepting this sacrifice" would be to imitate Dante's *Divine Comedy*, "the old Dante-Beatrice story, in which the poet had to pass through the fire before he could enter paradise and join the woman he worshipped. . . . love between man and woman can be truly happy only when each is a free and autonomous being, dependent not upon the other but upon God. . . . It was necessary for me to pass through the purgatorial fires of a horrifying psychosis before I could set foot in my promised land of creative activity."⁶¹ Powell also points out that, in Boisen's 1930 psychosis, he identified the "family-of-four" in emotional, romantic relationships with Batchelder and Dunbar, in which Boisen wondered if he was to give up both as well as leadership in the clinical education program that he masterminded and founded.⁶²

Powell and Richard Coble have also interpreted Boisen's "family-of-four" as pointing toward a mature mutuality as Boisen sought to grow away from emotional dependence—specifically, in his lifelong struggle to grow from dependence on Batchelder to maturity in his highest loyalties. Coble interprets the "family-of-four" as Boisen's attempt at a corrective pointing to "mercy and mutuality" rather than the "the imperfect morally blackmail[ing] the strong and the perfect for their love by manipulating their pity." While he attributes this to his own treatment of Batchelder, he also takes it as a challenge to grow and become more than what he was, an insight not just for himself but potentially useful to others as well, "to correct the balance of the world."⁶³

Powell sees this vilusion as "the splitting and unifying of groups to be a non-accidental significant norm," as the clinical pastoral education movement splintered along the lines of philosophy, personality, and geography. Boisen did not wish them, or others, to be "antagonistic or assimilated, he did want them to be productively confronting each other and engaged in dialogue." Powell also sees relevance of the "family-of-four" vilusion for caring relationships in which the caregiver does not approach from a position of superiority but "the necessity of speaking with authority and presence from a position of accepted vulnerability." And as encouraging realism and courage for people sick in mind, soul, and/or body: "'acceptance without surrender'—the acknowledgement of one's own imperfection without allowing it as an excuse—the acknowledgement of one's imperfection while searching for insights and understandings of potential value to both oneself and those outside."[64]

HOW OTHERS EXPERIENCED BOISEN'S MENTAL ILLNESS

For many, Boisen was an alien and alienating personality, difficult to relate to and understand when well, all the more so in psychosis. This task and his task were made all the more challenging, and his feat of overcoming was all the more impressive against the backdrop of the deep stigma that exists around mental illness. Psychologist Stephen Hinshaw writes that the stigma of mental illness, "a term conveying a deep, shameful mark or flaw related to being a member of a group that is devalued by the societal mainstream," is so pervasive a cultural marker that it often is applied without notice or critique: "what for example, is the worst thing that one can be called in modern society? Think of the following terms: crazy, nuts, loco, wacko, psycho, off your rocker, out of your mind, mental case, schizo, deranged—just a few of the synonyms and slang phrases for mental illness, which rival ethnic, racial, and sexual epithets as sources of ridicule. Some of these words are among the first used by young children to discount and dismiss disliked peers."[65]

Boisen's observers bring differing perspectives, experiences, and vantage points on him both when he was well and when he was ill. A fairly consistent view depicts him as an intense, taciturn, man who was prone to be misinterpreted by others. Fred Eastman, Boisen's loyal friend, gave him detailed and frank advice during his 1920 hospitalization. During their correspondence, Eastman notified Boisen of developments in psychology in Europe—especially Sigmund Freud's views that mental illness may not necessarily be an organic, permanent, and hopeless condition and that Freud's treatment methods were gradually being introduced in the United States. As Boisen attempted to negotiate with his physicians at Westboro State Hospital for treatment in accordance with Freud's new methods, his intensity got the best of him.

As Eastman mediated between the hospital and Boisen, Westboro superintendent W. E. Lang wrote Eastman: "He still believes that the recent experience through which he has been passing is part of a plan which has been laid out for him and that he has not suffered from any mental illness. This mistaken idea is sufficient to tell us that he is still in need of hospital treatment."[66] As Eastman tried to facilitate Boisen's release to a hospital using the new Freudian psychoanalytic methods,[67] he counseled Boisen regarding a pattern he had observed before in his old seminary friend:

> Please remember that it is of the utmost importance that you do not cross them or give them reason to think that you are opposing them. In a letter I had from Dr. Lang telling me that you could not come to our house for a weekend, he said "He believes that the recent experience through which he has been passing, is due to a plan which has been laid out for him and he has not suffered from any mental illness." I think I know exactly the cause of such a statement. Your answers to their questions meant one thing to you but another thing to the doctors. It reminds me of the time you were being examined for ordination. You repeatedly said in answer to questions, "I take an agnostic position on that subject." That word "agnostic" meant one thing to you, but quite a different thing to the preachers who were examining you. Just so in this case.[68]

As the year progressed, Boisen was unable to procure his release to Bloomingdale and suffered a relapse. Eastman delicately suggested:

> You and your welfare are the main consideration. In the first long letter . . . I pointed out the evidently neglected field of service right there in Westboro, the sort of service you are making a beginning at it the photographic and social celebration work you have told me about lately. It is not possible that your greatest opportunity lies right there, and that if you leave it, it may not be yours again? It would of course mean a real sacrifice on your part, but after all haven't most people made real sacrifices in order to accomplish real results?[69]

A chastened Boisen responded: "Your letter reminds me of a remark you once made when President Wilson had just fired a man from the Cabinet. You said that letter was so beautifully written that you would be willing to be fired yourself just to receive such a letter." Rebuilding his case that "functional" mental illnesses need not necessarily be permanent and irretrievable conditions, he pleaded with his friend: "I feel therefore that I am not ready to be junked yet."[70]

While Boisen's communications with Eastman indicated a hallmark intensity, it was leavened with humor as well. Some observers have opined that Boisen's affect became flatter and heavier as the decades rolled. Psychologist Paul Pruyser, an occasional acquaintance of Boisen's, reminisced that "there is an awful psychiatric expression referring to chronic schizophrenic patients, who have made a good hospital adjustment, or sometimes have been discharged to live on the outside. . . . 'burned out case.' This phrase came into my mind time and time again when I talked with him and saw him act. He was not without humor and delicacy, but something had happened to his feelings and their expression." Pruyser knew Boisen in Boisen's final years: "one felt somehow in the presence of a man preparing himself for death. This certainly augmented my sense of reverence towards him, but again, made it difficult for me to invest myself in him."[71]

Boisen started photographic and recreational projects as an inpatient at Westboro Hospital. He put these experiences to work as a chaplain and clinical educator at Worcester and Elgin State Hospitals. Boisen and his students created several pictorial yearbooks at both institutions. Invariably included were group photos of Boisen and his "theologs." The students clustered around Boisen exhibited differing affects and facial expressions, some looking forward, some looking to left or right or at each other, many grinning or smiling. Boisen, a slightly overweight, large, middle-aged man with a receding salt-and-pepper hairline, starred forward with intense determination—smiling only in rare instances. Other photos depict him gazing forlornly down at his typewriter.[72]

As Boisen's more severe acute illnesses manifested, he behaved in deeply disturbing ways. Carroll Wise, one of Boisen's early students, observed his descent into the abyss in 1930:

> During the short trip to the hospital, he was preoccupied. After we were settled in his office, he began talking. First, he wanted assurances that I would be loyal to him. He told me that I occupied a special place in the scheme of things. Then he unfolded a series of ideas we had heard him discuss before in relation to the case histories of patients. The world was facing a great catastrophe, but all was not lost. He revealed that he had a great part to play in restoring order. He was in line with the prophets, John Bunyan, George Fox, and Jesus. I was to be the son he never had. Then he repeated an idea he'd spoken of before. That sex was much more than an individual matter. It had social and cosmic significance. He felt he had failed greatly as he had not married, and he did not have a son. When he died, the Boisen name would go out of use as a famous name. He was the last, and his great failure was that he did not continue the family name. This had some relationship to his ideas of the "family of four." To bring harmony back into the world, I was to be his son. The clinical training movement would be

the agency through which we would work. This had all been revealed to him. This was followed by a story of great guilt and depression. He had committed what was to him the most abominable sin—masturbation. He deserved to be castrated. Self destructive fantasies came out strongly. I confess I got frightened. Boisen lived by himself in a rooming house in the city of Elgin. It was not difficult to visualize him performing a self-destructive act. It was not difficult to see him becoming violent toward others. He would be a hard man to handle, especially in a psychotic condition—What to do?[73]

Florid examples of Boisen in full psychosis have been used to exclude him from the mainstream of the profession he created as well as in justifying dismissive treatment of him personally. Edward Thornton, the first comprehensive historian of the clinical pastoral education movement, addressed "the fathers" of the movement: William Keller, who, in 1923, founded a short-lived clinical educational program that pre-dated Boisen's 1925 effort. Richard Cabot, who was instrumental in providing Boisen with the investigative and interviewing tools as well as the financial support and social contacts critical to getting the program off the ground. Last, and least (but too prominent to be overlooked entirely), was Boisen, who "must stand in the history of clinical pastoral education in a chapter by himself. In a sense this is symbolic of the way Boisen lived—essentially alone. . . . Boisen stands in history, as in life, somewhat apart, a problem to others as well as to himself." Thornton rhetorically asks if Boisen's entire program was little more than "a grand rationalization of a psychotic way of coping with life."[74]

Clinical pastoral education orthodoxy largely repeats the Thornton thesis of stigmatizing and dismissing its father. James Dittes compares Boisen to other autobiographers, such as Carl Jung, whom Dittes credits as writing "for others, to instruct them in what one has learned or wants to have learned, perhaps to offer oneself as a model, or perhaps as an advance scout." For Dittes, as with Thornton, Boisen fails the grade: "Jung welcomes and trusts the unconscious imagination; Boisen fears it. Jung celebrates mystery; Boisen strives for control. Jung has transcended his psychic turbulence by immersing himself fully into it; Boisen is a man still sadly trapped in his pathology because he has stayed alien to it."[75] Boisen's biographer, Robert Leas, mocks his love for Batchelder, stigmatizes her by proxy, and then reduces both to two-dimensional figures: "She represented a mysterious, mediumistic figure who never became a real person. Imagine, Boisen, the rigid, preoccupied, and distant personality on the one hand and Alice, the 'guardian angel,' the 'unreachable star,' the 'guiding hand of God' on the other—not a match made in heaven."[76]

Some of Boisen's students and acquaintances realized he would be denied a fair hearing in death as well as in life. The day after Boisen's death, Seward Hiltner, a prominent Boisen student and professor at the University of Chicago, went to the typewriter and committed twelve pages of remembrances of his mentor and friend. He admitted that Boisen could be a difficult personality, quoting Boisen's first boss at Worcester State Hospital regarding clinical pastoral education: "It must have had real strength,'... 'to get where it has with all the unattractive personalities who started it.' He meant Boisen.... where conviction was concerned, Boisen could set friendship aside." He was also capable of surprising charm aided by the very intense focus that at times contributed to his troubles: "I recall the first occasion when Boisen was in our home after my marriage. My wife had been hearing, ever since we met, of this great teacher of mine, with all the stories and folklore that had grown up about him. She would have been prepared, I think, if he had been gruff, or had sat all evening in a corner, or had given a lecture over dessert. When he left, she said spontaneously, 'He is charming,' and he was! He listened to her better than I have been able to before or since!" While it is possible that Hiltner is exaggerating Boisen's charms, he also points to the denigration critical colleagues treated him.[77]

Boisen was the prominent figure in the founding of clinical pastoral education and in the emergence of health-care chaplaincy as a profession unique and distinct from the parish—regardless of any effort to obfuscate those facts. He provoked visceral feelings, many of them negative, but, as Hiltner demonstrated, many positive as well. In 1968, only a few years following Boisen's death, Henri Nouwen, who devoted the bulk of his graduate study in psychology and theology as well as two unfinished doctoral dissertations to the study of Boisen's life and work, wrote wisely and presciently that "he was a forgotten man, by many remembered more because of his idiosyncrasies and schizoid personality than for his contributions in the field of the psychology of religion and pastoral psychology. But perhaps there is need for time and distance to be able to see the full stature of the man whose obvious weaknesses obstruct a clearer view of him."[78]

Within the institutional chaplaincy and clinical pastoral education world, Boisen gained a "folkloric" standing, to borrow Hiltner's phrase. Views on Boisen, however, are almost always filtered by how the viewer sees and experiences mental illness—a land that is, indeed, alien, perplexing, foreign, and frightening. Boisen's, repeated, sojourns in the "little-known country" of what we would probably call schizophrenia or schizoaffective disorder today brought him—and often those associated with him—the special stigma and shame often visited on the mentally ill.

Boisen, and his prodigious life work, cannot be understood apart from his experience of his mental illness. His illness was exemplified in intense focus to the extent of loss of context and perspective. As his ill episodes progressed, intense focus morphed into hyperactivity, hallucinations, and at times deeply bizarre and self-destructive behavior that required hospitalization. In the midst of his illnesses appeared "vilusions," such as the "family-of-four," the meaning of which he attempted to discern, if there was a meaning to be discerned, throughout his life.

As always, Boisen looked to Dante and his *Divine Comedy* as a parable in which to find meaning for his life both in illness as well as in health. Boisen had his "Beatrice(s)": First, Batchelder, and secondarily the brilliant Dante scholar Dunbar, who helped bring order, meaning, and peace to the chaos. Boisen experienced his illnesses as the inferno appointed for him before he could enter the paradise of revelation not just for himself but also for others who would visit their own little-known countries.

NOTES

1. Vacek, *Madness*, 168–69. In fact, Boisen was remarkably open about his struggles with mental illness from his early proposals for clinical education projects in the mid-1920s through his 1960 autobiography *Out of the Depths*.

2. John Harley Warner, "Ideals of Science and Their Discontents in Late-Nineteenth Century American Medicine," *Isis* 82, no. 3 (1991): 454–79, 460.

3. Bert Hansen, "America's First Medical Breakthrough: How Popular Excitement About a French Rabies Cure in 1885 Raised New Expectations for Medical Progress," *American Historical Review* 103, no. 2 (1998): 373–418; John E. Lesch, *The First Miracle Drugs: How the Sulfa Drugs Transformed Medicine* (New York, NY: Oxford University Press, 2007), 3–4. In 1932 Germany's I. G. Farben Company filed a patent application on a red dye that became the antibiotic drug Prontosil. Prontosil represented the first of sulfonamide antibiotics that provided "miracle" cures to a wide range of bacterial infections. The "therapeutic revolution" contributed "heavily to the opening of what was widely referred to as an era of miracle drugs, with its attendant optimism and raised expectations of medicine."

4. Anton T. Boisen, "A Project for the Investigation of the Religious Aspects of Certain Types of Mental Disorders" (Unpublished Manuscript, March 25, 1924), Series 2, Box 1, Folder 5, Boisen Papers, Chicago Theological Seminary. See also, Anton T. Boisen, "A Project for the Study of Certain Types of Mental Disorder from the Religious Standpoint" (Unpublished Manuscript, no date), Series 2, Box 1, Folder 1, Boisen Papers, Chicago Theological Seminary.

5. Boisen, however, realized he would need to strike a balance between claiming authority from his own experience of mental illness, "written by a patient, whose training had made him an impartial observer who was able to form critical judgments concerning the facts which he saw," and a self-indulgent exhibitionism that could "lay me open to the charge of still having a morbid interest in myself which is just as well to avoid." This balance of Boisen as experiencer opposed by the charge of researcher bias has featured prominently, both, in Boisen's advocates and critics in the decades

to follow. Boisen to Fred Eastman, November 12, 1922, Series 2, Box 3, Folder 27, Boisen Papers, Chicago Theological Seminary.

6. Paul Hoff, "The Kraepelinian Tradition," *Dialogues in Clinical Neuroscience* 17, no. 1 (2015): 36.

7. Bernard A. Fischer and William T. Carpenter, "Will the Kraepelinian Dichotomy Survive DSM-V?" *Neuropsychopharmacology* 34, no. 9 (2009): 2081–87; Nick Craddock and Michael J. Owen, "The Kraepelinian Dichotomy—Going, Going . . . But Still Not Gone," *The British Journal of Psychiatry* 196, no. 2 (2010): 92–95.

8. Robert Charles Powell, *Anton T. Boisen (1876–1965): Breaking an Opening in the Wall Between Religion and Medicine* (Buffalo, NY: Association of Mental Health Clergy, 1976), 8, fn. 45; Powell, "Whatever Happened to 'CPE,'" March 18, 1999. Powell references Dr. Milton H. Erickson, who treated Boisen in 1930 and remained his personal confidant in Boisen's later years. Powell also cites observations offered by psychiatrists David Shakow and Paul Pruyser and chaplain Carroll Wise.

9. Carol North and William M. Clements, "The Psychiatric Diagnosis of Anton Boisen: From Schizophrenia to Bipolar Affective Disorder," *The Journal of Pastoral Care* 35, no. 4 (1981): 264–75.

10. Curtis W. Hart, "Notes on the Psychiatric Diagnosis of Anton Boisen," *Journal of Religion and Health* 40, no. 4 (2001): 423–29.

11. *Statistical Manual for the Use of Institutions for the Insane* (New York, NY: American Medico-Psychological Association and National Committee for Mental Hygiene, 1918), 24.

12. *Desk Reference to the Diagnostic Criteria from DSM-5* (Washington, DC: American Psychiatric Association, 2013), 63.

13. Boisen, *Out of the Depths*, 9, 100–1, 107, 112–14. In his letter to Norman Nash, Boisen quotes from Dante Alighieri's *Divine Comedy*, which Boisen appears to have viewed as a template for his own experience of illness and revelation. The *Divine Comedy* is also an interest he held in common with his first clinical student, Helen Flanders Dunbar.

14. In 1906, the Rev. Dr. Elwood Worcester founded the "Emmanuel Movement" at Emmanuel Episcopal Church in Boston, Massachusetts. The Emmanuel Movement influenced Boisen's programs as well as other spirituality-based healing movements, such as Alcoholics Anonymous. Worcester was a unique figure at the turn of the century in traveling to Germany for cutting-edge training in psychology. See Allison Stokes, *Ministry After Freud* (New York, NY: The Pilgrim Press, 1985), 17–36.

15. Boisen to Ellwood Worcester, December 11, 1921, Box 1a, Folders 9, 10, Boisen Papers, Chicago Theological Seminary.

16. Boisen hints at an, almost monastic, asceticism that was foreign both to the evangelical Protestantism of his youth and even more so to the liberal Protestantism and clinical pastoral education movement of his mature years. Boisen, in his 1952 interview with Francis McPeek, affirmed that he neither drank nor smoked; he ate "what was put before him" and gave little thought to physical pleasure. Most of his modest income he gave to his project and to fund his students' work. Anton T.

Boisen, Interview by Francis McPeek, 1952, Audio Recording, ACPE Papers, Emory University, Decatur, GA.

17. Boisen to Fred Eastman, in "A Portion of the Case Record" (Unpublished Manuscript, no date), Box 1a, Folder 13, Boisen Papers, Chicago Theological Seminary.

18. Boisen and Bryan's friendship and correspondence continued for decades to follow. In 1949 Bryan writing, "I have in you one of the most loyal friends." William Lowe Bryan to Boisen, January 8, 1949, Series 2, Box 2, Folder 7, Boisen Papers, Chicago Theological Seminary. Boisen also dedicated his 1960 autobiography *Out of the Depths* to the memory of his "teacher and friend."

19. Boisen, *Out of the Depths*, 46–47.

20. Sex and sexuality and the impetus to "tell" were critical to Boisen's experience of mental illness, and his quest for healing he hoped would aid him and others. In the 1950s as Boisen worked on his autobiography—he consulted old friends. He commented to Fred Eastman:

> What does disturb me is your impression that my treatment of the masturbation problem is likely to be disturbing and that I seem to treat it as a deep dark secret. This troubles me especially because I cannot leave it out, as you suggest and be true to the facts in the case. . . . Most of the work on the Kinzie Report was done in Wylie Hall at Indiana University, the building which was named for our family (on Boisen's maternal side). . . . I am reminded that two major turning points in my life had to do with the handling of the sex problem and that in both cases the solution came in the prompting "Do not be afraid to tell." What puzzles me is what there is in my treatment of the problem which leaves the impression that I am emotional about it. Is it that I have not used the word "masturbation"? If that is the case, my reply would be that I did so in the interest of accuracy. The word "masturbation" is used rather loosely. I wanted to distinguish between phantasy [*sic*] and physical manipulation as factors, also between actual orgasm and erotic excitation.

The day after writing to Eastman, Boisen consulted Helen Flanders Dunbar, who suggested Boisen's autobiography and his study of sex and sexuality in the first place. Regarding the issues he wrote to Eastman, Boisen confided, "It is often painfully personal. My sister, when I showed it to her, was horrified. On the other hand, am I not in the position of one who has returned from an exploring expedition in a little-known but important region, and am I not under obligation to report on what I have found?" He also noted to Dunbar, "I was somewhat startled to learn that the Kinzie Report had been fabricated in Wylie Hall . . ., the building named after my [maternal] grandfather, I have often wondered what he would have thought about it, but my feeling is that he would have approved." Boisen to Fred Eastman, March 26, 1957, Box 3, Boisen Papers, Chicago Theological Seminary; Boisen to Helen F. Dunbar, March 27, 1957, Box 1a, Folder 7, Boisen Papers, Chicago Theological Seminary. Seward Hiltner, professor at University of Chicago Divinity School and Princeton Theological Seminary and one of Boisen's earliest students, engaged Kinsey regarding his work. Like Boisen, he essayed an appreciative critique of Kinsey's work and engaged Kinsey in collegial and respectful correspondence and expressed a perspective consistent with that of his former mentor. R. Marie Griffith writes, "Hiltner voiced his agreement with certain values expressed in the [Kinsey] report, such as 'reducing hypocrisy, trying to eliminate any unnecessary suffering, and the like,' but disagreed with other principles embedded in it, such as the presumption that human beings were wholly like other animals in their sexual appetites or 'that what exists must therefore be so important that it is in some measure what ought to be.'" R. Marie Griffith, "The Religious Encounters of Alfred C. Kinsey," *The Journal of American History* 95, no. 2 (2008): 349–77, 357.

21. Boisen, *Out of the Depths*, 77–78.
22. Boisen, *Out of the Depths*, 79.
23. Anton Boisen, A Statement of Belief, in "A Portion of the Case Record" (Unpublished Manuscript, no date), Box 1a, Folder 9, Boisen Papers, Chicago Theological Seminary.
24. Boisen to Fred Eastman, August 28, 1921, in "A Portion of the Case Record" (Unpublished Manuscript, no date), Box 1a, Folder 9, Boisen Papers, Chicago Theological Seminary.
25. Fred Eastman to Boisen, December 4, 1935, Series 2, Box 3, Folder 29, Boisen Papers, Chicago Theological Seminary.
26. Carroll Wise also gives additional hints regarding matters troubling Boisen. In the summer of 1930 Boisen supervised an abnormally large group of students "about 15 or 16, which by today's standards would be completely unheard of. He had a couple of people in the group, particularly one woman, who gave him no end of trouble and he didn't know how to handle her . . . [regarding Boisen's personal and emotional turmoil] . . . the students knew nothing about [it], but we knew something was happening." Interview with John Thomas, Carroll Wise, Al Sherve, no date, Audio Recording, ACPE Papers, Emory University, Decatur, GA.
27. Powell, *Anton T. Boisen*, 6–7; Boisen, *Out of the Depths*, 209.
28. Boisen, *Out of the Depths*, 52.
29. Alice Batchelder to Boisen, July 30, 1920, Box 1a, Folder 4, Boisen Papers, Chicago Theological Seminary.
30. Alice Batchelder to Boisen, November 29, 1930, Box 1a, Folder 4, Boisen Papers, Chicago Theological Seminary.
31. Alice Batchelder to Boisen, November 19, 1928, Box 1a, Folders 4, Boisen Papers, Chicago Theological Seminary.
32. Paul Batchelder to Boisen, June 24, 1937, Series 2, Box 7, Folder 72, Boisen Papers, Chicago Theological Seminary.
33. Boisen to Paul Batchelder, August 13, 1956, Paul Batchelder to Boisen, November 25, 1961, Series 2, Box 7, Folder 72, Boisen Papers, Chicago Theological Seminary. Paul Batchelder and Boisen's relationship displayed mutual esteem and respect in spite of significant personal and philosophical differences. Batchelder writing in response to reading Boisen's autobiography: "Naturally, I do not agree with all of the conclusions which you draw from your work and your personal experiences; you look at the world from the standpoint of a social scientist and a Christian, while my viewpoint is that of a physical scientist and a materialist, unable to believe in an 'intelligence beyond our own' or in a future life beyond the grave." Paul Batchelder to Boisen, October 2, 1960, Series 8, Box 2, Folder 61, Boisen Papers, Chicago Theological Seminary.

34. Paul Batchelder to Boisen, August 28, 1956, Series 2, Box 7, Folder 72, Boisen Papers, Chicago Theological Seminary.

35. Robert Charles Powell, *Healing and Wholeness: Helen Flanders Dunbar (1902–1959) and an Extra-Medical Origin of the American Psychosomatic Movement, 1906–36* (Ph.D. Diss., Duke University, 1974), 79.

36. Boisen, *Out of the Depths*, 154–55.

37. Boisen, "A Portion of the Case Record" (Unpublished Manuscript, no date), 127d, Box 1a, Folder 13, Boisen Papers, Chicago Theological Seminary.

38. Boisen, "A Portion of the Case Record" (Unpublished Manuscript, no date), 130, Box 1a, Folder 13, Boisen Papers, Chicago Theological Seminary. In editing *Out of the Depths*, Boisen expressed reluctance to identify Dunbar as the "other woman" in his life. He wrote his editor Eugene Exman:

> I have assumed that we could not avoid recognizing that such a person was involved in my break-down of 1930. I have assumed furthermore that her identity would be known to anyone who was at Worcester in that period. . . . I think, that about the only change I have made is to recognize that [sic] fact that Dr. Dunbar was a very important factor in the beginnings of the clinical training movement and in my own life, instead of barely mentioning her. I believe I have also made it clear that there was nothing in our relationship which needs to be concealed.

Boisen to Eugene Exman, March 24, 1960, Series 8, Box 2, Folder 59, Boisen Papers, Chicago Theological Seminary.

39. Boisen, "A Portion of the Case Record" (Unpublished Manuscript, no date), 130a, Box 1a, Folder 13, Boisen Papers, Chicago Theological Seminary.

40. Boisen, "A Portion of the Case Record" (Unpublished Manuscript, no date), 130c, Box 1a, Folder 13, Boisen Papers, Chicago Theological Seminary.

41. Boisen, "Portion of the Case Record" (Unpublished Manuscript, no date), 130d, Box 1a, Folder 13, Boisen Papers, Chicago Theological Seminary.

42. Boisen, "A Portion of the Case Record" (Unpublished Manuscript, no date), 132a, Box 1a, Folder 13, Boisen Papers, Chicago Theological Seminary.

43. Boisen to Alice Batchelder, 1930, in "A Portion of the Case Record" (Unpublished Manuscript, no date), 132a, Box 1a, Folder 13, Boisen Papers, Chicago Theological Seminary.

44. Alice Batchelder to Boisen, October 22, 1930, in "A Portion of the Case Record" (Unpublished Manuscript, no date), 132d, Box 1a, Folder 13, Boisen Papers, Chicago Theological Seminary.

45. Boisen, *Out of the Depths*, 169–70. Boisen's project in clinical pastoral education started modestly at Worcester State Hospital in 1925 with four students; two finished the summer course, Dunbar being one of the two. By 1930, Boisen's project experienced explosive growth, Boisen's center in Worcester alone having educated thirty-five students. Several of Boisen's early students, such as Donald Beatty, Carroll Wise and Philip Guiles, quickly moved on to found new clinical training centers in New England and the Mid-Atlantic. Robert D. Leas, *Anton Theophilus Boisen: His Life, Work, Impact, and Theological Legacy* (Macon, GA: Journal of Pastoral Care Publications, Inc., 2009), 104–5.

46. Leas, *Anton Theophilus Boisen*, 104–5.

47. Dr. Richard Clarke Cabot was a prominent, and socially connected, physician in private practice and affiliated with Massachusetts General Hospital and Harvard University. Cabot's deep-and-wide influence in the medical profession included his foundational work in hospital social work and in backing clinical pastoral education. Cabot provided Boisen with training as well as financial backing and social contacts critical to getting his project off the ground. Cabot and Boisen, however, disagreed on the treatability of mental disorders. Boisen held an optimistic prognosis for the potential amelioration, or even cure, of "functional" mental illnesses. While Cabot, in Allison Stokes' words, "support[ed] his work with the mentally ill. . . . he did not feel 'that a religious worker could do anything beyond giving comfort and consolation.'" While Cabot reflected the pessimism of his day, it also reflected personal, painful, experience with one "of his brothers [who] from the age of eighteen had recurrent attacks of manic-depressive psychosis, and Cabot was sure that this was of chemical origin." Stokes, *Ministry After Freud*, 48–51; Christopher Crenner, *Private Practice: In the Early Twentieth-Century Medical Office of Dr. Richard Cabot* (Baltimore, MD: The Johns Hopkins University Press, 2005).

48. Guiles was an early student of Boisen, having done clinical education with him in summer 1928. By 1930 he sided with Cabot in advocating Boisen's removal. The Boisen controversy quickly mutated into a complex of controversies that splintered Boisen's original Council for the Clinical Training of Theological Students into factions that pitted Dunbar and the New York-based Council for Clinical Training (CCT) against Cabot and Guiles' Institute for Pastoral Care (IPC). The difference between the two groups largely revolved around strong personalities behind them. CCT moved in a more psychoanalytic direction and tended to be more favorable to Boisen's early proposal to develop career chaplains in institutional, especially state hospital, settings. IPC focused on ministry in general hospitals, cooperative efforts with seminaries, and in training future parish clergy in practical pastoral skills. By 1932, Boisen resumed his work in clinical education and research at Elgin State Hospital in Illinois, founding the Chicago Council for the Clinical Training of Theological Students. Only in 1968 did the various clinical education tribes merge into a single Association for Clinical Pastoral Education. Edward E. Thornton, *Professional Education for Ministry: A History of Clinical Pastoral Education* (Nashville, TN: Abingdon Press, 1970), 46, 52, 58, 76–83, 181.

49. As Guiles and Cabot moved to oust Boisen from his own training program, Dunbar, CCTTS's medical director, in Powell's words, "beginning in early 1931 progressively seized control of the counsel on Boisen's behalf." What is not clear is whether she was doing this, at least solely, "on Boisen's behalf" or Dunbar, an ambitious and capable professional in her own right—was doing this for herself. As Guiles later opined, "Cabot despises Dunbar partly because she has outsmarted him on most occasions." Powell, *Anton T. Boisen*, 18, 35, fn. 149. Guiles also noted Boisen's "relationship of an emotional nature" toward Dunbar, "which had a marked influence on the recurrence of mental illness in the fall 1930" and fed some of the drama behind early clinical pastoral education. Powell, *Anton T. Boisen*, 35, fn. 139.

50. Leas, *Anton Theophilus Boisen*, 130. Carroll Wise attested to Dunbar's visits with Boisen during his 1930 hospitalization as salutary toward recovery: "She would come up from New York to visit him and they would have talks, I, of course know nothing about what went on in these talks, but Boisen commenced to improve after she had been up there a couple of times." Interview with John Thomas, Carroll Wise, and Al Shervy, no date, Audio Recording, ACPE Papers, Emory University, Decatur, GA.

51. Boisen to Helen F. Dunbar, September 26, 1950, Box 1a, Folder 7, Boisen Papers, Chicago Theological Seminary.

Boisen to Helen F. Dunbar, March 18, 1958, Box 1a, Folder 7, Boisen Papers, Chicago Theological Seminary. Boisen is referring to the "pet" name, "Theophilus," Boisen's middle name, by which Dunbar referred to him. Powell, *Anton T. Boisen*, 13.

52. Boisen, *Out of the Depths*, 168.

53. Anton T. Boisen to Marie Boisen, July 22, 1922, Box 1, Folder 12, Boisen Papers, Chicago Theological Seminary.

54. Boisen to Helen F. Dunbar, March 18, 1958, Box 1a, Folder 7, Boisen Papers, Chicago Theological Seminary.

55. Boisen, *Out of the Depths*, 176–77.

56. Boisen, *Out of the Depths*, 176–77.

57. Boisen, *Out of the Depths*, 204, 207.

58. Boisen, *Out of the Depths*, 79–81.

59. Boisen, *Out of the Depths*, 81–82.

60. Boisen, *Out of the Depths*, 206.

61. Boisen, *Out of the Depths*, 207–8.

62. Powell, *Anton T. Boisen*, 17.

63. Richard Coble, "Maneuvers in the Depths: The Politics of Identity in Anton Boisen's Pastoral Care," *Pastoral Psychology* 63 (2014): 409–10.

64. Powell, "Whatever Happened to 'CPE,'" March 18, 1999.

65. Stephen P. Hinshaw, *The Mark of Shame: Stigma of Mental Illness and an Agenda for Change* (New York, NY: Oxford University Press, 2007), xi.

66. W. E. Lang to Fred Eastman, December 30, 1920, in *Out of the Depths*, p. 109.

67. Bloomingdale Hospital in White Plains, NY. Boisen, *Out of the Depths*, 107.

68. Fred Eastman to Boisen, January 7, 1921, Box 1a, Folder 10, Boisen Papers, Chicago Theological Seminary.

69. Fred Eastman to Boisen, August 20, 1921, Box 1a, Folder 10, Boisen Papers, Chicago Theological Seminary.

70. Boisen, *Out of the Depths*, 128–33.

71. Paul Pruyser to Henri Nouwen, August 15, 1967, Box 290, File 333, Henri Nouwen Papers, John M. Kelly Library, University of St. Michael's College, Toronto, ON.

72. "Clinical Experience for Theological Students, Worcester State Hospital, 1928," Series 2, Box 2, Folder 2, Boisen Papers, Chicago Theological Seminary; "The Hospital Pictorial, Elgin State Hospital," August 31, 1933, Boisen Papers, Kansas Historical Society, Topeka, KS.

73. Leas, *Anton Theophilus Boisen*, 128–29.

74. Thornton, *Professional Education for Ministry*, 54–55.

75. James E. Dittes, "Boisen as Autobiographer," in *Turning Points in Pastoral Care: The Legacy of Anton Boisen and Seward Hiltner*, eds. Leroy Aden and J. Harold Ellens (Grand Rapids, MI: Baker Book House, 1990), 228–29.

76. Robert Leas, "The Biography of Anton Theophilus Boisen," *ACPE: Association for Clinical Pastoral Education, Inc.*, Last accessed September 30, 2018, www.acpe.edu/pdf/History/The%20Biography%20of%20Anton%20Theophilus%20Boisen.pdf.

77. Seward Hiltner, "The Heritage of Anton T. Boisen" (Unpublished Manuscript, October 2, 1965), Boisen Papers, Kansas Historical Society, Topeka, KS.

78. Henri J. M. Nouwen, "Anton T. Boisen and Theology Through Living Human Documents," *Pastoral Psychology* 19, no. 186 (1968): 63

Chapter 2

Searching for Meaning in the Madness

MEANING IN THE MADNESS

Attention to Boisen's illnesses has often obscured his vivid spiritual experiences. He encountered a plane of experience that he credited for giving him insight he did not previously have. Boisen experienced "abnormal condition[s], . . . Each one of these has marked a turning-point in my life and, along with abnormal and pathological elements which I have always recognized, it has brought me what I have regarded as most sacred and most authoritative."[1] Understanding Boisen as he would be understood starts with his experiences first of all and then proceeds to consider what, if any, elements of that experience give insight and what, if any, elements of that experience were "pathological."

Ann Taves revisits William James' study of religious experience. James' work in religion and psychology deeply influenced Boisen's views on spirituality and religion. James', and Boisen's, interest in religious experiential phenomena have tended to fall into disfavor during the last several decades. Taves credits James for examining religious experience within a larger psychological and cultural framework and not isolating it *sui genaris*, immune to a larger context. James did not reduce religion to psychology alone, "explain[ing] religious experience in psychological terms, while at the same time leaving open the possibility that it pointed to something more."[2] Taves' approach urges us to examine Boisen's experiences, and "other special things" as experiences that may be "deemed religious," and such individual and idiosyncratic events may even coalesce "as building blocks to create more complex formations . . . we typically refer to as 'religions' or 'spiritualities.'"[3]

Boisen's "special things" created neither a new religion nor a new spirituality—unless you regard clinical pastoral education as a "religion"—but his experiences were certainly special to him. His experiences were motivating enough to him, and others, to drive Boisen's life's work as well as the work of those who followed after him. In order for, at least some of, Boisen's experiences to be accepted as "special" and not dismissed as mere sickness, he would need to find people ready to accept them as such. Elwood Worcester was willing to search for meaning even amid madness.

The Rev. Dr. Elwood Worcester was an innovator and experiencer in his own right. He combined an innovative professional method in his own church-based work in psychiatric practice, with an unorthodox background and education. Worcester's own peculiar and profound experience with "special things," in Allison Stokes' words, "demanded that he work out a technique of his own."[4] Worcester wrote in his autobiography, "Fate denied to me boyhood and youth" and provided "a revelation which I could not deny or dishonor." He meditated on the words of Lao-Tzu: "My religion is to think the unthinkable thought, to speak the ineffable word, to do the impossible deed, and to walk the impassable way."[5]

His first "special thing" occurred at age six with the death of a beloved aunt and an imagination fired by a mischievous sibling:

> I pitied her profoundly because she was so still and unable to move and because she had been placed in a hideous, box-like bed. I was permitted to kiss her, and I can still feel the imprint of her cold, stiff lips against mine. I asked my sister Mary, what would happen to her and she told me that a hole had been dug in the ground in which she would lie forever and ever, and worms would feast on her. This gave me a sense of the horror and of the dreadfulness of life exposed to such vicissitudes, of which I never spoke, but which haunted me for years.[6]

Memories of this early, and intimate, experience with death:

> Followed me into my sleep and gave me nightmares, or rather a recurrent nightmare. For more than a year I dreamed from time to time that I saw bright flashes of light which terrified me because I knew what they presaged. In a few minutes a horde of robust, fat little devils, flitting on wings like bats and shining in their own light, would burst into my room and would disport themselves as they darted about. . . .Soon they discovered me cowering under the bedclothes and they would haul me out and begin to cuff and buffet me. . . .The fact that the scene of these nocturnal terrors was always Aunt Lizzie's house, not our own home, now indicates to me that they arose from my sight of her dead body.[7]

Worcester retained a lifelong interest and fascination with psychology and parapsychology and the ongoing relationship of the living with the dead. In the final chapter of *Life's Adventure*, "Psychic Research," Worcester confessed, "this is the chapter of my life which will encounter the most opposition and inspire the least sympathy."[8] Worcester wanted to determine if a connection between the living and the dead could be scientifically proven. For example, he facilitated a séance in an effort to connect Boisen with his departed father.[9] While Boisen participated in the experiment and late in life confessed an experience he could not explain, he shied away from the psychic and occult, which he found chaotic and unsettling. Boisen recollected on his séance experience:

> Did I myself actually hear those raps in Dr. Worcester's study? I think I can say yes. What I do remember is that I expressed a reluctance to become involved in the spiritistic phenomena in which Dr. Worcester believed so strongly and that in my subsequent conferences with him there were no other such manifestations. My attitude at that time was undoubtedly determined by my encounter with the "Unseen Guest" [a now obscure occult book] at Westboro. My present attitude with regard to spiritism is that religion pre-supposes the existence of a spiritual world and the survival of the personality, but I do not believe in attempts to communicate with miscellaneous disincarnate spirits. Such phenomena are unwholesome in that they make for a disorganized universe. The genius of the Christian religion may be found in the fact that prayer is directed to God in the name of Christ. This makes for an organized universe.[10]

Boisen found Worcester's peculiar technique of interacting with the dead unsettling and he did not pursue it further. Worcester's interaction with "special things" did not cease with his aunt's death. Litigation over her property, economic downturn, and his father's inability to liquidate business holdings wiped out the Worcester family fortune. Mounting health issues sapped the elder Worcester's previously robust ability to rebound from setback.[11] Worcester's father died when Worcester was seventeen. His mother began to lose her eyesight to glaucoma and a botched eye surgery "enduring so much pain that she was obliged to withdraw herself largely from us."[12] Worcester's sister, Mary, stepped into the breach; "always the leader," she responded effectively and inspiringly to catastrophe. Led by his sister, "a strange religious awakening had come to all the members of our family." Mary "became gentler, more spiritual, more beautiful, and she spent much time in solitary prayer." She often absented herself from home "until a late hour of the night." When Worcester went out to search for her, she was found "usually in some poor home, nursing the sick, watching beside some dying person, or praying with a group of poor people. . . . I idolized her."[13]

Worcester took on employment to aid his now destitute family: "I was sitting alone, filled with sad thoughts, eating my dinner out of a tin pail. . . . Suddenly, the yellow wall opposite me seemed strangely to brighten, and I knew that something was happening. . . . Much mystified, I returned to my dinner and in a few minutes, the phenomenon of light returned. This time it was accompanied by an audible voice and I plainly heard these words, 'Be faithful to me and I will be faithful to you.'"[14] Boisen was not alone in his experiences of the special; he drew on those who guided him as his guides drew on those who came before them.

Worcester went to college and pursued ordained ministry, but he pursued this goal via a technique of his own. Graduating from Columbia in 1886, Worcester longed to study in Germany, "to study under the greatest living teachers, and to devote myself to subjects—the Bible, philosophy, psychology—which even then I divined would be of most value to me in my future work." Before going to Germany, however, his bishop insisted he attend an approved Episcopal seminary in the United States to prepare for ordination. He acquiesced but proceeded on his own terms. Worcester studied for, and to the surprise and dismay of his professors and ecclesiastical superiors, tested out of, the first two years of the three-year seminary curriculum. After one year at General Theological Seminary in New York, Worcester, holding his bishop to his promise, received ordination and left for Germany.[15]

At the University of Leipzig, the Reverend Worcester studied the burgeoning field of psychiatry with leading lights in the field: Franz Delitzsch, Wilhelm Wundt, and Gustav Fechner. In 1889, he returned to America with his doctorate in hand.[16] After a long incubation, Worcester's vision came to fruition at Emmanuel Episcopal Church in Boston. In 1906, Worcester founded a clinic at the church dedicated to treating "assorted forms of 'nervousness' including alcoholism and other addictions."[17] Among Worcester's patients, Courtenay Baylor and Richard Peabody were treated, with varied success, for addiction and mental illness. Worcester entrusted many of these patients, in turn, to counsel others suffering like maladies.[18]

Recalling his first hospitalization at Westboro Boisen stated, "Most of the doctors, I think, are not religious men. Many of them regard religion as a superstition which is responsible for many of the ills they have to treat. Such men are not fitted to deal with religious problems. If they succeed in their aims, the patient is shorn of the faith in which lies his hope of cure."[19] In Elwood Worcester, Boisen met a critical person at a critical time; according to Robert Powell, Worcester was an "anchor—in that he believed in Boisen at a vulnerable time when almost no one else did."[20]

Numbering among Freud's forerunners, Worcester was an early adopter, if not a pioneer, of views departing from Kraepelinian orthodoxy that mental illness, and especially of the dementia praecox/schizophrenia spectrum, need not necessarily be permanent and organic conditions. Worcester's training and personal spiritual experiences and inclinations rendered him ready "to take Boisen himself entirely seriously, delusions and all."[21] Boisen's situation in late November 1921 was not encouraging. At that point he had been an inpatient at Westboro State Hospital for about a year and had suffered several relapses.[22] Boisen wrote for his unpublished case record that "the judgement of my family and of the friend [Fred Eastman] with whom I was in closest touch that I should remain in the institution for the rest of my days."[23]

Boisen knew of Worcester's Emmanuel Clinic in nearby Boston and suggested a consultation to his legal custodians: "the matter was taken up with Dr. Worcester . . . and my family agreed to abide by his judgement. Dr. Worcester stipulated that he must be given the full facts in the case. My mother and I therefore made formal request to the superintendent that Dr. Worcester should have access to the facts." While superintendent William Lang was unable to release Boisen's record due to confidentiality issues, Boisen recalls that "the superintendent was liberal in making possible the necessary conferences and they put no obstacles in the way of my plans."[24]

Boisen commenced his "interviews" with Worcester in early November 1921, which continued into summer 1922. The two remained in cordial professional and personal contact for the remainder of Worcester's life. Memorializing their first meeting, Boisen wrote: "many patients . . . have no physical trouble. They are just sick of soul. Now to the physicians here anything in the nature of automatisms, any 'voices,' any visions, even a belief in providence or divine guidance is *per se* evidence of insanity and justifies commitment. . . . Saul of Tarsus and George Fox would fare badly before a present-day psychiatric staff. Certainly, they exhibited phenomena of abnormality. But with them the abnormality was a source of power and strength."[25] Worcester viewed Boisen's case favorably and Boisen left inpatient care in early 1922. Boisen promptly enrolled at Harvard "to discover the interrelationship between mental disorder and religious experience."[26]

EXPERIENCE IN CONTEXT

In Elwood Worcester, Boisen found someone who believed in him, anchored him, and took him seriously. While Boisen's many vilusions contained, as Boisen readily admitted, delusion, many of his visions contained insight. Worcester was especially inclined to listen to Boisen and take his peculiar experiences seriously, having had like experiences himself. Boisen's vilusions, however, occurred within a larger life and cultural context. To better understand Boisen's vilusions, it is important to look to those who went before him and accompanied him. Worcester was one such experiencer. William James and George Coe's studies of religious experience provide insight into Boisen's vilusions. Boisen's life, times, and historical context are also important to consider as is James George Frazer's work on religion and the modernist-fundamentalist debate that raged within Boisen's variety of Protestant Christianity. Conflict between science and religion drove controversy surrounding Charles Darwin's *Origin of Species* in 1859 through the Scopes Trial of 1925—a courtroom extravaganza that coincided with Boisen's pioneering unit of clinical education at Worcester State Hospital.

Ann Taves points to William James' explicit influence on Boisen's life, work, and self-understanding. Both Boisen and James were scholars born and bred into the values of the classical liberal arts of the Victorian era. Boisen's family members, on the maternal side, were among the founders of Indiana University. His mother, Elizabeth Louisa Wylie, was one of the first women to graduate from Indiana and briefly taught art at the University of Missouri. His father, Hermann, German-born and educated, taught modern language.[27] Like James, Boisen was learned in the classics, in Latin and Greek, comfortable in moving freely among many areas of knowledge and expertise. Both were comfortable "where philosophy and psychology still mingled."[28] Boisen became increasingly a quaint anomaly as the twentieth century marched toward ever-narrowing specialization.

Boisen and James' commonalities extended beyond the academic, professional, and intellectual. Personal experiences and struggles that fueled the quest for understanding also paralleled. Like Boisen, James encountered his own "little-known country" of mental illness and transformed that experience to purpose, learning, and service. Daniel Pals writes, from "1867 to 1872, both during and after his medical studies, James wrestled with recurring, serious attacks of mental depression. As recounted in his letters, he became at moments even suicidal." Following years of drift, vocational uncertainty, and distaste for clinical practice as a physician, he obtained a teaching position. He also found his own "guiding hand," marrying "Alice Gibbens, a girls' schoolteacher . . . her even temper and exceptional patience brought happiness, stability, and children into his personal life. [James'] physical ailments did not disappear, nor did occasional further bouts with depression, but both became more moderate and manageable as the years moved on." James embarked on a long and prestigious career at Harvard, as a towering figure in his classic *The Varieties of Religious Experience*, and as a cofounder of pragmatism, often credited as a uniquely American contribution to philosophy and the understanding of religious experience.[29] James, along with Worcester, provides a pattern, an archetype, for Boisen as an experiencer and how to judge and channel experience.

James' influence on Boisen was explicit and deep—having presented and published papers on James' ongoing influence on, and significance for, the psychology and spirituality.[30] Boisen's themes and topics of study closely paralleled James'. Boisen took up many of James' historical examples of religious experiencers in his own works: George Fox, St. Paul, Ignatius Loyola,

Martin Luther, John Bunyan, and Augustine of Hippo feature prominently in James' *Varieties* and appear repeatedly in Boisen's many books and articles. Both Boisen and James invested themselves in "the prophet appearing as a mere lonely madman."[31]

Many of James' experiencers experienced "visions, voices, rapt conditions, guiding impressions, and 'openings,'" and James admits to "the psychopathic temperament in religious biography" of the subjects that interested him. James, however, did not equate all "rapt conditions" as positive experiences to be hailed and promoted.[32] James alludes to "delusional insanity, paranoia" as examples of "diabolical mysticism" which "spring[s] from the same mental level . . . 'seraph and snake' abide there side by side." "To come from thence is no infallible credential. What comes must be sifted and tested, and run the gauntlet of confrontation with the total context of experience, . . . Its value must be ascertained by empirical methods, . . . Once more, then, I repeat that non-mystics are under no obligation to acknowledge in mystical states a superior authority conferred on them by their intrinsic nature."[33] For James, the pragmatist, religious, and spiritual experience cannot be trusted as self-authenticating by the experience alone but rather tested against the practicalities of life lived and the practical results of the experiencer having had the experience and how that experience goes on to change the life of that person and other persons.[34]

Although Boisen did not study with James, he did study with who could be considered the next best thing. During his second year at Union Seminary, George Coe, a "thoroughly Jamesian psychologist of religion," joined the faculty. Coe combined an interest in religious experience and mysticism with a drive toward examining those experiences against empirical and practical observation. While at Union, Boisen enrolled in all the courses Coe offered, "as well as in his seminars on mysticism, religious experience, and scientific methods."[35] Coe became another lifelong friend and acquaintance of Boisen. Coe was personally and professionally uncomfortable with mental illness, subscribing to the generally prevailing physiological view of it. While Coe was explicit with his professional and even personal views in his correspondence with Boisen, Boisen consistently credited Coe as a steadfast supporter of his work.[36]

James and Coe, however, had significant differences. Those differences manifested themselves in Boisen's work. James was enthusiastic about the experiential, whereas Coe was not and viewed mental illness as outside his purview. Coe and James also differed in their evaluations of the pragmatic results of mysticism. Taves explains, "Coe's chief complaint against mysticism was that it was socially conservative. Thus, ironically, one of the basic disagreements between Coe and James was rooted in their assessment of the 'fruits' of mysticism. Where James judged religious experiences of this sort in terms of their ability to unify a divided self, Coe judged them in terms of their ability to promote social change."[37] Boisen's own interpretation of spiritual and mystical experience began with an individualist focus, which tended to hold his attention in the 1920s as his own personal experience was fresh. Later in his career, in the 1940s and 1950s, Boisen's attention moved toward sociology regarding the results of religious, spiritual, mystical experience especially in light of World War and the peril of nuclear annihilation during the early Cold War.

Viewing "mysticism" as an "unprecise and inconsistent" category, Coe quips that "psychologists feel free to use the term mysticism in any sense that suits their incidental purposes." Coe's "science" of mysticism influenced Boisen and how he would see himself as practicing "science." Trying to bring greater clarity where confusion reigned, Coe developed a rudimentary taxonomy of mysticism, "A Survey of the Mystical," that resembled Kraepelin's attempt to make a taxonomy of mental illness. Coe, for example, distinguished between mysticism as "experience" versus "deliberate practice" versus its "supposed source or content." He also distinguished between theistic, pantheistic, spiritist mysticisms and efforts toward mystical experience that could work on a spectrum from total and permanent absorption in the experience to mystical states directed toward limited durations and ends.[38]

Boisen's interests and experiences coincided with those of Worcester, Coe, and James. Boisen lived against a backdrop of growing and increasingly dramatized enmity between science and religion. The controversy over evolution tore Boisen's brand of evangelical Protestantism into warring camps of modernists and fundamentalists—inaugurating a cultural war that challenges American society to the present. While modernists, generally, favored a conciliation with Charles Darwin's evolution and cooperation with the scientific method, fundamentalists, generally, clung to a more literal interpretation of the words of the Hebrew and Christian scriptures.

Edward Larson insightfully observes that the modernist/fundamentalist debate often related to issues entirely outside interpretations of scriptural texts: "Many Americans associated Darwinian natural selection, as it applied to people, with a survival-of-the-fittest mentality." William Jennings Bryan, three-time presidential candidate, secretary of state, and a major figure on the "fundamentalist" side of the Scopes trial, condemned it as "the merciless law by which the strong crowd out and kill off the weak."[39] While the debate over evolution was at least as much a debate over social relationships in the present, the debate over Darwin smoldered from its beginnings in the 1860s and progressed to the point in the 1920s where "middle ground did exist . . . but gained little attention in the public debate." You are either for science or you are for religion—even though many Americans, in practice, were for both.[40]

Boisen's formative experiences pointed to a middle ground and a "both/ and" approach to science and religion. The Boisen and Wylie families bridged church and academy, modernist and fundamentalist:

> The faith of my fathers was, for me, at one with the authority of science. In the warfare between science and religion which waged so furiously during the later nineteenth century, my grandfather may have been on the conservative side. If so, he made no issue of it. I know that he accepted the scientific account of the age of the earth. I do not know his attitude on the theory of evolution. My father, ... joined the Congregational church and on that occasion he wrote out a statement of belief which shows that he was a thoroughgoing liberal.[41]

Boisen experienced, from an early age, his family striving to reconcile equal imperatives that others said could not be reconciled: in this case, the divide between science and faith. Boisen took up reconciliation during even more fractious times.

POWER OF MYTH AND SYMBOL

Understanding symbol, myth, and story is critical to understanding Boisen, his motives, and how he understood, and interacted with, his environment. Literature, poetry, mythology, and scripture were not just texts to be mastered; the words on the page were important because they participated in the experienced reality to which they alluded. Boisen often retuned to, meditated upon, these words:

> At the mid-point of the path through life, I found
> Myself lost in a wood so dark, the way
> Ahead was blotted out. The keening sound
> I still make shows how hard it is to say
> How harsh and bitter that place felt to me-
> Merely to think of it renews my fear-
> So bad that death by only a degree
> Could possibly be worse. As you shall hear,
> It led to good things too, eventually, ...[42]

The *Divine Comedy* was not just another story to the classically trained Boisen. In Dante Alighieri's already venerable verses, Boisen read the story of his own life. Boisen's devotion to Dante was already well established at the time of his travel to his little-known country at the mid-point of his life. Boisen, after being rebuffed by Alice Batchelder, as early as 1903, adopted

Dante as a "patron saint" and even kept a portrait of him in his room during the decades to follow.[43]

In his obsession with Batchelder, he saw himself in Dante and in Dante's progress from the hell realms to fulfilment in which Dante would no longer be dependent on his Beatrice. Henri Nouwen wrote that Boisen's obsession with Batchelder resembled "what Beatrice was for Dante and Regina Olsen for Kierkegaard. The woman he never married but who remained the source of his inspiration all through his life. Boisen himself is aware of the fact that the unreachable love was not only the main cause of his suffering but also the main motive for his creative work."[44]

As the *Divine Comedy* provided a mythic template for Boisen's search for love and work, so also a flower, the trailing arbutus, was a tangible symbol, a "grail" symbolizing the same quest. Nouwen finds that "the arbutus [for Boisen] suggest that more is involved than just an idiosyncratic hobby. This rare flower is a rich symbol which evokes associations with his mother, who told him about it, with the memory of his father, who discovered it, with the University of Indiana, which adopted it as the college flower, with Dr. William Bryan, who shared Boisen's love for it. The arbutus is in the background of his decision to study forestry, of his call to the ministry, and of his failure with Alice."[45] Boisen saw himself in Dante and viewed Batchelder as his Beatrice. As Helen Flanders Dunbar, a Dante scholar and expert on the interpretation of symbol, entered Boisen's life, it was telling that as Batchelder continued to ignore Boisen's gifts of bouquets, he would send those bouquets, of trailing arbutus, to Dunbar instead.[46]

Boisen lived, and experienced, an intensely symbol-driven reality. We see this with his lifelong adoption of the arbutus flower as his grail symbol and in his personal Dante journey as expressed in the *Divine Comedy*. His life was an ongoing progression from lower to higher loyalties, and this is how he, as a theologian and pastor, framed his view of the divine, of his God. Late in Boisen's life, Henri Nouwen arranged a personal meeting with Boisen. Boisen challenged Nouwen: "Who is God? What is your answer? [he] challenged me to a straight and open answer. When I asked him the same question he replied: 'God is the internalization of the highest values of our social relationship, and Jesus Christ is the man in which the apostles found these highest values represented.'"[47] Ross Snyder opines that for Boisen, finding God, peace, a resolved conscience depended on the "interiorization of a Significant Other, and of the significant symbol structure of one's society. This is the way *human* beings are made. This is the way mind, self, society is constituted. Conscience therefore is primarily a *loyalty* phenomenon. This Boisen learned from [Josiah] Royce. Its basis is caring, trust, in some Significant Otherness that for this person is *the* Significant Otherness. . . . a sense of guilt was a sense of isolation and estrangement from that which is supreme in our system of loyalties."[48]

Symbol was not a placeholder for something absent: to participate in the symbol is to participate in the reality itself. The arbutus grail participated in all that gave Boisen deepest joy and deepest pain at the same time. It is Boisen himself. The Dante quest was Boisen's quest from the hell of disloyalty and isolation—through his own "guiding hand," Alice Batchelder, and by many other sympathetic friends—to finally arrive at union with *the* Significant Other, requiring a full and mature realization of that state, the dross of lesser loyalties having been purged away.

Helen Flanders Dunbar—an intimate with Boisen in mutual professional interests and symbolic union via the arbutus and the Dante quest—understood symbol and understood Boisen. The faithful, as she points out through her biographer Robert Powell, often do not understand the power of symbol:

> "we have forgotten the meaning of symbolism" and how to use it. "If a symbol be taken literally it comes to inevitable conflict with scientific thought and becomes ridiculous. If a symbol be taken to have meaning in the realm of the intellect only and has failed to develop in the realm of the emotions or vice versa, infantile reactions persist in the personality which cause the individual to lose faith in himself and in the universe." She observed pointedly that "symbolism, which must remain the channel of religious growth, and is in itself a powerful technique, is given little attention in the theological curriculum and by exponents of the faith."[49]

Dunbar, in her magisterial exploration of Dante and medieval symbol, notes, "Symbolism, whether conscious or unconscious, always fundamental in thinking, became in the Middle Ages both the natural medium of thought and expression, and an instrument consciously developed as the truest means of penetration into the mystery of reality. It was such, in whichever branch of knowledge lay the seeker's interest: for all were united in their goal." Dunbar implicitly admits that whatever division there was, or was recognized as being such, between "science" and "religion" in the medieval era, it was much less than it was in the 1920s when she first wrote. Philosophy, natural science, theology, and psychology had yet to specialize into discrete spheres. Whereas Dante's mystery of reality was a unitary one, by the 1920s the biologist and the theologian both delved the "mystery of reality," yet had very different languages in which to describe it and tended to focus on very different aspects, often leading to conflict and misunderstanding.[50]

In the *Divine Comedy*, "the interpretation of the poem involves an outline of all known to the medieval mind of physical science, the science of human relationships, and the science of the relationship of the individual to the universe—with, if the validity of Dante's symbolic theory be accepted, the addition of all that is known today."[51] Yes, science has moved on since the Middle

Ages, as has religion; still, Dunbar argues that the symbols that drive story, myth, dreams, nightmares, and religion have a unitive power that transcends the ages and can be curative when used sensitively and with skill. She argues that the use of symbol, story, and myth not only is an individual endeavor but has power to move peoples, in Dante's case "as a consecrated messenger he must lead mankind in the same arduous journey, from the place where the Sun is silent, to the eternity of illumination where the Sun compels silence."[52]

Like Boisen's ascent from lesser to higher "loyalties," a similar ascent, with some diversions, is found in Dunbar's analysis of Dante: "Beatrice showed Dante in the Moon souls who, though now loving God perfectly and rejoicing in his will, on earth had wavered in the pursuit of their ideal. . . . they had allowed themselves to be diverted, albeit against their desire, from a greater to a lesser good."[53] Dante could settle with nothing less than the highest good and the highest loyalty; even his beloved Beatrice had to be surpassed in pursuit of and in achievement of the unitary goal.

> He who earlier could not so much as take his eyes from Beatrice, having so long mourned on earth his separation from her, in this second separation, although he perceives the distance, feels no remoteness and so no pain. . . . Having been guided by Beatrice through the ways of purgation and illumination, Dante, now prepared for the way of union, is no longer dependent on her symbolic presence. Moreover, it is only when Beatrice has left his side to take her place in the Rose, that Dante at last forsakes the *voi* of formal address for the greater intimacy of the *tu*.[54]

Boisen was intimately, and consciously, aware of his deep spiritual and psychological connection to the language of symbol and myth, especially as expressed in the *Divine Comedy*, and found a kindred spirit in Dunbar, who expressed a sympathy as deep as her knowledge of the language and spirit of symbol. Boisen's assessment of his voyage through the *inferno* was, at last, more optimistic than Dante's. In the work he dedicated to Batchelder, his Beatrice, Boisen wrote:

> Over the gates of his Inferno Dante Alighieri saw the legend, "All hope abandon, ye who enter here." As I read the *Divine Comedy* and the *Vita Nuova*, I get the impression that Dante himself had explored very thoroughly this inner world and that he has given us a marvelous first-hand account of what he saw. But he was perhaps too much influenced by medieval theology. At least I find no evidence of any hell of eternal torment, and the pictures which he gives us of what he saw within that ominous gate contain too much of suffering and agony to accord with that inscription. Suffering, as I see it, is remedial. As long as there is suffering there is hope.[55]

He further assesses, "It was necessary for me to pass through the purgatorial fires of a horrifying psychosis before I could set foot in my promised land of creative activity."[56] For Boisen, like Dante, the destination was silent unity with his highest loyalty:

Imagination, there on high—
Too high to breathe free, after such a climb—
Had lost its power; but now, just like a wheel
That spins so evenly it measures time
By space, the deepest wish that I could feel
And all my will, were turning with the love
That move the sun and all the stars above.[57]

Boisen progressed through his inferno knowing he was not the first and nor would he be the last to encounter the "purgatorial fires" of a "horrifying psychosis." He took some comfort in his suspicion that his own "patron saint" Dante Alighieri may have been able to identify with his plight.

BOISEN'S VILUSIONS: GROPING IN THE DREAMSCAPES

Boisen's visions and delusions were intensely and overpoweringly tangible and frightening:

> A patient is rarely brought before a staff meeting without being asked in some form or other if he has heard "voices." I suppose to such a question I would have to answer, yes. The ideas which I had in my delirium were all intensely real. Every idea which came into my head was itself reality, something objective and external to myself. That music I heard most distinctly. The black-cats and the poke-bonnets I picked up with my own hands. The horse-blanket I opened and then unfolded the linen cloths. I heard most distinctly that awful tap-tap-tapping on the walls and I smelled the smell of brimstone. There were therefore not only auditory, but also visual and tactual and olfactory hallucinations. Every idea which came to me was externalized. But always the real happenings registered in some way differently from the products of my imagination. . . . The unseen world becomes the real world.[58]

The visions, hallucinations, and delusions Boisen experienced, and suffered from, during his 1920 hospitalization are memorialized in his published autobiography as well as in his unpublished personal papers. Boisen notes that his vilusions were not story, metaphor, nor allegory when he experienced them. His experiences, in dreamscape/nightmarish language, were intensely and vividly "real" to his physical and mental perception. The physical toll of his first hospitalization was hinted at in his loss of approximately thirty pounds by Spring 1921.[59]

Boisen's vilusions, regardless of how outlandish, occurred within a broader context. Understanding that context helps in understanding Boisen as someone trying to transcend his "abnormal" state and as someone who succeeded in transforming his experiences into healing and new possibility for himself and for others. Boisen's vilusions were most prominently, and obviously, connected to the raging conflict between science and religion. They also reflect Boisen's struggle as an experiencer inpatient in a mental hospital and point to Boisen's struggle to transcend an individual as well as a sociological chasm. Many of Boisen's vilusions point to meanings that are less obvious but are echoed repeatedly in myth, religion, and storytelling relating to such things as deaths and resurrections, boon-giving objects, the moon, the sun, and fertility.

Claude Levi-Strauss' landmark work in structuralism can give us some hints in helping understand Boisen and his vilusions. Levi-Strauss inquires why the stories of religion, myth, dream, and storytelling "at first sight [appear] contradictory" in that so many of these stories contain fantastic, dreamlike, and downright mad elements. Yet, following in Carl Jung's footsteps, Levi-Strauss notes that the "apparent arbitrariness is belied by the astounding similarity between myths collected in widely different regions. Therefore, the problem: If the content of a myth is contingent, how are we going to explain the fact that myths throughout the world are so similar?"[60]

For Levi-Strauss, the language, and even logic, of myth is one way that people bring "some kind of order to what was previously chaos." One example of the "chaos" to which Levi-Strauss refers is the opposition between life and death in which death can strike at any time. Mythic "trickster" characters, such as the raven or coyote, serve as symbolic mediators between life and death. They, on the one hand, eat carrion, dead animals, but they do not themselves kill the animals they eat. The raven and the coyote appear in many Native American religions, spiritualties, and mythic systems as the trickster that closes uncloseable dualities. One of those dualities would have been the difference between cultivator/herbivores and hunter/carnivores; the larger and more basic duality would be the opposition of death and life. Coyote and Raven are the "tricksters" that reconcile what cannot be reconciled.[61]

Boisen observed, and encountered, the stresses of many dualities which seemly could not be reconciled. He observed America's cultural war between science and religion; he strove to live a productive life of service even though he was deemed "mad." He sought the love of a woman always a little out of his reach. Boisen, to borrow Levi-Strauss' structuralist notion, was a person prone to "trickster" symbol to resolve the irresolvable. Perhaps, during his decades of dedicated toil, and in the puzzle others have made of him, Boisen has graduated to something of a trickster in his own right.

Boisen's autobiography contains several vivid delusions from his initial hospitalization at Boston Psychopathic Hospital in October 1920, where he received acute treatment prior to his long-term hospitalization at Westboro State Hospital.[62] Along with his "family-of-four" vilusion (discussed previously), Boisen witnessed the vilusion that served as the keynote for his life's work:

> The next night I was visited, not by angels, but by a lot of witches. I had the room next to the one I had occupied before. There was, as I remember it, nothing in it but a mattress on the floor. It seems that the walls were of peculiar construction. There was, it seemed a double wall and I could hear a constant tap-tapping along the walls, all done according to some system. This was due, it seemed, to the detectives in the employ of the evil powers who were out to locate the exact place where I was. Then the room was filled with the odor of brimstone. I was told that witches were around and from the ventilator shaft I picked up paper black cats and broomsticks and poke bonnets. I was greatly exercised, and I stuffed my blanket into the ventilator shaft. I finally not only worked out a way of checking the invasion of the black cats, but I found some sort of process of regeneration which could be used to save other people. I had, it seemed, broken an opening in wall which separated medicine and religion. I was told to feel on the back of my neck, and I would find there a sign of my new mission. I thereupon examined and found a shuttle-like affair about three-fourths of an inch long.[63]

The "wall" between medicine and religion, science and religion, which Boisen perceived in his vilusion was a duality that he dedicated his life to closing. In this vilusion also appears a boon-giving object—the "shuttle-like affair" symbolizing power to begin his journey. Boisen, a classically trained and widely read scholar of the Victorian era, would have been familiar with a wide range of Greek and Roman mythology outside of the scriptures of his own religion. Boisen was familiar, indirectly at the very least, with the writing and themes expounded upon by James George Frazer who published his classic survey on religion and mythology *The Golden Bough* in 1890. Frazer's writings include multiple references to inanimate objects, stones, and amulets—some worn on the neck—credited with beneficial, consecratory, or curative powers.[64] Boisen's vilusions contained themes, and beneficial objects, that he had encountered in his deep and broad study of classic literature and mythology—parcel to classical Victorian education.

Boisen's "new mission" was in "[breaking] an opening in the wall which separated medicine and religion" in developing a new method of theological learning via clinical education with troubled people. He envisioned, and invented, modern health-care institutional chaplaincy as distinct from the parish, and in promoting humane and person-centered care for the mentally ill free from the stigma he had known. Robert Powell's compact and illuminating précis on Boisen's life, *Anton T. Boisen (1876–1965): Breaking an Opening in the Wall Between Religion and Medicine*, witnesses the power this vilusion had for Boisen and for those who have followed in his footsteps. Powell describes this "Prophetic delusion" as "patently delusional but highly significant in terms of Boisen's later career. . . . In view of the extremely productive course Boisen's life took after this episode, there is perhaps some justification for agreeing with an assertion he made in a letter soon after the gross disturbance cleared: 'The cure has lain in the faithful carrying through of the delusion itself'—which is exactly the task to which Boisen dedicated the rest of his life."[65]

Robert Leas credits the significance of Boisen's visionary event as encapsulating his already middle-aged life: "His long educational history, the memory of his father and his mother's influence, the many influences of life with grandfather Theophilus Adam Wylie and his mentor at Indiana University, Dr. William Lowe Bryan, teachers and friends, and the varying experiences in forestry, theological education at Union Seminary, church survey and the congregational pastorates." These experiences drove him to reconcile the realms of science, religion, and his own struggle with mental illness, with the drive to teach and serve as his kin had. Boisen required a mediator, perhaps even a "trickster" to reconcile the irreconcilable. While his vilusions were "a [source] of new ideas, new insights," Boisen still needed more, he needed friends, companions, and anchors, like Elwood Worcester, for him to not only "trust in his intuition" but also have the capacity and support to operationalize it.[66]

Leas insightfully points to the backdrop of the modernist/fundamentalist controversy and the Scopes Trial both in assessing Boisen's vilusions and in considering the challenges and opportunities confronting Boisen's early work. Christian scripture, and the book of Revelation in particular, uses the metaphor of "Lamb" and "Lamb who was slain" in reference to Jesus of Nazareth, a particularly fertile and potent symbol for Boisen.[67] During Boisen's "gross" illness (to borrow Powell's word) at Boston Psychopathic, he had many vilusions centered on the fate of a lamb he thought to be wandering the hallways of the hospital. Boisen "heard what seemed to be a choir of angels. I thought it the most beautiful music I had ever heard. . . . shortly afterward I heard something about a little lamb being born upstairs in the room just above mine. This excited me greatly and next morning I made some inquiries about that little lamb." After some time of searching for the lamb and exchanging "certain tokens left by the angels" with other patients in the hospital for information about the lamb, "The idea came, 'The doctors were very much interested in it and they immediately killed it and preserved it in alcohol because of its scientific interest.'"[68] Even if some dark humor can be detected in this vilusion, it points to Boisen's distress regarding his religions ability to credibly dialogue with science as well as his own ability, as a person of faith, to successfully navigate his own inferno.

Many of Boisen's vilusions focused on his own fate and effort to make sense of his madness:

> I seemed to be in some labyrinthine tunnels deep down in the recesses of the earth. Part of the time I was drugged with what I was told was "bismuth." This, it seemed, was the drug they used to preserve the old Egyptian mummies. . . . I found myself wandering through these subterranean tunnels until at last way down deep I came upon a horse-blanket within which was wrapped up some peculiar white linen fabric. These it seemed were some most sacred relics. They were connected with the search for the Holy Grail and represented the profoundest spiritual struggle of the centuries.[69]

As his vision continued, he perceived himself as "now imprisoned and exploited by a lot of unprincipled medical men and nurses. The only way of escaping was by having my head cut off."[70]

Boisen's vilusions were filled with symbolism reflective of his Christian faith. Being in "the recesses of the earth" echoed Jesus' burial that preceded his resurrection. Images of deaths and resurrections suffused not only Boisen's Christian faith but also the mythology with which he would have been familiar. Frazer's *Golden Bough* recounts many mythic gods, goddesses, and heroes that die and revive.[71] As Boisen traversed the underground tunnels "way down deep," he found "some most sacred relics" which included "some peculiar white linen fabric." Christian scriptures speak of Jesus' body being wrapped "in a clean linen shroud, and laid . . . in . . . [a] . . . tomb."[72] Whereas the "Holy Grail" may refer to the cup Christ used at his Last Supper (Last Supper references also appear in Boisen's vilusions), the Grail provenance had life in a mythic context wider than, and predating, the Christian context. Joseph Campbell catalogues a wide range of "grails" besides the cup of Christ. "Grails" include a wide variety of dishes, bowls, cups, stones, and other objects that render aid to, or empower, the searcher in completing their quest. Even the quest itself can be interpreted as a "grail." For example, Dante suffering the pain of his *inferno*.[73] Of these grail references, Christian and otherwise—especially noteworthy in Boisen's love for Dante's works—Boisen was explicitly aware.

Boisen's vilusions also frequently recount lunar imagery and gender dysphoria. Levi-Strauss notes how the relationship of the sun and the moon across many mythologies is often likened to the relationship of the male and the female. It is common, but not universal, that the sun is associated with the male and the moon with the female and fecundity.[74] Merete Jakobsen provides another example, in Greenlandic shaman taking a journey "to the Moon Spirit/Moon Man mainly to deal with the fertility of the society. . . . The other travelling he has to perform is the journey to the Land of the Dead, to make contact with the deceased or to bring back souls that have gone astray."[75] Boisen envisioned his own arduous trip to, and ordeal in, the moon:

> Then I found myself in the Moon. The idea of being in the Moon had been present almost from the beginning of the week. Now this became an outstanding feature. The Moon seemed ordinarily quite far away, but really it was very near. The medical men knew about it and they had perfected a way of spiriting people away and burying them alive in a cell in the Moon, which in the meantime some designing person, a sort of double, would take their place in this world. Everything was run in a very strange way in the Moon. It was done in the most scientific manner. It seemed that it was the abode of departed spirits and all the interests were frankly and openly concerned with the problem of reproduction and of sex. Really it was quite appalling. It seemed that upon one's advent in the Moon the sex was likely to change and one of the first things the doctors tried to determine was whether you were a man or woman. They had certain delicate instruments for determining that. When they examined me, I heard them say in great surprise, "He is a perfect neutral." It seemed that the needle was not deflected in either direction. . . . At one time I succeeded in climbing into the sun, but through some clumsiness, I managed to destroy the balance of things and my friends and relatives in the sun suffered heavily in consequence.

Boisen's fixation with the moon continued for several weeks following his initial hospitalization and continued briefly after his transfer from Boston Psychopathic to Westboro:

> I saw it (the moon) centered in a cross of light. I took that as proof that I was right in ascribing great importance to what was happening to me. The cross stands for suffering. Therefore the Moon knows and the Moon is suffering on my account. But on Wednesday night, as I lay awake on the sleeping porch speculating on this dire portent, I made a discovery. When I changed my position to a certain spot, the cross no longer appeared. The explanation was simple. From that particular spot I was looking at the Moon through a hole in the wire screening! That discovery was a big help toward recovery.[76]

While Boisen is aware that the perceptions he describes having experienced were, at least for most people, out of the ordinary, his visions, perceptions, delusions had root in a deeper cultural, perhaps even biological, wellspring than simply the product of his own disturbed mind. Boisen struggled with the role of sex and sexuality—especially in regard to Alice Batchelder, the love of his life. Unrequited romantic interest and desire factored to a lesser extent in regard to his relationship with Helen Dunbar. In Boisen's dreamscapes regarding the moon also appears the symbol of the cross—self-explanatory to Boisen—as he traversed the *inferno*. He also notes the delusion loosening its hold on him as he begins his descent toward reality as most people experience it. His task then turned toward trying to determine what, if any, significance his vilusions could have for himself and others.

"THE PROPHET JONAS" BENJAMIN MICKLE, BOISEN'S PERSONAL PROPHET

William James, opined that a prophet often first appears as a "mere lonely madman." This must have been Boisen's appearance upon his release from custody at Westboro State Hospital. As Boisen's work and research grew, he wondered what differentiated prophecy from insanity. Boisen looked to, and often reflected on, an early and favorite patient, a kindred "mere lonely madman." Benjamin Mickle featured prominently in Boisen's published and unpublished writings from Boisen's early work at Worcester State Hospital in the mid-1920s through an article Boisen published in 1960 in *Pastoral Psychology* which appeared toward the end of Boisen's career and long life. Mickle's indelible mark on Boisen was likely due to the similarity of Mickle's experiences and ideations to Boisen's own. Boisen, in Glenn Asquith's words, "had great respect and appreciation for this man and his potential."[77] He also viewed Mickle as a prophet regarding Boisen's own potential. Boisen nicknamed him "The Prophet Jonas" in discerning the difference between insight and insanity. Boisen in one of his studies on Mickle rhetorically asks why "other religious eccentrics" of his time would be "allowed full liberty" while Mickle was confined to a State Hospital when "the charge against him was nothing more serious than that of vagrancy."

Boisen's recollections of Mickle, although always sympathetic, continued to soften as the decades progressed. Boisen's initial writings focus closely on Mickle not being able to traverse the chasm between insanity and service due to his inability to successfully recruit believers to his vision. While Boisen did not reverse his earlier conclusions, he increasingly appreciated the strength, comfort, and power to persevere his visions gave Mickle, an impoverished and homeless African American man who grew up in Georgia and South Carolina, to carry on with joy, purpose, and hope.

In his early case studies, Boisen points to social acceptance, or lack thereof, as the chief indicator on whether an experiencer would successfully bridge the gap between madness and inspiration. Boisen expressed: "The answer is that he had no followers. If there had been even two or three who shared his faith and believed in him, that would have been sufficient to save him from being committed." Boisen admits in his files that Mickle was capable of physical violence—which provided reason enough for Worcester Hospital to deny release in spite of Boisen's advocacy on his behalf—the main difference between Boisen and Mickle is that Boisen had people who believed in him and advocated for him at crucial moments in his life's journey.[78]

Boisen noted that he was able to build rapport with Mickle by "seeing things thru Mickle's eyes, making use of his language," including taking seriously his faith in "the Man Above" (Mickle's euphemism for the divine) and that "the Man Above 'mashed his foot' and gave him orders." He gained at least some level of trust and esteem from Mickle by showing esteem and respect for Mickle's experiences that were hitherto dismissed. Boisen noted in an early case study: "here is a man who has given up everything in obedience to his religious faith and has embarked on a great adventure. His psychiatrist is struck by the fact his life is completely unified around what he conceives to be God's will for him. And yet he comes to grief. He is adjudged insane and confined to an institution. What is the matter with his religion?" Boisen credited Mickle's religious problem in having "no true sense of perspective." Mickle's experiential realm left "little room in his universe for others beside 'me and God.'" Besides this, Boisen found it difficult to offer Mickle constructive criticism and convey that "his motivation was self-centered and included an element of hostility."

In Mickle, Boisen seemed to find value in balancing personal spiritual experience with empathy with others and in endeavoring to find a wider, pragmatic, social validation and context for that experience to operate. Boisen tangentially refers to Mickle's race but does not delve into how discrimination and lack of opportunity could play into denying Mickle the recognition that Boisen eventually achieved. While Boisen found Mickle deeply instructive, and clearly liked him personally, Mickle, for Boisen, was the pattern of the experiencer who forever remained trapped in his own experience—he was a man who travelled to a little-known country, or a "Moon" of his own, and never fully returned to tell and make productive use of it.[79]

Part of Mickle's problem in operationalizing his experience rested with Mickle personally, and this was the focus of Boisen's interest and investigation, but part of it also rested with Mickle's lack of opportunity due to race and class. In addressing Mickle specifically, Boisen is primarily interested in the role of experience and illness in the life of individual persons—consistent with Boisen's own interests and focus in late 1920. Boisen showed greater interest in the sociological ramifications of his work in the 1930s onward. As Boisen's career progressed, he turned increasingly to how illness and experience impacted larger social dynamics. Boisen was cognizant of larger racial and economic factors. While Boisen viewed America, and particularly Protestant America, as offering "relative freedom from the hatreds and the exploitive imperialism in which the European and Asiatic [*sic*] peoples are enmeshed. Our hands are indeed far from clean. Our record in the treatment of the Negroes [*sic*] is disgraceful. The attitude we have shown toward them, . . . would be fatal to any hope of betterment." While Boisen used terminology and expressions common to his era, he shows growing awareness of how Mickle's opportunities were limited, in part due to Mickle personally but also attributable to the systemic racism and lack of access that limited his scope of possibility.[80]

Boisen continually revisited his favorite prophet. He noted Mickle's diagnosis in the dementia praecox range—to use Kraepelinian diagnostic language and how Mickle described the experience of his "acute disturbance," which "usually begins with a period of preoccupation and sleeplessness during which the patient is intensely concerned about his own role. There is a narrowing of attention which is conducive to creative mental activity but unfavorable to balanced judgment."[81] Boisen's affinity for Mickle is undoubtedly due to their marked similarity in experience of illness and spirituality. Boisen intently inquired into his prophet's experience of prophecy and pathology:

> Mickle's chief delight . . . his conversations with the Man Above. [who] would appear to him, especially at night, and bring him comfort and counsel and warning. Sometimes he would bring a choir of angels to sing to him. . . . When he got good signals, he was happy. When for any reason the signals were not functioning, or when they were disquieting, he would be irritable and cross. I asked him once if these signals sounded like my own voice in talking to him. His answer was, "No, he tell me things to tell you. He speak much like a natural man, but he don't speak like a natural man. When God speak to me, it ain't no idea that comes into my mind. There's a man down in here (pointing to his chest). But the Spirit don't talk like you talk. He don't say no dozens of words. I don't hear him with my ears. I hears him here." (He points to his chest.) . . . Frequently in talking with Mickle, a far-away look would come into his eyes and he might explain, "He's talking to me now." This was likely to happen when for any reason he was deeply moved.[82]

Late in his life, Boisen wrote, "For me, Mickle always seemed a work of art or, better perhaps, an artist himself." In Mickle, Boisen started "my business to talk with patients who are said to 'hear voices.' I have found that most of them, if left to themselves, will describe this experience in different ways.

The commonest term is 'voice,' but most such patients make a sharp distinction between such voices and those they hear with their ears."[83]

While the early lessons Boisen drew from his prophet related to how, as a spiritual experiencer, he could navigate life as a productive, and free, person, Boisen's later memories of Mickle soften and he appreciated his experiences for their own value. Boisen recalled frustration in his apparent inability to get Mickle to change course once he set upon one: "When he "got a mad on," he would fight like a tiger, hurling flowerpots and swinging swabs with reckless abandon. He could not be persuaded that the Man Above would have given him two good fists if he were not to use them in fighting." While Mickle may not have been able to socialize his unique experiences the way Boisen was able to, Boisen admired how his prophet's visions gave him the strength to carry on in spite of all reason to experience the contrary:

> He had found something which enabled him to bear up and keep going in the face of devastating frustrations and disappointments. . . . the Man Above had a plan for him and that this Man Above was in full control. As to the signals, the medieval mystics had to learn the lesson that some of the ideas which came surging into their minds could hardly be from God. They assumed that they must come from the devil. Perhaps we of today need to learn the converse lesson, that all auditory hallucinations do not necessarily come from the devil but may represent the operations of the creative mind.[84]

Boisen's use of, and assessment of, his own personal prophet followed in the footsteps of Jamesian pragmatism. Boisen's assessment of Mickle, initially, was concerned with how Mickle—and by extension all experiencers including himself—would be able to find a socially acceptable context and use for his experience (outside of incarceration in a State Hospital). Boisen's initial assessment that the difference between prophecy and insanity depended on the acceptance accorded it by society seems to be naïve at best and cynical at worst. Yet, even then he hit upon a theme of importance. The more general theme was that experience, illness, and wellness all operate within a larger social context beyond the experiencer. If that special experience, "special thing," is to have significance beyond the individual, it will depend on how others view and are able to access that experience. Boisen's early assessment of Mickle undoubtedly also reflects, consciously or not, the lessons Boisen drew from his prophet. While Boisen did have experiences and heard "voices" in a way reminiscent of Mickle, Boisen, consciously or not, seems to have taken the lesson that he could not "narrow his attention" so tightly as to shut out reality as most people understand it. He had to adjust his own creative, and sometimes "mad," mind and vision in such a way as to be able to interact with those around him who may not share his mystical nature.

As time passed, Boisen saw career success, and his memories mellowed of a favorite and formative patient. His writings grew more appreciative of Mickle's visions for the practical effect they had for a single, marginalized man who did not have access to education, social contacts, and a second chance. Mickle's "Man Above" spoke to him, companioned him, cared about him, gave him a purpose and a vision, when so many of the others around him gave him none of these things. While Boisen believed in Mickle when nobody else would, Boisen's faith was not enough.

While Boisen suffered from bouts of severe mental illness, he was also a spiritual and religious experiencer. He saw, and experienced, his environment and context in ways different than others. His vivid dreamscape/nightmarish visions revealed an inflamed psyche but also envisioned reconciliations of what could not be reconciled. His vilusions prophesied a new and creative solution to culture war. They propelled him to delve into what was happening within his own mind and soul but also to use that introspection in an effort to be of service to others. Boisen understood he would need help if he were to successfully navigate the arduous return from his little-known country. He would need examples and mentors, and these he found in William James, Elwood Worcester, and even in his own personal prophet, Benjamin Mickle. They taught him what a vision of special things could achieve and provided warning of the pitfalls that would come of getting too trapped in the vision—of visiting the "moon" and not being able to find his way back home.

While Boisen's visions and delusions—"vilusions"—may have been peculiar, they were not entirely unique nor *sui generis* to him. This is not to imply that they were insincere experiences nor that they were, in some form, "plagiarized." Rather, Boisen's experiences were informed by a larger cultural context, some of which he may not have been consciously aware but much of which he was aware. His experiences also occurred within a larger social and interpersonal context. He lived within a wider ad hoc community of experiencers, even though they may not have thought of themselves as such nor have been perceived by others as such. Boisen also came to realize, on a practical level, that he would need to socialize his special experiences so he could gain some level of mastery over them and so they could become beneficial to himself and others.

NOTES

1. Boisen, *Out of the Depths*, 112–13.
2. Taves, *Religious Experience Reconsidered*, 4–5.
3. Taves, *Religious Experience Reconsidered*, 8–9.
4. Stokes, *Ministry After Freud*, 19.

5. Elwood Worcester, *Life's Adventure: The Story of a Varied Career* (New York, NY: Charles Scribner's Sons, 1932), 75.
6. Worcester, *Life's Adventure*, 4.
7. Worcester, *Life's Adventure*, 5.
8. Worcester, *Life's Adventure*, 314.
9. Worcester, *Life's Adventure*, 314–37. Psychic research involving séances and use of mediums to study communications between the living and the dead were somewhat more mainstream research during the Victorian era, and many of Worcester's citations date from the 1870s—from Worcester's youth. As Worcester, himself, acknowledges, his interest in and ongoing pursuit of psychic phenomenon fell into disrepute among most mainstream psychologists well prior to the 1930s. See Ann Taves, *Trances, Fits, and Visions: Experiencing Religion and Explaining Experience from Wesley to James* (Princeton, NJ: Princeton University Press, 1999), 166–206, 247–49.
10. Boisen to Paul Batchelder, August 13, 1956, Series 2, Box 7, Folder 72, Boisen Papers, Chicago Theological Seminary. In fall 1921 Boisen had an appointment with Worcester. He recalled a dream regarding his boyhood and his father: "there came a sharp rap. Dr. Worcester said: 'Did you hear that?' That comes when there is anything important." Anton T. Boisen, "A Portion of the Case Record," Box 1a, Folder 13, Boisen Papers, Chicago Theological Seminary. Boisen's friend Fred Eastman unadvisedly sent a copy of a now obscure occult book: *Our Unseen Guest* (New York, NY: Harper & Brothers, 1920). Boisen became fixated on spiritism and communication with the souls of the dead, which were the foci of the book. Boisen's new obsession triggered a relapse and delay in Boisen's release. Fred Eastman to Boisen, March 11, 1921, Series 2, Box 3, Folder 26, Boisen Papers, Chicago Theological Seminary; Boisen, *Out of the Depths*, 114.
11. Worcester, *Life's Adventure*, 37–38.
12. Worcester, *Life's Adventure*, 39.
13. Worcester, *Life's* Adventure, 40.
14. Worcester, *Life's Adventure*, 44–46.
15. Stokes, *Ministry After Freud*, 19; Worcester, *Life's Adventure*, 76–78.
16. Stokes, *Ministry After Freud*, 20; Worcester, *Life's Adventure*, 88–91, 97.
17. Katherine McCarthy, "The Emmanuel Movement and Richard Peabody," *Journal of Studies on Alcohol* 45, no. 1 (1984).
18. McCarthy, "The Emmanuel Movement and Richard Peabody."
19. Boisen, *Out of the Depths*, 101–2.
20. Robert Charles Powell, *e-Mail Message to Author*, May 10, 2016.
21. Powell, "Whatever Happened to 'CPE,'" March 18, 1999.
22. Boisen, *Out of the Depths*, 79.
23. Boisen, "A Portion of the Case Record" (Unpublished Manuscript, no date), Box 1a, Folder 13, Boisen Papers, Chicago Theological Seminary.
24. Boisen, "A Portion of the Case Record," Box 1a, Folder 13, Boisen Papers, Chicago Theological Seminary.
25. Boisen to Ellwood Worcester, November 20, 1921, in Boisen, *Out of the Depths*, 138–39.

26. Boisen, *Out of the Depths*, 142.
27. Leas, *Anton Theophilus Boisen*, 9–10, 17, 29.
28. Taves, *Fits, Trances, and Visions*, 306.
29. Daniel L. Pals, *Nine Theories of Religion*, 3rd edition (New York, NY: Oxford University Press, 2015), 189–91, 215–16.
30. Taves, *Fits, Trances and Visions*, 306.
31. James, *The Varieties of Religious Experience*, 270.
32. James, *The Varieties of Religious Experience*, 376–77.
33. James, *The Varieties of Religious Experience*, 337–38.
34. Pals, *Nine Theories of Religion*, 220–22. Daniel Pals notes difficulties in applying Jamesian pragmatism due to different perspectives on what constitutes a desirable outcome. He likens this problem to assessing the "value" or "good" of the French Revolution—many leftists viewing it as, overall, an at least necessary event, many rightist and Catholic historians seeing it as "bad."
35. Powell, *Anton T. Boisen*, 7.
36. Powell, *Anton T. Boisen*, 7; George Coe to Boisen, September 1, 1921, in Boisen, *Out of the Depths*, 133–34.
37. Taves, *Fits, Trances, and Visions*, 302.
38. George A. Coe, "The Mystical as a Psychological Concept," *The Journal of Philosophy, Psychology, and Scientific Methods* 6, no. 8 (1909).
39. Edward J. Larson, *Summer for the Gods: The Scopes Trial and America's Continuing Debate over Science and Religion* (New York, NY: Basic Books, 1997), 26–27.
40. Larson, *Summer for the Gods*, 119–20.
41. Boisen, *Out of the Depths*, 39.
42. Dante Alighieri, *Dante: The Divine Comedy. A New Verse Translation by Clive James*, ed. and trans. C. James (New York, NY: Liveright Publishing Corporation, 2013), Book I: Hell, Canto 1, vv. 1–9.
43. Anton T. Boisen, "Out of the Depths: Supplement" (Unpublished Manuscript, no date), Box 1a, Folder 8, Boisen Papers, Chicago Theological Seminary; Anton T. Boisen, "BEATRIX" (Unpublished Manuscript, no date), Box 1a, Folder 10, Boisen Papers, Chicago Theological Seminary. Boisen wrote, "This poem by Victor Laprale was given me by my chief Professor Kuersteiner in 1903 at the time I was trying to decide upon my course with reference to Alice. It made a deep impression upon me and it was an important factor in my decision not to give up. Hence an identification with the poet Dante and the picture of him which I kept for many years in my room."
44. Henri Nouwen, "Anton T. Boisen and the Study of Theology through 'Living Human Documents'" (Unpublished Manuscript, no date), Box 1, File 4, Henri Nouwen Papers, John M. Kelly Library, University of St. Michael's College, Toronto, ON, 42.
45. Nouwen, "Anton T. Boisen and the Study of Theology," 49.
46. Powell, *Healing and Wholeness*, 201.
47. Henri Nouwen, "BOISEN" (Unpublished Manuscript, August 1964), Nouwen Papers, Special Collections, John M. Kelly Library, University of St. Michael's College, Toronto, ON.

48. Ross Snyder, "The Boisen Heritage in Theological Education," *Pastoral Psychology* 19, no. 186 (1968): 12.

49. Powell, *Healing and Wholeness*, 256.

50. H. Flanders Dunbar, *Symbolism in Medieval Thought and its Consummation in the Divine Comedy* (New York, NY: Russell & Russell, 1961), 24–25.

51. Dunbar, *Symbolism in Medieval Thought*, 25.

52. Dunbar, *Symbolism in Medieval Thought*, 102.

53. Dunbar, *Symbolism in Medieval Thought*, 36.

54. Dunbar, *Symbolism in Medieval Thought*, 92.

55. Boisen, *The Exploration of the Inner World*, 15–16. In his 1952 recorded interview with Francis McPeek, Boisen alludes to a closing of dualities in his experience: "joy that comes through pain, life that comes through death, blessing that comes through adversity." Anton T. Boisen, Interview by Francis McPeek, 1952, Audio Recording, ACPE Papers, Emory University, Decatur, GA.

56. Boisen, *Out of the Depths*, 208.

57. Dante, *Dante: The Divine Comedy*, Book III: Heaven, Canto 33, vv. 162–68.

58. Boisen, "A Portion of the Case Record" (Unpublished Manuscript, no date), Box 1a, Folder 13, Boisen Papers, Chicago Theological Seminary.

59. Louise Boisen to Fred Eastman, June 10, 1921, Box 8, Folder 80, Boisen Papers, Chicago Theological Seminary.

60. Claude Levi-Strauss, *Structural Anthropology*, Vol. 1 (New York, NY: Basic Books, 1958), 208.

61. Levi-Strauss, *Structural Anthropology*, 224–25.

62. Boisen, *Out of the Depths*, 87.

63. Boisen, *Out of the Depths*, 91. Boisen implies that the "shuttle-like affair" on the back of his neck was likely a cut or injury that a physician attempted to treat the next day.

64. James George Frazer, *The New Golden Bough* (New York, NY: A Mentor Book, 1959), 57–59.

65. Powell, *Anton T. Boisen*, 8.

66. Leas, *Anton Theophilus Boisen*, 86–87; Powell, *e-Mail Message to Author*, May 10, 2016.

67. Revelation 5:12.

68. Boisen, *Out of the Depths*, 89–91.

69. Boisen, *Out of the Depths*, 93.

70. Boisen, *Out of the Depths*, 94.

71. Frazer, *The New Golden Bough*, 273–470.

72. Matthew 27:59–60.

73. Joseph Campbell, *The Masks of God: Creative Mythology* (New York, NY: Penguin Compass, 1968), 530–54.

74. Claude Levi-Strauss, *Structural Anthropology*, Vol. II (New York, NY: Basic Books, 1958), 211–21.

75. Merete Demant Jakobsen, *Shamanism: Traditional and Contemporary Approaches to the Mastery of Spirits and Healing* (New York, NY: Berghahn Books, 1999), 88.

76. Boisen, *Out of the Depths*, 100–1.

77. Anton T. Boisen, "Inspiration in the Light of Psychopathology," *Pastoral Psychology* 11, no. 107 (1960). See also Asquith's prefatory remarks on Boisen's 1960 republished article. Glenn H. Asquith, Jr., ed., *Vision from a Little Known Country: A Boisen Reader* (Macon, GA: Journal of Pastoral Care Publications, Inc., 1992), 113. Boisen frequently used his copious notes on, and interview transcriptions with, Mickle as teaching material. Anton T. Boisen, "The Prophet Jonah" (Unpublished Manuscript, no date), Series 5, Box 1, Folder 23, Boisen Papers, Chicago Theological Seminary; Anton T. Boisen, "JONAS" (Unpublished Manuscript, no date), Series 5, Box 1, Folder 24, Boisen Papers, Chicago Theological Seminary; Anton T. Boisen, "A Modern Jonah: A Case Study by A. T. Boisen" (Unpublished Manuscript, no date), Series 4, Box 3, Folder 17, Boisen Papers, Chicago Theological Seminary; Anton T. Boisen, "What Makes a Man Go Crazy," *The State Hospital—Elgin, ILL. MESSENGER* 21, no. 3, January 17, 1953, Series 4, Box 3, Folder 19, Boisen Papers, Chicago Theological Seminary.

78. Anton T. Boisen, "The Prophet Jonas" (Unpublished Manuscript, no date), Box 1, Folder 24, Boisen Papers, Chicago Theological Seminary. See also, Glenn Asquith's notes, Boisen, "Inspiration in the Light of Psychopathology"; Asquith, *A Boisen Reader*, 113.

79. Boisen, "The Prophet Jonas," Box 1, Folder 24, Boisen Papers, Chicago Theological Seminary.

80. Anton T. Boisen, *Religion in Crisis and Custom: A Sociological and Psychological Study* (New York, NY: Harper & Brothers Publishers, 1955), 258–59.

81. Boisen, "Inspiration in the Light of Psychopathology," 16.

82. Boisen, "Inspiration in the Light of Psychopathology," 13.

83. Boisen, "Inspiration in the Light of Psychopathology," 14–15.

84. Boisen, "Inspiration in the Light of Psychopathology," 18.

Chapter 3

How Boisen Interpreted His Experience and Illness

Boisen struggled with determining which special things were helpful versus those that were not. Having struggled with illness and inspiration in his own life, he felt himself "hardly in position to form an intelligent judgement regarding the meaning of these experiences until after we have made a study of religious experience at its best and have considered the significance of the frequent association of the mystical and the pathological."[1] For Boisen, illness and experience, and the pathological and the mystical were often closely associated, so much so that it may be hard to tell where the one ends and the other begins.

Heather Vacek shows how Boisen's work invited religious workers, especially Protestants, to claim greater authority and responsibility in the medical arena—especially in the shunned area of mental illness. But especially "important to him was the authority of experience," and "Proper treatment, he held, started with correct diagnosis, and . . . redefined some illnesses as spiritual problems instead of medical concerns."[2] Thus, Boisen challenged a common assumption of his day that mental illness had its source in the irreversible organic, physical malfunction in the brain and challenged a common assumption even of the present that mental disorder is strictly a medical concern.

Boisen's interests had sociological as well as individual ramifications. Although he is most often associated with the plight and experiences of individual persons, he wrote extensively on sociological issues as well. His earlier, pre-1920, work included employment by the Presbyterian Church in a survey of rural and small-town churches. During World War I Boisen accompanied U.S. expeditionary forces with the Young Men's Christian Association (YMCA), a para-church organization dedicated to education and welfare. Upon his return to the States, he wrote a substantial unpublished manuscript documenting the YMCA's, in Boisen's opinion, largely unsuccessful and ill-placed, efforts to provide religious ministration to U.S. military abroad. Boisen's concern with the individual emerged sharply in 1920 with his own hospitalization and his effort to try to understand what happened to him and to provide treatments and insights useful for other sufferers via the clinical pastoral education experiment. In the 1940s and 1950s sociological concerns returned to the fore as Boisen studied the plight of conscientious objectors in World War II and with his sociologically oriented 1945 monograph "Religion in Crisis and Custom."[3]

Illness and inspiration, individual and the social, revolved in a tightly bound matrix, somewhat echoing Boisen's "family-of-four" vilusion—the one category quickly bleeding into the other. The four relate to each other in intimate and complex ways. Boisen examined illness and experience in the life of the individual. He noted that these states exist relative to, and in relation with, the larger community in which the individual resides. Larger communities, likewise, are deeply and intimately affected by the visions and sufferings of each individual and even the corporate whole can exhibit the phenomena of illness and insight that are often attributed to individuals.

In 1965, shortly after Boisen's death, Seward Hiltner noted the difficulty in trying to interpret his old teacher's approach and experience, which tended to confound and perplex the pastors and psychologists who most often read Boisen's works. He wrote: "The old-fashioned liberals were baffled by the pietistic element; the neo-liberals were puzzled by both the pietism and the mysticism; mystics could not understand the devotion to empirical and scientific inquiry; scientists could not quite reconcile themselves to the mysticism and the mental illness; and so on. Boisen did not always make it easy for the theological critic."[4]

INSPIRATION, ILLNESS, AND THE INDIVIDUAL

Boisen attempted to study his experience of illness and mysticism in a systematic, "scientific," manner. The case study was the bedrock method for how Boisen studied his patients and for how he tried to gain understanding of himself. Glenn Asquith notes that Boisen was wary about placing "too much emphasis on the precipitating factor of a disturbance, because he was convinced that acute disorders were the result of the *accumulation* of inner stresses throughout a person's developmental history."[5] As a result, Boisen developed highly detailed interview templates to collect a broad and deep set of empirical data. Boisen surveyed such areas as a patient's childhood, adolescence, and growth to maturity; relationships with other family members and friends; sexual experiences; vocation; leisure activities and hobbies; and social class and background, and not just how the disorder initially manifested itself. From this base data the case study proceeded to evaluation and assessment. Psychologist Paul Pruyser noted that Boisen did not settle with "one-shot impressions" but scrupulously sought as wide, deep, and systematic a portrait as he could develop.[6]

His joint project with Helen Dunbar to produce a questionnaire on schizophrenic thinking exemplifies Boisen's systematic effort to collect information regarding individual experiences of inspiration and illness. Boisen and Dunbar started with introductory questions on what brought a patient to the hospital, the initial manifestation of illness, and then proceeded to the patient's "unusual experiences," "Sense of the Mysterious and Uncanny" that may have prompted, or at least played part in, eliciting a diagnosis. The questionnaire continued to assess if the patient experienced a sense of peril to self or others and what the patient's sense of personal responsibility, erotic involvement, philosophy of life, as well as religious concerns were. The questionnaire proceeded to ask if the patient held any particular significance for inanimate objects, such as the sun, moon, stars, fire, rocks. The agenda for the interview, or interviews, "may be closed with a consideration of the patient's plans and ambitions," pointing toward the possibility of new directions for the patient's life as a result of the experience. The preface suggested the "questions are not to be used in a mechanical way." It encouraged the interviewer to internalize the content well enough to have a natural and personally engaged conversation. With a goal of drawing out content without excessive focus on the patient's literal responses, the questions "begin with some natural points of contact and proceed by easy transitions, following the patient's leads, . . . centered upon what he is thinking and feeling rather than what he actually says."[7]

Boisen's most thorough and polished case study is the one he produced on himself in his 1960 autobiography.[8] Boisen essays a comprehensive telling and interpretation of his life story and how he interprets his experiences of illness and insight. *Out of the Depths* "sought to present a simple, factual account. It has told the story of my life with a minimum of reflection and interpretation."[9] Only in the concluding chapter does Boisen provide a more explicit self-interpretation. Boisen recalls having "passed through five psychotic episodes during which my thinking has been irrational in the extreme . . . I believe I can say that, severe though they were, they have for me been problem-solving experiences."[10]

Boisen interpreted his illnesses as resulting from unresolved life problems. He attributed his unrest around sex, sexuality, and especially Alice Batchelder as "the basic conflict."[11] He recalled, in detail, his adolescent fixation on sex that he experienced as problematic.[12] Boisen, the scientist, had few reservations discussing highly personal matters in great detail. Batchelder was his foremost fixation. While she factors hardly at all in any of his other writings—except for a cryptic dedication to "A.L.B." in *Exploration of the Inner World*, published shortly after Batchelder's death—she is the central figure in Boisen's own personal case. Batchelder was Boisen's lodestar, a mate always out of reach and for which he viewed himself unworthy but also the muse and inspiration for "the work" upon which her letters frequently urged him to refocus his attention. She is central from their first meeting in 1902, to her premature death in 1935, and remained an ongoing object of his thoughts up to his own death, thirty years later.

Boisen viewed his episodes of mental illness as efforts to overcome lapses in personal and spiritual development "analogous to fever or inflammation in the body. They are attempts at cure and reorganization which are closely related to certain recognized types of religious experience."[13] Drawing upon his youthful crisis of Easter Day of 1898, Boisen recalled that his favorite professor from Indiana University William L. Bryan offered a theory of his case that Boisen found helpful. Bryan, drawing upon John Dewey, posited "that in the acquisition of skill, the curve of progress showed a tendency to strike certain levels and stay there, perhaps even to drop a little, until suddenly there would come an abrupt upward turn which would continue for time with diminishing acceleration until again a dead level was found." Boisen likened his episodes, and perhaps by extension those of others, to these "plateaus" of learning. Some expressions of mental illness, he interpreted as efforts by the mind and soul to make "an abrupt upward turn" toward a new, higher, and more functional level of personal and spiritual development.[14]

Boisen attributed his Easter Day crisis to arrested "development [that] had been checked by the presence of instinctual claims which could neither be controlled nor acknowledged for fear of condemnation." He sought balance in "the prompting 'Do not be afraid to tell,' . . . socializing the difficulty, and it did so on the level of what for me was abiding and universal. I was now at one with the internalized fellowship of the best, the fellowship which is represented by the idea of God." In this instance, dealing with this plateau of personal and spiritual development involved confessing his, almost certainly erotic, fixation to a trusted friend who served as a link to acceptance by the ultimate. Boisen's favorite professor, William L. Bryan, served as that representative of the fellowship of the best—and by extension, Boisen's experience of the divine.[15]

Illness, for Boisen, usually started with what he called an "automatism." An "automatism" for Boisen was an "idea, or thought structure, which after a period of incubation in the region of dim awareness, leaps suddenly into consciousness." Boisen was often vague by what he meant by "automatism." He implies that he experienced "automatisms" as a form of deep concentration, or perseveration, over which he experienced imperfect control. An automatism started as an idea or a pattern that could be an intentional focus of these thoughts and interests but slipped into the "abnormal" when it left conscious control or regulation, resulting in behaviors that, at times, resulted in his hospitalization.[16]

The "automatism" was a symptom, an experience, that lies at the crossroad between illness and inspiration: "abdication of reason before the authority of the automatism is, then, distinctive of the abnormal condition, especially in its acute forms. A better way to express it might to be to say that critical judgment, though never absent, ascribes undue validity to the automatism, or insight, and feeling displaces reason and common sense. The unseen world of fantasy and feeling becomes the supposedly real world." In other words, Boisen acknowledges that his "automatisms" led him to lose reason and common sense and act in ways that others did not regard as reasonable. The "automatism," however, "is not only in the experience of schizophrenics. It is to be found also in the creative activities of poets and inventors and scientists."[17] A difficult task, for Boisen, as well as his patients—like Benjamin Mickle—was in finding ways to tame the "automatism" and socialize what insights it may bring for service not only to oneself but to the world.

Boisen's experience of illness and inspiration led him to believe that the automatism could only be tamed and channeled by discussing it openly and thoroughly, no matter how painful or awkward, with trusted others, his "fellowship of the best." Confession, and confrontation, did not mean indulgence nor fixation on the self. Successful resolution of mental illness exhibited itself in "freedom in my association with others which I had not felt before; I found new interest in my work, and increased effectiveness." In other works, a good outcome accorded with Jamesian pragmatism. It produced greater ability to operate as a social being and to contribute to that society through valuable work and work that the "fellowship of the best," wider society, verified as having value.[18]

Boisen lived, and advocated, an asceticism derided by the clinical pastoral education movement that he founded. He retorted, "The solution offered by some of our chaplain-supervisors was that of getting rid of the conflict by lowering the conscience threshold. There were even those who accepted the later teachings of Wilhelm Reich, advocating a freedom quite at variance with the basic insights of the Hebrew-Christian religion."[19] As clinical pastoral education became increasing student-, instead of patient- and person-centered, Boisen wrote to Fred Kuether, "my emphasis has been more upon the understanding of the patients than upon the personal counseling of students. I proceed upon the assumption that in dealing objectively with persons in trouble, trying to see their problems in the light of his own reactions, the student gets help in understanding of his own difficulties. It has been my policy to let the student work out his own problems except in so far as he comes to me for help."[20]

Against a backdrop of stigma and pessimism within the medical community and the broader culture, Boisen interpreted his experiences with mental illness in a new way. He acknowledged the medical communities' view that some mental illnesses may be "organic" and that science, let alone theology, may not be able to bring cure to such instances. He pressed to acknowledge, at least the possibility, that not all mental illnesses need be permanent incurable conditions nor a result of some defect of character. Boisen interpreted his initial experience with mental illness as an effort to confront and overcome a "plateau" in spiritual and personal development. As the plateau was scaled and overcome—Boisen perceived that the spiritual and psychological struggle had the potential of yielding new insight and healing. The individual struggle with mental illness—a struggle that had the potential of yielding insight and inspiration for self and others—was never a totally individual concern. The healing of individuals was an imperative for the larger society, and the insights that individuals could have could only be confirmed (or disconfirmed) in relationship with others, with Boisen's "fellowship of the best." Thus, for Boisen, the focus was always a holistic view of the patient and how the patient fit into and interacted with the community in which she or he lived.

SOCIETY IN RENAISSANCE, SOCIETY IN CRISIS

Most studies on Boisen focus on the relevance of his writings for individuals; Boisen was at least as much interested in the wider social and cultural ramifications of mental illness and spiritual experience that transcended the merely religious. In the sociological context, how churches did, or all too often did not (or ineffectively), minister to the mentally ill was a primary interest. Boisen's pre-1920 theological writings, published and manuscript, were almost exclusively devoted to how church and para-church organizations either ignored or ineffectively served the communities in which they resided. As the Great Depression progressed and World War II approached, he turned increasingly to sociological and psychological questions of how churches can better serve and work with the mentally ill as well as other excluded and stigmatized groups, such as conscientious objectors[21] and racial minorities.[22]

While religion is central to Boisen's concern and focus, he is also concerned with the wider social ramifications of religious communities failing to serve their communities effectively. His sociological surveys, as early as 1916, recorded church decline, anticipating loss of "social capital" such as that examined by sociologists many decades later.[23] While Boisen's studies recorded, in some cases, numerical decline, they also point to a softening and weakening of civic participation similar to Robert Putnam's "hollowed out" religious and secular institutions that may appear functional at first glance but do not bear out, under closer scrutiny, a robust life outside the nominal demands of formal membership.[24]

Putnam proposes that "faith communities in which people worship together are arguably the single most important repository of social capital in America."[25] His perspectives on "social capital" resonate closely with Boisen's notion of the "fellowship of the best." For Putnam, the "positive consequences of social capital—mutual support, cooperation, trust, institutional effectiveness"—are critical to making functional civic communities as well as healthy and fulfilled individuals.[26] Likewise, for Boisen, social capital and individual health and well-being are inextricably related. It is, at the very least, much more difficult for individuals to live healthy and fulfilled lives unreconciled with their larger "fellowship of the best" within which support, sympathy, belonging, cooperation, trust, and love may be found.[27]

As with his studies of individuals, Boisen endeavored to be thorough and "scientific" in his studies of sociological groups and in his compilation of raw data for use in supporting his discussion and tentative conclusions. Shortly out of seminary, Boisen, along with Fred Eastman, who factored significantly in Boisen's recovery from his 1920 breakdown, commenced work for the Presbyterian Board of Home Missions. Boisen and Eastman conducted a systematic survey of small-town and rural churches in several U.S. states. Drawing "upon my forestry experience and ma[king] use of the sample-plot method," Boisen "chose a number of representative school districts, and with the aid of trustworthy informants I made a list of persons over twelve years of age, together with information regarding their health, education, occupation, church affiliation, and church attendance. I also questioned the church leaders regarding what they were trying to do." Boisen and Eastman wrote up the results of their surveys into reports on the state of the community. The reports discussed the role of churches they found in their "sample-plot" and how those churches may, or may not, have been meeting the concrete or perceived needs of the people living in their catchment basins.[28]

Seward Hiltner alluded to the breadth, depth, and diversity of Boisen's interests—often seeing relations and connections where others did not. Boisen's first major scholarly contribution occurred not in theology, nor pastoral care, but in sociology. Drawing upon interviews he conducted in six counties in New England, the Midwest, and in the Border States, Boisen diagnosed a decline in rural church communities. While Boisen equivocates that "The data upon which these conclusions are based are, of course, not sufficiently comprehensive to make them absolutely convincing," the tentative result of his interviews indicated to him that the number of "those who have lost interest in the church varies directly with the liberalizing of popular religious opinion" that as the fear of "the hell pictured by Jonathan Edwards" declined, so also did membership and interest in churches.[29]

Boisen constantly related the fate of the individual to the fate of the larger society in which he or she lived. Individual salvation and social salvation were inextricably intertwined, and the good that churches could bring transcended the theological. Boisen took some solace in "a significant and hopeful fact that even in the more liberalized sections the better-educated and the more public-spirited are still, for the most part, interested in the church, and the chief losses are among those in whom the altruistic and social interests are poorly developed."[30] Still, Boisen feared that those "whom the church has lost its hold are now, for the most part, outside of any organized social activity. They are no longer interested in anything except their own families, their own work, and their own pleasures."[31]

Boisen prefigured a very modern loss of social capital, a "salvation," that for him was as much this worldly as other-worldly. While Boisen feared for "the church's task in saving or socializing the individual man," he argued that "the old message of eternal punishment and the vicarious atonement" would no longer be sufficient to the task—nor, he argued, should it have to be. Rather, "the hell of wrong habit, of diseased will, of misused opportunity, and of guilty conscience" should provide enough negative motivation. Left unclear, and in fairness outside the scope of his thesis, was how his country churches should remake themselves into "organization[s] in which men are associated at their highest level, in order to guarantee the survival of the values which they desire in their personal life and in their social order" and not offer little more than (after-) "life insurance . . . by accepting a creed, attending worship, and partaking of the sacraments."[32]

By the late 1930s Boisen inquired if major social upsets such as economic depression or world war could serve as creative crises on par with Boisen's interpretation of his own personal crisis of 1920. At the close of World War II, Boisen wondered about the potential of spiritual awakening coming from the crisis of war. He posited: "It is, of course, not to be assumed that crisis periods are always attended by religious quickening—far from it. . . . Any mental hospital can furnish numberless instances of malignant reactions in the face of these turning points in life; also of desperate attempts at reorganization which are more or less successful."[33] While Boisen's article "What War Does to Religion" was largely a speculative "thought piece," he bases his speculation on his own wartime experiences and observations as a YMCA staffer accompanying U.S. Expeditionary Forces during World War I.[34]

Recalling campfire stories of allied atrocities, he doubted that war had "quickening" power. Boisen's World War I informants related their interrogation of a German soldier until "they tickled him with the bayonet until he died. . . . Or consider again a story which went the rounds of the Forty-second Division about a group of twenty-four German prisoners taken by the "Alabams." They were sent to the rear but only four reached their destination. The guards had drawn cards to decide which prisoner they would shoot next. Such stories could be multiplied." While Boisen grants that not all war stories are accurate, what concerned him at least as much was the attitude behind them; he opined in them "a bloodthirstiness which was perhaps more pronounced among the women—at least to hear them talk—and among the people back home than among the fighting men. Human life is cheap in wartime." Boisen doubted war's ability to bring the kind of spiritual transformation he sought—"a marked tendency to think in terms of black and white, to magnify the motes in the eyes of the enemy and to ignore the beams which obscure our own vision. War breeds hatred, and hatred bars the door to love and truth." The hate and absolutism that Boisen attributed as the hallmarks of war seemed to him an unlikely milieu for spiritual transformation, at least not the kind of transformation he sought.[35]

The 1920 Scopes trial coalesced Boisen's views and insights regarding the relationship between mental illness and religious experience of the individual and how it related to ineffective, or nonexistent, ecclesiastical ministry to and with people who needed help. Boisen, a theological "liberal," enthusiastically accepted, endorsed, and made effort to utilize science and the scientific method in his own work and viewed it as critical to Christianity's long-term survival, let alone its thriving.[36] As such he seemed an unlikely defender of William Jennings Bryan, the attorney arguing on behalf of Tennessee's anti-evolution statute. Yet, this he did in publishing an article defending, at least some, aspects of conservative evangelicalism:

> Mr. Bryan's group is, it is true, still primarily concerned with the sick soul, and undoubtedly they are doing some good, . . . It gives to him through prayer all that suggestion and autosuggestion can do as a means of re-education and far more besides. And it surrounds him with the fellowship of the believers. But it is *treatment without diagnosis*. My Liberal friends, however, supply *neither treatment nor diagnosis* [italics are Boisen's]. . . . they have nothing to substitute for Billy Sunday's message. For the soul that is sick they have no gospel of salvation. There is as yet no body of men working together with the enthusiasm of discovery in the effort to formulate the laws of the spiritual life, with which religion must ever be primarily concerned.[37]

Boisen warmly remembered the evangelical and Pentecostal churches of his own youth in rural Indiana and their tent revivals that promoted an emotional and experiential faith that transcended intellectual assent in a "born-again" reorganization of life. In comparison, the liberal mainline churches, of Bloomington and elsewhere, tended to focus on education and social action—activities that Boisen viewed as both relevant and needed. These, more cerebral, approaches, however, did not convey the ineffable visceral experience that triggered the personal and spiritual transformation Boisen experienced and thought may be helpful, if not necessary, for many individuals as well as the communities in which they lived.

Boisen viewed born-again "holy roller," "treatment without diagnosis" churchmanship as well-meaning, but misplaced, engagement with the mentally ill and people facing spiritual and emotional crisis. Still, "treatment without diagnosis" was better than no treatment, neglect, shame, and stigma. Such were the charges Boisen laid against his fellow "liberals." Boisen's conservative "treatment without diagnosis" versus liberal "neither treatment nor diagnosis" he repeated, almost *ad nauseam*, as a mantra in his writings on church engagement, or lack thereof, with mental illness in the decades to come.

Boisen's comparison of "holy rollers" against "churches of custom" is based primarily on a systematic "sample plot" study of churches in Indiana and Tennessee.[38] As he hypothesized that crisis could motivate individuals toward engaging and solving problems, he analogized that the same dynamic may be at work in corporate examples. He credits "the rise of the Holy Roller churches of my own native town and of the county in which it is located. . . . sprang up among the underprivileged as a reaction to the social crisis induced by the economic distress of that period."[39] "Churches of custom" in his home town typically were "composed in large part of persons connected with the university and of those who make some pretensions of 'culture.' . . . Their chief feature is a sermon, some thirty minutes in length, dealing with some problem relating to the conduct of life and appealing to the intelligence and loyalty of the congregation."

Whereas, old-line, established churches tended to appeal to erudition, custom, tradition, and decorum, the churches of "the new group," the "holy rollers," provided haven to those of lower-income and lower social status; "they have found little satisfaction in the formal type of service . . . and, rightly or wrongly, they have felt that they were not wanted. They have therefore organized churches of their own."[40] Boisen generalized that

> their services are characterized by spontaneity and enthusiasm. All the new churches believe that one has to be "converted" in order to be "saved" and that this conversion must be followed by a "second baptism" or "sanctification." Five of them [of thirteen in total of Boisen's "new" group] go further and teach that the believer must in addition be "baptized by the Holy Spirit" and give evidence thereof by "speaking with tongues," as the early Christians did on the Day of Pentecost."[41]

Thus, Monroe County's "new" churches represented a corporate effort in problem solving analogous to Boisen's individual case. The problems his "holy rollers" faced were social exclusion found in lower educational status in a university town and furthermore in economic crisis and displacement of the Great Depression in the 1930s. For Boisen, the enthusiastic, experiential religion of the "new" churches provided spiritual sustenance that the intellectual, and often arid, "churches of custom" did not.

As with his personal prophet, Benjamin Mickle, Boisen admired and respected the experiential and heartfelt religion of those he studied but with which he did not entirely identify. Boisen's "holy rollers" as a community, like Mickle the individual, were "making religion real" for themselves and others in "the intensity of their religious faith they feel themselves to be instruments of God," when, so often they were made to feel valueless.[42] Boisen, however, reflecting personal experience, warned that not all "special things" were of divine origin. "The tendency to ascribe to a divine source the idea that flashes into the mind is as old as the human race and it is not without justification. Certainly, new and creative ideas do come in just this way. So also do ideas that are valueless and ideas that are disturbing and dangerous."[43] Boisen warned that the "otherworldly emphasis among the Pentecostals call attention to a common tendency to divorce religion from social action" and to "withdraw from the world and its problems." He mourned cases where "leaders of reform movements have abundant reason to know that there are multitudes of unstable individuals who seek in attempts to reform the system and escape from the need of reforming themselves. But always it is a misfortune when religious zeal stops short of its practical task of bringing the kingdom of heaven down to earth. It seems equally unfortunate when those who are in a position to work for social betterment lose touch with the church."[44] Boisen sees the individual and the social, illness and inspiration as tightly and inexplicably connected.

Boisen's interests and energies, predictably, returned to fashioning ways of helping individuals in crisis. Boisen suggested that individuals may have once "'hit the saw-dust trail' to find salvation or cure" in a religious revival experience as a response to personal crisis. He advised that new and supplemental methods were needed, especially for liberal Protestants, to address the spiritual needs posed by mental illness and social crisis in a way that united the scientific with the experiential. In the near aftermath of the Scopes extravaganza, Boisen was not afraid to reflect, openly, on his own personal witness: "Here again I may speak from personal experience. Within the past three years it has been my misfortune, or perhaps my privilege, to spend a year as a patient in a hospital for the insane. It is this experience which has radically changed my point of view with reference to the church's task."[45] Boisen's social advocacy was irreducibly rooted in his own individual experience of illumination amid illness.

A larger "fellowship of the best" could treat and accompany individuals in crisis—likewise spiritually strengthened individuals composed that "fellowship of the best." Boisen affirms that the impulse behind "Mr. Bryan and his friends" support for scriptural literalism was understandable even if he viewed the literalist position, itself, as logically and factually undefendable. The fallout of Darwinian evolution, he granted, shook the faith of many: "the breaking down of the old traditional authority does destroy popular faith with a resulting loss of influence on the part of the church and the disruption of the old moral safe-guards." For Boisen, these "old moral safe-guards" meant not only morality but also the entire edifice of experiential, spiritual cures, resources, and remedies for what Boisen viewed as spiritual ailments. Thus, "the church must have an *authoritative message* [italics are Boisen's]." That "authoritative message," however, could not be scriptural inerrancy nor nostalgic retreat to an era and mentality Boisen saw as no longer suitable to modernity.

Rather, Boisen accused "the liberal group . . . precisely in the fact that it has not yet gone far enough. *It has merely surrendered the authority of the tradition without freeing itself from the traditional point of view* [italics are Boisen's]." By this Boisen meant that liberal Protestants needed to expand their focus beyond "the traditional disciplines, the scriptural languages and literature, church history, systematic theology and homiletics" and encompass "*the human personality in either health or disease or the social and economic forces which affect it* [italics are Boisen's]." The problem facing, especially liberal, Protestantism was in projecting "a living and prophetic message and speak with the authority of those who are divinely inspired. . . . As a group the liberal group is without authority or conviction, and its attitude is apologetic, not enthusiastic and aggressive."[46]

The solution could not be addressed by seminary curriculum reform alone. The corporate task, especially for his own liberal Protestantism, was to "awaken" "those whom I have called the "unawakened." These are the persons, usually fairly well adjusted in the vocational, social and sexual fields, who have never really come to terms with their ultimate loyalties. . . . but go through life absorbed all too often in the petty, the trivial, the selfish, and even in that which makes them loathsome in their own eyes. . . . it may be necessary to disturb their conscience in regard to the quality of the life they are living."[47] Churches of his youth utilized the camp revival to "convict"— convince individuals and communities of their alienation from God and need for reconciliation not only on an intellectual level but on an experiential level. Modern religion would need to find a way to recall women and men to their deepest and highest loyalties of integrity within, and with persons and society without.

For Boisen, a "new evangelism" was needed to build realized, and healed, individuals and communities. For this to happen, religion would need to enlist, and cooperate with, science and psychology in "our growing knowledge of human nature and its problems and it must recognize that the task of reconstruction is merely begun when an individual is awakened to his need. . . . and a force of workers equipped to give the needed help."[48] While Boisen's early clinical pastoral education programs and manuals on pastoral care may offer some hints on practical efforts—it may be relatively easy to give the reasons for why a spiritual renewal may be needed—it is more difficult to tell someone how to do it.[49]

In 1936, he wrote in expansive language that often confused, bemused, or alienated his more academically inclined readers. As the globe slouched toward fascism and world war, the "how" of spiritual renewal and revitalization may have eluded him, but the "why" did not: "Once more I am standing on the threshold of the limitless unknown, face to face with death and life. It is not merely personal fate that is at stake. I see unfolding before me the great drama of the ages. Amid all the interplay of forces and against the dark background of the selfish and the cruel and the lustful, I see continually manifesting itself a great and loving Spirit, at work in the homely aspirations and loyalties of ordinary folk as well as in the heroic endeavors of prophet and leader."[50]

This "family-of-four" of the individual and the larger community (or communities) in which she or he lives and the interplay of inspiration mixed with and opposed to illness are critical to how Boisen interpreted his visit to his "little-known country" experience of mental illness mixed with experiential inspiration. As Boisen experienced his own illness, he also noticed the mentally ill as omnipresent in the communities in which he lived and studied. Illness manifested itself in individuals in crises related to alcoholism, depression, bipolar disorder, and, his favorite, "dementia praecox." So also he viewed economic depression, war, and growing isolation and loss of community as critical social crises in need of some resolution that begged a conversion of soul, for communities as well as individuals.

Inspiration and illness often manifested together in crises that demanded resolution and healing that included, yet transcended, the intellect. For Boisen, right relationship with one's highest loyalty in the "fellowship of the best" manifested spiritual attainment. This fellowship manifested itself in unselfish and, if need be, sacrificial dedication to the common wealth. How the individual lived out that loyalty and fellowship was up to them so long as it was done loyally and in fellowship and not merely to indulge personal whim, caprice, or pleasure-seeking.

Boisen's focus returned to working with individuals in crisis. As individuals could be aided in confronting and negotiating their own plateaus of development, this spiritual growth could also provide leaven for the lump of society. Many individuals suffered crisis demanding resolution, as was the case with Boisen. Boisen proposed that the only resolution for social decay, narcissism, and excessive individualism that ignored the common good was to have a cataclysmic spiritual experience that would restore relationship between individual and community. Invariably, Boisen's solution to crises both individual and social was spiritual renewal—an ineffable, experiential event that resembled the "born-again" experiences he recalled witnessing in his youth and that he studied again in his "holy rollers."

Boisen posited the need for spiritual experience and renewal repeatedly throughout his career, yet, he provided few direct answers on how to achieve it—for individuals or for communities. His emphasis on the "living human documents" via his clinical education program—of studying actual human beings confronting real-time spiritual problems—is likely his best known and most enduring answer on how to follow a path for which he gave no clear map.

NOTES

1. Boisen, *The Exploration of the Inner World*, 10–11, 57. "Exploration of the Inner World" was Boisen's most highly regarded contribution to the field of chaplaincy and the relationship of spirituality and psychology. Boisen consistently, and rather dogmatically, differentiated mental disorders that were the result of an "organic" or physical problem with the brain—with which he was not interested against disorders "of the problem-solving variety" where no observable disease process could be verified.

2. Vacek, *Madness*, 90–91.

3. Anton T. Boisen, *Religion in Crisis and Custom: A Sociological and Psychological Study* (New York, NY: Harper & Brothers, 1945).

4. Seward Hiltner, "The Heritage of Anton T. Boisen," *Pastoral Psychology* 16, no. 158 (1965): 6.

5. Glenn H. Asquith, Jr., "The Case Study Method of Anton T. Boisen," *The Journal of Pastoral Care* 34, no. 2 (1980): 94.

6. Asquith, "The Case Study Method of Anton T. Boisen," 89–94; Pruyser, "Anton T. Boisen and the Psychology of Religion," 215.

7. Helen F. Dunbar and Anton T. Boisen, "H.F.D., A.T.B., Schizophrenic Thinking Psychiatric Examination" (Unpublished Manuscript, no date), Series 4, Box 1, Folder 140, Boisen Papers, Chicago Theological Seminary.

8. Boisen, *Out of the Depths*.

9. Boisen, *Out of the Depths*, 198.

10. Boisen, *Out of the Depths*, 201–2.

11. Boisen, *Out of the Depths*, 198.

12. Boisen, *Out of the Depths*, 46. An example of Boisen's unflinching detail regarding his own life: "The 'transgression' referred to was that of a psychically induced orgasm. Concerning my problem, I may say that it had to do chiefly with erotic fantasy derived for the most part from reading. Actual orgasm was not frequent,

and when it did occur it resulted usually from psychic stimulation. The fantasies were always of the opposite sex."

13. Boisen, *The Exploration of the Inner World*, 29–30.
14. Boisen, *Out of the Depths*, 47–48.
15. Boisen, *Out of the Depths*, 48–49.
16. Boisen, *Out of the Depths*, 203.
17. Boisen, *Out of the Depths*, 203.
18. Boisen, *Out of the Depths*, 49.
19. Boisen, *Out of the Depths*, 186.
20. Boisen, *Out of the Depths*, 190.
21. Anton T. Boisen, "Conscientious Objectors: Their Morale in Church-Operated Service Units," *Psychiatry: Journal of the Biology and Pathology of Interpersonal Relations* 7, no. 3 (1944): 215–24.
22. Boisen, *Religion in Crisis and Custom*, 82–83, 259.
23. Robert D. Putnam, *Bowling Alone: The Collapse and Revival of American Community* (New York, NY: Simon & Schuster, 2000).
24. Putnam, *Bowling Alone*, 72.
25. Putnam, *Bowling Alone*, 66.
26. Putnam, *Bowing Alone*, 22.
27. Anton T. Boisen, "The Problem of Sin and Salvation in the Light of Psychopathology," *The Journal of Religion* 22, no. 3 (1942): 288–301. Boisen published this article in 1942 as his interests shifted back toward the sociological ramifications of his work and experiences. Here he speaks of salvation in a context of "confession and forgiveness. Man is, therefore, a social being, and the idea of God is the symbol of that fellowship of the best apart from which we cannot live and of which our standards of value are merely a function. Salvation or cure is, then, not a matter of the correction of faulty habits or of the resolution of conflicts but of restoration to this fellowship."
28. Boisen, *Out of the Depths*, 65–68.
29. Anton T. Boisen, "Factors Which Have to Do with the Decline of the Country Church," *American Journal of Sociology* 22, no. 2 (1916): 178–79, 191–92.
30. Boisen, "Factors Which Have to Do with the Decline of the Country Church," 191.
31. Boisen, "Factors Which Have to Do with the Decline of the Country Church," 191.
32. Boisen, "Factors Which Have to Do with the Decline of the Country Church," 192.
33. Anton T. Boisen, "What War Does to Religion," *Religion in Life* 14 (1945): 2.
34. Anton T. Boisen, "Notes of a Camp Follower in the World War" (Unpublished Manuscript, December 22, 1922), Series 15, Box 6, Folders 10, 11, Boisen Papers, Chicago Theological Seminary.
35. Boisen, "What War Does to Religion," 9.
36. Boisen, *The Exploration of the Inner World*, 236–37. Boisen observes, based on data collected in his own early church surveys with Eastman, that "Even though the conservative attitude might succeed in holding the lines a little longer, it offers no

solution. . . . For this reason, I hold that a shift from faith in a revealed religion to an empirical basis, which is responsible for so much of the present confusion, must be not merely accepted but eagerly furthered."

37. Anton T. Boisen, "In Defense of Mr. Bryan: A Personal Confession by a Liberal Clergyman," *American Review* 5 (1924): 323–28. Boisen, at first, proposed publishing under the title, "In Defense of Mr. Bryan: A Personal Confession by a Disciple of Dr. Fosdick." The title associating Boisen and his views with the renowned liberal clergyman, and Boisen's old classmate at Union Seminary, Harry Emerson Fosdick. Fosdick wanted no part in the Scopes controversy. Protesting a draft copy that Boisen thoughtfully sent him, he wrote: "This article would be an attack in the rear, and a very serious one indeed. The plain fact is that you have used Mr. Bryan's name and mine for advertising purposes in order to get across your message, which is a very important and true one. But you are quite mistaken when in your letter you say that 'nothing which I have said here reflects in the slightest degree upon you.' I know well enough that you did not intend that it should, but unquestionably it will be taken up by my enemies and used in most serious ways." Harry Emerson Fosdick to Boisen, February 19, 1924, Series 2, Box 3, Folder 32, Boisen Papers, Chicago Theological Seminary; Anton T. Boisen, "In Defense of Mr. Bryan: A Personal Confession by a Disciple of Dr. Fosdick" (Unpublished Manuscript, no date), Series 1, Box 7, Folder 25, Boisen Papers, Chicago Theological Seminary.

38. Boisen, *Religion in Crisis and Custom*, 8; Anton T. Boisen, "Religion and Hard Times," *Social Action (A Magazine of Fact): Published by the Council for Social Action of the Congregational and Christian Churches* (15 March 1930): 8–30.

39. Boisen, *Religion in Crisis and Custom*, 8.
40. Boisen, *Religion in Crisis and Custom*, 16.
41. Boisen, *Religion in Crisis and Custom*, 16–17.
42. Boisen, "Religion and Hard Times," 33.
43. Boisen, "Religion and Hard Times," 32.
44. Boisen, "Religion and Hard Times," 34.
45. Boisen, "In Defense of Mr. Bryan," 326.
46. Boisen, "In Defense of Mr. Bryan," 324–25.
47. Boisen, *The Exploration of the Inner World*, 280.
48. Boisen, *The Exploration of the Inner World*, 281.
49. In 1946 Boisen published a brief practical guide for pastors on interviewing parishioners. Anton T. Boisen, *Problems in Religion and Life: A Manual for Pastors with Outlines for the Co-operative Study of Personal Experience in Social Situations* (Nashville, TN: Abingdon-Cokesbury Press, 1946).
50. Boisen, *The Exploration of the Inner World*, 295.

Chapter 4

My Friends Are Coming to Help Me

The idea came, 'Your friends are coming to help you.' I seemed to feel new life pulsing all through me. And it seemed that a lot of new worlds were forming. There was music everywhere and rhythm and beauty. But the plans were always thwarted. I heard what seemed to be a choir of angels. I thought it the most beautiful music I had ever heard.[1]

In 1920 Boisen experienced a vilusion of friends coming to help him. It is unlikely that Boisen was, at least consciously, alluding to the aid of others in operationalizing his visions. Still, it would have been impossible for Boisen to implement his complex vision without the aid and collaboration of friends and allies.[2]

Anton Boisen's work alternated between the individual and the social. His pre-1920 work was primarily sociological. From 1920 through his official "retirement" in 1938, his focus tended toward the individual. Following 1938 Boisen pivoted back to the corporate and sociological ramifications of his work. He was profoundly aware that mental illness and religious experience were not only individual conditions but resided in, and were confirmed by, relationship with other people and the communities they formed. Heather Vacek has studied American Protestant efforts to practice "hospitality" toward mental illness and the mentally ill. Christopher DeBono has examined Boisen's contributions to Catholic cultural competency in conducting psychiatric chaplaincy.[3] As mental illness and wellness and spiritual experience are socially conditioned, Boisen depended on the collaboration and aid of his "friends" to transform madness to vision.

Edward Thornton explains that Boisen's vision revolved around two overarching goals. He wanted to (1) explore religion from a psychological angle, including "one's own development and identity; . . .not only about ecstatic religious experience, but also about professional functioning in ministry." (2) He wanted to revolutionize professional education for ministry through empirical, clinical, observation: "For this he believed there was no better laboratory than the mental hospital and no better library than 'living human documents.'"[4] In so doing, Boisen sought not only to better understand his own visions and delusions and those who had experiences similar to him but also to revolutionize theological education and pastoral care through working with the observed experiences of actual people in crisis.

Boisen implicitly realized that his experience and personality made him difficult for others to identify with and understand. Henri Nouwen wrote that "Boisen was a man with few close friends, lonesome all through his life and suffering from a mental illness that was hardly understood. Only through the publication in 1960 of his biography . . . did the real nature of his pain and isolation become known, even to his colleagues and friends."[5] In spite of Boisen's acclaimed isolation and loneliness, he was not without friends who aided his work. Nouwen pointed to "significant others" who provided critical aid and support to Boisen's work, and to him personally, who made operationalizing his visions possible. Among these "significant others," Nouwen lists William Lowe Bryan, Boisen's professor at Indiana University; Raphael Zon, his supervisor with the U.S. Forest Service; and Alice Batchelder, the not entirely requited love of his life.[6] Bryan and Batchelder gave Boisen the spiritual and psychological center to keep on task with his projects. Zon provides but one example of not only a personal friend but a teacher who gave him the analytical tools grounded in the scientific method to build a program of inquiry and instruction. Other "friends" like Seward Hiltner built upon Boisen's work for future generations, especially in bringing Boisen's notion of clinical training in closer cooperation with theological schools.[7]

Nouwen's insights on Boisen point to the critical role of friends and colleagues in making his work possible. Boisen's friends provided not only the tools he needed to commence and continue his work but also the psychological center to stay on task. Boisen's experience and project parallel the early Mental Hygiene movement, which was intimately tied to the personal life and experiences of Clifford Beers, its founder, who in many ways prefigured Boisen's life, experiences, and work. However motivated, intelligent, and creative Boisen and Beers may have been, these individuals needed sympathetic helpers to carry on the work. Seward Hiltner, a student and steadfast sympathizer, built upon Boisen's work and integrated it more closely with the work of traditional theological schools during Boisen's lifetime and in the decades after his death.[8]

Glenn Asquith's prefatory comments on Boisen's 1960 article *Inspiration in the Light of Psychopathology* hint at the emerging role of community, imaginative reinterpretation, a sort of "friendship" toward the mentally ill and mental illness as a possible means toward healing. In this article, Boisen cites a favorite patient, Benjamin Mickle, whose "auditory hallucinations 'may represent the operations of the creative mind." While Boisen's suggestions may, as Asquith suggests, prefigure R. D. Laing and Thomas Szasz' efforts toward "deinstitutionalization" of the mentally ill, Boisen did not hold that all hallucinations were beneficial or to be encouraged nor did he imply that all such experiences were under the individual's control.[9] While some voices and visions may be hallmarks of creativity and inspiration, some were "paranoiac" and "medieval mystics had to learn the lesson that some ideas which came surging into their minds could hardly come from God." The difference "depends entirely upon the value of their message and of their achievement."[10]

Boisen elaborates, "In every mental hospital, . . . we find patients who believe that God has spoken to them, that he has given them some important mission to perform and that they have some important role to act out."[11] Yet, not all are misunderstood geniuses to be left to their own devices in a society that may not be able to accommodate their idiosyncrasy without harm to self and/or others. Boisen gave Mickle the benefit of the doubt in advocating for his release from custodial care, but he also admitted that it was Mickle's "fighting proclivity which kept him in the hospital and blocked my efforts to set him free."[12] Still, Boisen saw value in Mickle's bizarre experiences and behavior, and in Mickle personally, who "seemed a work of art or, better perhaps, an artist himself" who reframed the world in which he lived that often treated him with neglect and cruelty.[13]

Boisen's vision for engagement was a two-way street. While, on the one hand, larger communities must be challenged to accommodate the odd or unusual, on the other hand that individual is tasked to cooperate in their own accommodation. David Steere cited Boisen as prefiguring "behavior or 'reality' therapy," and more recent Cognitive Behavioral Therapies in "discard[ing] the 'excuses' attached to 'being sick.'" In religious terms, "Sin was a matter of broken relationships to be restored. And whether we describe these experiences as sin or sickness, the person must finally assume responsibility for making restoration and getting well."[14]

A RECEPTIVE CONTEXT: AMERICAN PROGRESSIVE REFORM

No matter how committed Boisen was to forward his visions in socially useful ways, his efforts would have gone nowhere save for a context and other people who were ready to accept his visions as visionary and accept him as more than a madman. Boisen's first hospitalization coincided with the waning days of the Progressive Era, a time that heralded reform of medicine, medical education, and treatment of the mentally ill. Boisen fortuned upon a context that was ready to hear him and take him seriously. Ronald Numbers notes that Boisen's era coincided with a "reformation" of American medical practice and education that sought to "increase the quality of medical practitioners." Data establish that due to tightening regulatory standards, "between 1910 and 1920 the number of medical schools declined from 155 to 85, and it continued falling for the next two decades." The schools that survived attrition included "rigorous scientific and clinical training" in their curricula.[15]

The case study was a hallmark of Progressive Era education across the arts and sciences that bled into medicine as well. By Boisen's time, the case study tradition was already well established. In 1870 Christopher Columbus Langdell introduced the case method at Harvard University School of Law via his *Selection of Cases on the Law of Contracts*. Langdell introduced the case method in having his students study law by reading published court opinions showing how law was made by court deliberations over live controversies at bar.[16] Many decades later the case study method had spread to several other areas of inquiry. Boston physician and Harvard professor Richard Cabot, already well familiar with the case method in multiple didactic contexts, was shocked to discover that the case method was foreign to theological and pastoral education and that most seminary faculty assumed pastoral skill was an innate quality that "could not be taught."[17]

Cabot urged the creation of "a clinical year in the course of theological study" in the tradition and method of case and clinical study already well-established in law and medicine. Cabot observed from his frequent encounters with theological students at Harvard Yard, "I have known medical students and theological students, their ideals and hopes, they seem to me astonishingly alike. . . . the majority want to be of use to their kind, in man-to-man personal relations." In order to apply theological and religious ideas to concrete problems of actual people in crisis, Cabot proposed:

> Not a medical year or a sociological year, but a year of practice in applying their religious beliefs in the attempt to encourage, to console, to steady human souls and to *learn from them* [sic] as well as from failures in attempting to help them. . . . no one need fear to intrude upon the almshouse if he goes there with the sincere desire to bring a little companionship and cheerfulness into lives that are often very lonely and depressed. Visitors to old people in the almshouses, to the sick in hospitals, to the insane in asylums, are sorely needed.[18]

Cabot's proposal to extend the case method to the study of pastoral care and theology drew upon methods already prevalent in Progressive Era education. It also addressed the emerging recognition of the need to provide more than custodial care for the sick, the vulnerable, the insane, and for others in crisis. As Boisen wrote in his first published article (1923) following his hospitalization at Westboro, "I am under no illusion as to the present equipment of the average pastor for such work. His academic preparation has not included the consideration of such problems. He finds himself quite at a loss when he meets them in actual life."[19]

Christopher DeBono establishes a subtle shift from strictly "custodial care" to a more holistic vision "which sought to support the totality of the individual with a concern for such issues as their health, legal, social welfare, as well as the 'religious welfare' of the hospitalized patient." Boisen's visions, proposals, and programs for theological education fortuitously coincided with "a new clinical vision" that sought to reform and transform the teaching and practice of medicine.[20]

Gerald Grob, in his study of mental illness in the Progressive Era, notes that "between 1900 and 1940 a self-conscious mental hygiene movement replaced an older prescriptive and didactic tradition."[21] The new clinical vision emerged not only from authoritative figures but also from, and in relationship with, those subject to the clinical vision. This "self-conscious mental hygiene movement" is inextricably connected with the founding of the National Committee for Mental Hygiene in 1909 and the life of Clifford Beers, its founder.[22]

Beers' life and experience parallel Boisen's in significant ways. They were born in the same year, 1876; Beers attended school at Yale; and upon graduation in 1897 (the same year Boisen graduated from Indiana University), he briefly held a succession of jobs in New York City. Beers' clinical-level symptoms manifested earlier than Boisen's. A suicide attempt and ongoing deterioration in his psychological condition resulted in a stay of over three years in various mental hospitals. Upon discharge in 1903, Beers found improved mental stability, employment, and increasing success in the business world. As success compounded, Beers resolved to write a book about his experiences and found a movement to help others struggling from mental illness and improve conditions in mental hospitals.[23]

As Beers' vision for a movement and a book crystalized, his mood became, in Grob's words, increasingly "elated." Beers' elation increased to the point where he agreed to his brother's advice to seek hospitalization. During Beers' month-long hospitalization, he worked on the nucleus of a manuscript that was the basis of his 1908 book *A Mind That Found Itself*.[24] The effect of this book Grob describes as "comparable to that of *Uncle Tom's Cabin*" in drawing attention to abuse and inhumane treatment in mental hospitals and in agitating for more humane conditions.[25]

Like Boisen, Beers was classically educated and had a period of wandering and unsatisfying employment that culminated in a major personal crisis. Following hospitalization, he reentered society propelled by a vision. Although, Beers, as Boisen, suffered from some ongoing mental instability, he was aided by loyal, sympathetic, and often very patient friends who helped him operationalize a vision. Beers relied on the advice of his brother. He also benefited from the financial, social, and personal support of William James, a fellow visionary and sufferer from mental illness, who staunchly backed Beers' work until James' death in 1910.[26]

Boisen's first employer at Worcester State Hospital was also critical to implementing his ideas. The "enlightened administration" of Dr. William A. Bryan consistently, and fearlessly, experimented in operationalizing a humane clinical vision.[27] Bryan's efforts at Worcester Hospital included an attempt "to organize a 'community council' made up of representatives from various religious and social welfare organizations, in the hope of easing the transition from institution to community." Bryan's effort in this regard met limited success and tepid response even from Beers: "Most people, he noted, considered a mental breakdown 'a sort of disgrace' and regarded recovered patients 'with some suspicion.' He therefore questioned 'whether the organizing of ex-patients, even those who may be willing to join such an organization, will be in their interest.'"[28] Bryan hired Boisen, the former mental patient, to be chaplain at Worcester during increased cultural tension and conflict between "science" and "religion." As Bryan received blowback from his colleagues on the eve of the Scopes trial, Bryan retorted, "I would hire a horse doctor if he could help my patients."[29]

A MERE LONELY MADMAN LEAVES THE HOSPITAL

Before Boisen could help Bryan's patients, he needed a home, training, contacts, and a job. For these to happen Boisen needed friends and sympathetic allies willing to give him a chance. Boisen's friends and contacts, established prior to his 1920 crisis, as well as those he soon met, were critical to giving him the chance he needed.

Boisen gained a conditional release from Westboro State Hospital in January 1922. His release was coordinated through his mother, who was Boisen's legal guardian; Fred Eastman, Boisen's long-time friend from Union Seminary; and Norman Nash, a faculty member at Episcopal Theological School in Cambridge, Massachusetts, and Boisen's former supervisor when he worked for the YMCA during World War I. Nash suggested that Boisen contact Ellwood Worcester's Emmanuel Clinic in consultation on his case. With Boisen's permission, Eastman and Nash turned over their correspondence to Worcester for his opinion on Boisen.[30] Nash aided Boisen in finding housing at the Episcopal seminary and in enrolling in courses.[31] He also aided

Boisen in enrolling as a special student at Andover Theological Seminary, which was then affiliated with Harvard University.[32] Eastman, Nash, and Worcester were critical in giving Boisen the emotional and material support he needed to leave custodial care and start a new life.

Boisen needed tools and education to breach the "wall" between science and religion. His germinating notion of empirical, research-informed, work with spiritual experiencers and the mentally ill and in promoting a new kind of theological education required tools appropriate to his work and vision. Fortuitously, Boisen did not have to start completely from scratch. He already held a graduate degree in divinity from Union Seminary in New York and possessed education and practical experience in the scientific method via a forestry degree from Yale and in his work with Raphael Zon a significant figure in the foundation of the U.S. Forest Service.

Decades after leaving the Forest Service, Boisen continued his dialogue, and friendship, with Zon. Zon, however, was often puzzled by Boisen's subject matter. Having reviewed a manuscript Boisen sent him, Zon replied:

> I am impressed with the smooth flow of your English and the richness of your vocabulary. The reading of the paper, however, did not evoke in me concrete reactions within the range of my own experience, and therefore left me somewhat in a hazed state of mind. This is probably because you are dealing in ideas and concepts too remote from my own intellectual evolution, and in terminology not entirely understandable to me. You will have to translate these ideas to me in some simpler form, more on the mental level of my capacity to grasp abstractions.[33]

While Zon expresses his inclination to the concrete and the practical, which was inherent to his nature, he also underlined his friendship and colleagiality with Boisen as a person. Noting an upcoming meeting with the Department of Agriculture at Chicago's Hotel Stevens, Zon proposed, "I naturally would like to see you and talk with you."[34] While Zon did not always understand Boisen's subject matter, as the decades moved on, he did provide him with a solid foundation in practically oriented research and the scientific method. Perhaps even more importantly, Zon was among the cluster of sympathetic, and often patient, friends who listened to and made time for a man whom others dismissed.

Boisen already possessed sophisticated knowledge and methods for his proposed work, yet, Ellwood Worcester and Richard Cabot were critical in providing the remaining equipping and contacts necessary for Boisen to begin his new work at Worcester State Hospital. Many of Boisen's friends and confidantes were connected by class, profession, and family. Norman Nash suggested that Boisen consult with Ellwood Worcester and his Emmanuel Clinic.³⁵ Ellwood Worcester had professional and familial ties to Boston physician and professor, Richard Cabot, a critical factor in gaining Boisen the training, contacts, and financing he needed. Cabot taught courses in pastoral care at Boston's Episcopal Seminary, and this placed him in proximity to Ellwood Worcester. This tie was reinforced by Cabot's collegial association with fellow physician Alfred Worcester (Ellwood's cousin), who collaborated with Cabot on his article and advocacy for clinical training for theological students.³⁶ Although Cabot was a staunch "organicist," that mentally ill persons were physically so by brain structure, and could not be expected to "get better" with or without treatment, he was willing to give Boisen the benefit of the doubt holding that Boisen's "one attack of mental disease," possibly, provided qualification to work with the mentally ill.³⁷

Who Cabot was, in Victorian and Progressive Era Boston, was at least as important as his profession or anything he could teach or tangibly give. Christopher Crenner reminds us that Richard Cabot, in the 1920s, practiced in a medical profession different than that of today. As professional expectations and state regulations tightened, "American medicine in Cabot's day was a rapidly changing profession with fluid boundaries, but a great number of social strata separated its various practitioners." Richard Cabot commanded resources and respect, "as much by reason of his membership in a socially elite Boston family, the Cabot's, as he did by reason of being a physician."³⁸

Cabot's class and social standing admitted Boisen to contacts and material backing that Boisen could not marshal on his own. Boisen's vision and ripening interests coincided with Cabot's changing professional interests and aspirations. As early as 1893, Cabot wrote to Ella Lyman, his future wife, anticipating he would "practice medicine till 45 or till I can live on my income, then I will cultivate other fields." By his late forties, Cabot, indeed, ramped down his medical practice. After service in World War I, Cabot saw 229 patients in 1919 and only 40 in 1920.³⁹ Cabot also met with private professional disappointment. His private notes traced his divergence from traditional medical practice to his being passed over in 1912 for the coveted Jackson Professorship of Medicine at Harvard Medical School. While "Cabot's public good sportsmanship on this occasion drew general praise," his personal notes reflected his disappointment and suspicion that he was member of a profession where he did not, at heart, really belong. Cabot noted, as medicine evolved, "The great men in medicine are interested in Disease. I was happier teaching ethics." Cabot's evolution propelled him toward Boisen's humanitarian interests.⁴⁰

Cabot partnered with Alfred Worcester in warning against hewing too closely to the emerging disease model at the cost of developing a fuller knowledge of, and relationship with, the patient. Alfred Worcester, like

Cabot, valued the medical role of skillful diagnosis yet prioritized the ongoing therapeutic relationship between doctor and patient:

> Worcester expressed no particular criticism of the tools and techniques required here for diagnosis. What seemed to trouble him was how the requirements of making a diagnosis altered the doctor's interactions with patients. The doctor was so deeply absorbed in the immediate technical goals that he sacrificed an ongoing therapeutic influence over his patient. Worcester reportedly claimed proudly that his own patients often got well "without the luxury of diagnosis."[41]

Alfred Worcester's primacy of the therapeutic relationship also reflected medical realities of his times. Crenner explains that physician "unalloyed authority" reflected a reality that followed Cabot's (and Alfred Worcester's) time and is coming into question in our own time as we see a reclamation "of the patient's capacity as a discriminating client of the physician's services." Cabot, and Alfred Worcester, at least implicitly, understood that they were collaborators with an active patient with agency all their own. "The patients who frequented his office were often quite active and opinionated about their medical care. They selected Cabot from a variety of practitioners," Alfred Worcester, certainly, and Cabot likely to a lesser extent, valued the active role of the patient and saw this as a positive in the facilitation of healing and wholeness.[42] This collaborative emphasis coincided with Boisen's goals and aspirations and provides an image of medicine that is in many ways surprisingly modern.

Cabot's support for, and collaboration with, Boisen and his early work went beyond the philosophical. Cabot provided critical aid and advocacy in Boisen gaining the tools and credentialing he would need to engage his work. Cabot's influence was indispensable. Recently released from a mental hospital, Boisen may not have seemed the most promising, or desirable, of students. Cabot and Nash encouraged his graduate studies at Andover and at Harvard, where he took courses in social ethics with Cabot, abnormal psychology with William McDougall, the case study method and the psychology of belief with Macfie Campbell (who had previously examined and treated Boisen in his illness),[43] and did applied case work as a social worker with Susie Lyons at Boston Psychopathic Hospital, where Boisen had been recently treated.[44] Charles Hall related that Cabot "would take Boisen to a professor, introduce him and say, 'He is going to be in your class.' It was almost impossible to say no to Cabot."[45]

Cabot's influence rounded out Boisen's access to the analytical tools he needed. The courses Cabot sometimes strong-armed Boisen into, incidentally but critically, put him in contact with colleagues, contacts, and friends who supported, aided, and partnered with his work for decades to come. Cabot,

McDougall, Campbell, and Lyons were early advocates and supporters of Boisen's work on exploring the intersection of religious experience and mental illness. Psychologist David Shakow was a fellow student with Boisen in taking classes with McDougall and Campbell. Shakow later collaborated with Boisen and team-taught courses with him at Boston University.[46]

Cabot, and his associates, gave Boisen critical professional and financial aid at a critical time. Boisen also needed the focus to keep on task with his massive and unwieldy constellation of projects that faced uncertain prospects and was spearheaded by a person many doubted. Alice Batchelder (1880–1935) was a critical person in giving Boisen the psychological center and focus he required to stay on task. Little is known about Batchelder besides the following gleanings:

> Born in 1890 in Portsmouth, NH, the daughter of Charles E. Batchelder (1849–1894), a Harvard graduate and lawyer, and Nellie M. Dearborn (1855–1908), the daughter of a New Hampshire merchant. She graduated from Smith College in 1901, and had apparently intended to enter teaching, but from 1902 until 1918 she held various executive posts in the Young Women's Christian Association. From 1918 until the last years of her life, she worked with the credit department of the Continental and Commercial National Bank of Chicago. Alice seems to have been in continual ill health from about 1928 on, and in mid-1935 she was found to have cancer. She died on Dec. 2, 1935, while Boisen was in the midst of his last acute psychotic episode, a brief one apparently precipitated by the news of her impending death.[47]

Batchelder's presence in Boisen's life was sporadic, and often testy, from their first meeting in 1902 to her death in 1935. However, she seemed to emerge in critical times in his life and work. Her often abrupt, even scolding, letters abjured him to be "sane and normal" and continually returned to the refrain "forget thyself" and return to "the work." The work in which Boisen was engaged and to which Batchelder, repeatedly, redirected, and reoriented him toward was his work of spiritual engagement with the mentally ill and mental illness and building his project of a new kind of theological education based on practical cases.[48]

Boisen's relationship to Batchelder was, indeed, puzzling. Henri Nouwen offered it possessed aspects, on Boisen's side, of "an adolescent love affair," in which Batchelder appeared, at least in Boisen's writings, a Melchizedek-like figure without "a history and a future. She seems without parents, brothers and sisters; only good, with wisdom, courage and unswerving fidelity—more a guardian angel than a woman of this world, more an unreachable star than an attractive girlfriend."[49] Nouwen also puzzles over Batchelder's often humiliating treatment of Boisen in her making "it clear that she did not love him, by not answering his letters, not allowing visits, by cool receptions and blunt refusals. Boisen is honest enough to show how all the initiative was on his side and how he constantly had to ask for permission even to write to her. It was 'a one-sided affair.'"[50]

Boisen pursued Batchelder for decades, to the point of what could be considered stalking today. While the evidence indicates that Boisen did not mean harm and seemed oblivious to the threat a tall, large, sometimes odd-behaving man could project, Batchelder's less-than-enthusiastic greeting is understandable. As Nouwen points out, Boisen often did not relate to Batchelder as a fully realized person in her own right. He was, however, aware of her family and work responsibilities, having visited her at home in New Hampshire and Chicago. Boisen also explicitly saw Batchelder as his Beatrice of Dante's *Divine Comedy*, as the one who could direct him to his highest loyalty. While this does not excuse aspects of Boisen's behavior that Batchelder did not welcome and may have perceived as threatening, it does give a window into his view of Batchelder as well as his regard, if not fixation, for her.

The relationship between Batchelder and Boisen may have reflected a sort of unconventional "love," especially toward the end of Batchelder's life. There seemed to have been some cognizance on part of both of the "therapeutic" role of the relationship. Batchelder setting conditions on Boisen's writing and making it clear that it was for his benefit, and not hers, that the relationship, such as it was, continue. Nouwen speculates, "It seems as if she sensed that Boisen needed her, if not as a wife, then certainly as a point around which to center his life."[51] As peculiar, and puzzling, as Boisen's relationship to Batchelder may have been, he clearly credits her as the critical focus of his life and work, without which there would have been "no new light upon the interrelatedness of mental disorder and religious experience. Neither would there have been for me any clinical training movement."[52]

At critical moments Boisen had supportive friends who contributed the contacts, training, and personal focus required to engage his work. This does not detract, however, from Boisen's agency and commitment to his vision. In an early proposal to continue his case work and study on "types of mental disorder from the religious standpoint" at Boston Psychopathic, Boisen noted to Macfie Campbell that he had already "refused a position as research worker with the Social Sciences department at Chicago Theological School which would have meant a salary of three thousand and field expenses." Boisen further advertised his commitment to his work already underway in Boston, promising Campbell "to contribute to the Hospital as much as possible and to tax its resources as little as possible." And to the extent actual expenses exceeded his anticipated budget, Boisen proposed "to pay the excess cost of the travel out of my own pocket."[53]

While Boisen's proposal to Campbell "came to nothing," his initial work at Boston Psychopathic did catch the attention of Professor Arthur Holt at Chicago Theological Seminary—the seminary that was already attracted to Boisen's perspectives. Holt, Boisen recalled, commissioned and financed Boisen's early study of Pentecostal religious experience among African American churches in the Roxbury section of Boston. Boisen's work in Roxbury provided the nucleus for Boisen's later writing on "Holy Roller" Pentecostal groups.[54] Holt was intrigued with Boisen's emerging case approach to studying psychopathology and religious experience, and it was he who was critical to Boisen gaining a faculty affiliation, suggesting "that the strategic point of attack lay in the theological schools." Holt facilitated Boisen's academic affiliation that provided him further luster along with the extensive professional and social contacts that Cabot already furnished. Holt even went as far as offering "to back the project himself" if Boisen could find no other backer.[55] Hannah Curtis, director of Social Work for the Massachusetts Department of Mental Diseases, provided Boisen's lead to a job. She was the one who informed Boisen of a potential opening at Worcester State Hospital.[56] While Boisen was not able to bring to fruition his idea for case work at Boston Psychopathic, his growing credibility and contacts were sufficient for William Bryan at Worcester State Hospital "to try out a chaplain."[57]

Christopher DeBono marvels that "a mere one and half years after being discharged Boisen started work as a clinical chaplain and researcher at Worcester State Hospital." His work was not as a church pastor who, incidentally, visited the hospital but as a fully integrated part of a medical and therapeutic team, where he had access to patient records, the right and duty to visit patients throughout the hospital, and the opportunity to participate in staff meetings deliberating on patient cases.[58]

Boisen was aware that his appointment was not without controversy and not without potential risk for his new employer. His earlier, failed, proposal to Boston Psychopathic revealed to him the latent, to frank, suspicion held by many in the psychiatric community to religion and religious workers. Writing to Fred Eastman, Boisen lamented, "I have just run into another obstacle. I am refused permission to do any case work at the Psychopathic Hospital. And this case work was to have been the basis of my year's work. The reason is not I think a personal one but a ruling that no one who is not an advanced medical student is to be permitted on the wards." While Boisen did not have sufficient standing within the medical hierarchy to gain access to patients and their records, his conversations with his professor, and former attending psychiatrist, Macfie Campbell drew out the ambivalence of the medical community in mixing psychology with religion: "when I was talking with him said that religious workers have no concern with psychiatric problems and that the medical profession did not look with favor upon their stepping over the line as [Ellwood] Worcester had done."[59]

In summer 1924 he commenced his work at Worcester as controversy over the relationship between science and religion fermented and as the Scopes trial in Dayton, Tennessee, loomed. Boisen remained aware of the utility of the press in forwarding his vision and agenda. However, these attempts could backfire:

> One of my early experiences at Worcester was an encounter with the press. It so happened that at the time I arrived Worcester's morning newspaper was engaged in writing up the hospital. The reporter wanted a story from me. Dr. Bryan approved but stipulated that I should prepare the copy and let him see it. This I did and then gave it to the reporter. The morning paper used it without change, but the headline writer got busy. In glaring type the morning paper proclaimed, "Worcester Hospital Appoints Soul Healer." And the evening paper rewrote the article on the basis of the headline. Since that time, I have been wary of publicity and have made it a policy to rely for publicity upon articles in scientific journals rather than upon newspapers and magazines.[60]

He, briefly, drew the ire of prominent Protestant liberal Harry Emerson Fosdick, one of Boisen's former classmates at Union, when Boisen proposed publishing an article (which he thoughtfully submitted to Fosdick for comment prior to publication) publicizing Boisen's own ideas and studies on religious experience titled "In Defense of Mr. [William Jennings] Bryan by a Disciple of Dr. Fosdick." Fosdick responded that publication "would have to be over his dead body."[61] In spite of the controversy, and Bryan taking "a good deal of chaffing from his fellow superintendents," Boisen's boss stood resolutely by his decision to retain a minister of religion on staff. Heather Vacek explains that Bryan was not a "churchman" and that his interest "was therapeutic, not religious." As a therapist, his primary interest was the welfare of those under his charge, and "he allowed that spiritual care might help patients recover" and that Boisen could be of assistance in reaching that overarching goal.[62]

ORIGINS OF CLINICAL PASTORAL EDUCATION

As friends and collaborators were critical for Boisen in inventing professional institutional chaplaincy, his collaborators were critical to his mission of developing and growing a new kind of theological education. While Boisen often gave Cabot credit for the idea, Robert Powell provides evidence of a more complex mutual influence. It was politically wise to give his connected sponsor "ample credit." Yet, Powell notes that Charles Graves, who lived in the same dormitory with Boisen in 1923–1924, had dialoged with him on the possibility of clinical study at Worcester Hospital, but passed on the opportunity.

Boisen had a knack for getting people, who personally and professionally differed, to work together. In an audio interview on the development of clinical pastoral education, John Thomas mentioned that Boisen "had an amazing capacity to involve men [sic] from other disciplines." Carroll Wise picked up on Thomas' lead: "Dr. Cabot thought psychoanalysis stunk . . . but here he was working with Dr. Hill and Dr. Dunbar. Boisen was a genius at this kind of thing."[63] Furthermore, in later years, Boisen mentioned that, Arthur Holt, his friend and colleague at Chicago Theological Seminary, "had as much to do with the initiation of the program at Worcester as did Richard C. Cabot. Furthermore, the Chicago Theological Seminary was the first school to open its curriculum to classroom teaching in this field."[64] Powell provides evidence that Boisen shrewdly deprecated his own role, perhaps with more calculation than he has been given credit, in order to flatter patrons and facilitate dialogue between professionals who otherwise would have little to do with each other due to sharply, at times toxically, incompatible philosophy and personality.[65]

Regardless of the origin of clinical pastoral education as an idea, Boisen was acutely aware that he needed to add value that hospitals recognized as beneficial if not necessary. Boisen recalled the boredom of his own incarceration. Citing a letter he wrote to hospital administration at the time: "between half past five and six o'clock, [we] washed, dressed, took breakfast, and helped with the ward work. This was completed before nine o'clock. At ten we took half an hour's walk. The rest of the day we've been chiefly occupied in doing nothing."[66] Boisen's era marked an increased recognition that warehousing patients was neither sufficient nor humane, and that improved therapeutic effort was needed. However, most state hospitals suffered "a dramatic lack of trained personnel. . . . Anyone who was willing to be of help could easily find work in this understaffed setting. Boisen was aware of this and realized that the simple help which theological students could give in terms of ward-work and recreational activities was already enough to convince hospital authorities of their value. And they would probably be willing to forgive them their scientific aspiration and theological perspectives, certainly if these hobbies were practiced outside the regular working hours." Boisen's early "theologs" worked long hours—ten hours per day as ward attendants, study and case conferences off the clock.[67]

Donald Beatty started his long connection with Boisen in 1927, commenting on clinical educations early years at Worcester:

We had to justify our place and indeed our presence in the hospital by assuming many responsibilities now shared or carried on by other workers. In addition to worship services, pastoral calling, and individual interviewing, we conducted choirs, managed ball teams, promoted plays and pageants and outdoor carnivals for patients, published the hospital newspaper, took patients out for walks and hikes, managed the hospital library, sometimes the canteen, and generally made ourselves useful.[68]

While Boisen and his theologs had to "pay the bills," figuratively, in providing work and services the hospital deemed useful, literally finding money to make budget was also an ongoing challenge. Decades later, Fred Eastman recalled, "financing of this work constituted one of Boisen's major problems. The hospital could pay his modest salary and a limited amount for attendants' wages. It also provided room and board for the students. Other expenses had to be solicited from outside sources."[69]

Boisen's single-minded, to obsessive, commitment fueled his search for money. As mentioned previously, he turned down full-time employment with Chicago Theological Seminary because it would detract from his vision of pastoral care and research with the mentally ill and his emerging vision for clinical theological education. Robert Leas notes that Boisen sacrificed to provide for his vision, "he had limited needs personally. . . . lived a very spartan life." At Elgin State Hospital, where he lived and worked from 1930 until his death in 1965, he occupied a one-room apartment on campus, often ate at the hospital cafeteria, drove an "old beat-up Ford automobile," and contributed a handsome share of his own salary to fund his students. Francis McPeek, an early Boisen student and friend, "remembered when he was at Elgin that he occasionally received a check from Boisen to help with his student expenses."[70] Seward Hiltner, one of Boisen's prominent students, attested that Boisen had sharp elbows in pursuing his goals, recalling that Worcester superintendent William Bryan "had to say no on many occasions to Boisen's single-minded devotion to getting the budget he needed for his work. He meant that, where conviction was concerned, Boisen could set friendship aside."[71]

When direct budgetary appeals failed, he demonstrated ingenuity in partnering with other hospital projects that, coincidentally, forwarded his agenda and also in relentlessly publicizing his project and in cultivating outside donors. A significant opportunity crossed Boisen's path in 1927 when Roy G. Hoskins initiated a groundbreaking study of endocrinology and schizophrenia at Worcester Hospital. Boisen's former classmate David Shakow was also involved in this study that featured early cross-disciplinary collaboration between psychology and psychiatry.[72] While Hoskins was primarily interested in the physiological aspect of the 173 patients studied, Charles Hall notes that "the hospital gave Boisen a free hand to study the same patients from a different perspective." Namely, how "conflict and stress" may factor into the emergence of serious mental illness and how religion and spirituality may factor into patient outcomes.[73] Partnership with Hoskin's prestigious and well-funded project brought scientific credibility and institutional prestige to his own endeavors. Hoskin also provided additional contacts in the broader scientific and medical community that aided Boisen and his theologs who went on to have careers not only in pastoral care but in diverse areas as psychology, medicine, law, and social work.

Richard Cabot and early theologs Philip Guiles and Helen Dunbar were prominent among people who aided in early fundraising. Financial woes became acute in summer 1928 as it became obvious that Boisen could not personally underwrite the eleven students expected for the summer session. While Guiles' and Cabot's critical financial assistance relieved many concerns, dependence on these two sources carried attendant problems as well. Guiles was son-in-law of wealthy Detroit businessman H. B. Earhart, who suggested that Boisen incorporate his project, which he did in 1930. Guiles' fundraising acumen propelled through Cabot's contacts and aid from his father-in-law's charitable foundation brought needed finance. Guiles' and Cabot's control of the purse provided occasion to point up conflicts between the opinionated and demanding characters among whom Boisen had built a tentative alliance centered on a common cause.[74]

The relationship between Guiles and Dunbar soured quickly. While the precise reasons for the enmity are unclear, it seemed to emanate from differences in personality and in ambition for control within the emerging clinical pastoral education project. By 1932, the relationship between the two, according to Edward Thornton, had reached such heights of acrimony that Dunbar unilaterally declared New York City the headquarters of the organization and Guiles founded a separate clinical training organization separate from Dunbar.[75] Guiles and Dunbar were starkly dissimilar personalities. Thornton describes Guiles as "vivacious, outgoing, and thoroughly disorganized." Dunbar, he describes as "ambitious, cold and calculating, noncommunicative, and basically rather shy."[76] Dunbar's legendary discipline and organizational skills, along with her familial social contacts, produced rapid financial dividends for the New York program. According to Robert Powell, "Taking the social register entirely seriously . . . she quickly doubled the contributed income to the council."[77] While ambition and personality seem to have played a significant role in the conflict—Dunbar was a rarity in her era as a professional woman with a divinity degree, a Ph.D., and a medical degree, during a time when such "ambition" from women was unexpected and often frowned upon.

Whiles Guiles, and Cabot, provided administrative acumen and fundraising for a fledgling project that badly needed it, they also demanded the influence they felt their financial contributions had bought them. While Cabot provided, and facilitated, critical funding according to Nouwen "probably related to his personal sympathy with Boisen and his loyalty to his movement.

But he never could change his mind regarding the organic basis of all forms of mental illness." Cabot felt his opinion confirmed in Boisen's relapse and hospitalization in 1930.[78]

Cabot resorted to financial blackmail. As Boisen exited Worcester, and as Dr. Bryan selected Carroll Wise to take over the program (to Guiles' chagrin), "Wise visited Cabot in his New England home, Cabot sat down with him at the fireplace and wanted to "do business." He made it clear to Wise that he only was willing to continue his financial support of the Worcester program if Wise abandoned his and Boisen's ideas about the psychogenic interpretation of mental illness. It was obvious for Wise that he couldn't change his mind on this matter and that stopped Cabot's support."[79]

RELAPSE: MY FRIENDS CAME TO HELP ME

Boisen suffered a relapse into psychosis in 1930 and again in 1935 which required his temporary hospitalization and absence from work. While Boisen returned from both breakdowns to resume a successful career—either relapse could have ended him professionally and ruined his personal reputation. His recovery and return to work depended on the staunch and timely support of understanding friends and colleagues who believed in him or at least believed in the importance of his vision and work.

Fred Eastman and Alice Batchelder were prominent among Boisen's personal friends and contacts who provided the support and direction he needed to stay on task and focused on his projects. Eastman was a true friend through Boisen's life. He communicated thoughtfully and at length, unafraid to offer criticism and candid advice and counsel, and did so when he had nothing to gain from it. During his initial hospitalization in 1920, Eastman counseled Boisen to avoid conflict with his doctors when he disagreed with them about the nature and course of his illness. He also posed practical questions: "What thought have you given to the practical and bread-and-butter aspects of the future? How can you make a living while you pursue your study?" He also offered solutions that may have contributed to Boisen's vision: "My original suggestion still holds: become chaplain of some nervous hospital. . . . The practical question is can the authorities be sufficiently convinced of this to provide a salary for it? That is a task for you to work out." As he dialogued with his friends, including on his obsessions with Batchelder, "your problem will never be solved until you can forget all about yourself and Miss B.[achelder] and everything else and lose yourself in your service to those around you. You have yourself preached on the text 'he that would save his life must lose it' and can follow out that line of thought without any sermon from me."[80]

As Boisen's 1920 hospitalization at Westboro progressed and Boisen's prognosis for recovery and release looked increasingly grim, Eastman offered,

> You and your welfare are the main concern. In the first long letter—at least one of the first I wrote to you there—I pointed out the evidently neglected field of service right there in Westboro, the sort of service you are making a beginning at in the photographic and social celebration work you have told me about lately. Is it not possible that your greatest opportunity lies right there, and that if you leave it it may not be yours again? . . .Are you sure in your own mind that you can be more useful outside than there?[81]

Eastman, in a sense, may have been right from the beginning. Boisen found his work and vision in institutions for the mentally ill. First, as a committed inpatient, second, as a committed servant.

Boisen's friendship with Batchelder rarely featured the esteem and affection seen in his letters with Eastman. The nature of Batchelder's aid and support lies in her constant redirecting of Boisen to "the work"[82] While her views of, and feelings toward, him may have softened in later years, she abjured Boisen: "I have explained so often and so explicitly that I have no love to give you, and not even friendship unless it can be on a sane and normal basis" when Boisen moved from "the work" to suggesting a more intimate relationship.[83] In 1930, nine years after Eastman's advise that Boisen "lose" himself in service to others Batchelder, more tactfully this time, suggested he "forget thyself" as she opined him getting "too much absorbed by the perplexing question of 'relationships'" at the expense of his work.[84]

1930 was a busy, mostly successful, but fraught year for Boisen. He saw success in incorporation and growth of his project, and he noticed the emergence of professional and personal relationships with Dunbar and Batchelder—the two women in his life. As these significant events coalesced, Boisen suffered a relapse. Boisen's 1930 breakdown culminated in a visit to "Dr. Cabot. Of that visit I recall that I identified with my father, inquiring about myself in the third person. Dr. Cabot was much alarmed and saw to it that I was at once hospitalized."[85] While Cabot may have been willing to entertain continuing Boisen as a behind-the-scenes researcher, he would no longer tolerate him interacting with students in the clinical program.[86] Boisen wrote contemporaneously, "Guiles has put it very frankly, that I must learn to look upon myself as an 'emeritus' and keep out of the way. He wants me to be comfortable, but my usefulness is at an end, except in so far as I can continue the research work. Now he may be right, but I do not think he is."[87] While Cabot's voice and influence were prominent both in his own right and in his new role as president of the newly incorporated Council for Clinical Training, his voice did not overrule all. While Guiles sided with Cabot,

Dunbar—perhaps out of loyalty and affection for Boisen, perhaps to forward her own ambitions, likely a combination of both—ensured that Boisen would not be sidelined entirely.[88]

Dunbar's support for Boisen included support for him in traversing his episodes of illness and in gaining greater understanding of them. She first suggested that Boisen write his own personal case record, which he did in nucleus in 1928.[89] This personal case study was a vestigial version of what would eventually be published in 1960, his autobiography *Out of the Depths*. There appears to have been real affection, perhaps even romance, between Dunbar and Boisen during this time. Dunbar also used her medical and psychological training in attempting to treat Boisen as well: "The writing up of my case record was one of the things Helen suggested, and the section on the earlier years was in fact written more or less under her guidance. I think it is fair to say that Helen undertook to give me some sort of [psycho]analysis, encouraging me to discuss some rather searching questions."[90] Dunbar's aid in Boisen's case ended with Boisen's 1930 breakdown and the two assuming a more formal, and distant, relationship.[91]

Dunbar's and Boisen's relationship, wisely or not, crossed professional and personal realms. While Dunbar appears to have been, at the very least, trying to use her personal friendship and medical training to provide Boisen with sincere assistance, she also had professional motives and benefits from associating with Boisen and his work. As she became increasingly prominent in the clinical training program and eventually its medical director, she, in Powell's assessment, used the "Council for Clinical Training as primarily the educational arm of [her] work" in psychosomatic illness and holistic health.[92] While Dunbar may have had mixed motives in her relationship with Boisen, her aid also contributed to his recovery and his ongoing relevance in pastoral care and clinical training.

Boisen's students were critical to his success, the survival of his project, and his having an ongoing role in it. Following Boisen's 1930 psychosis, Cabot and Boisen were, at least tacitly, agreed that Boisen leave Worcester Hospital. At first, the two reached concord that Dunbar would be Boisen's successor at Worcester. As conflict among Boisen, Cabot, and Guiles increased, Dunbar's role grew within the Council, with her throwing her support to Boisen.[93] Dunbar's finesse was critical in Boisen's political survival; Guiles noted, "Cabot despises Dunbar partly because she has outsmarted him on most occasions."[94] Boisen's career survival depended upon several other students of his, including Donald Beatty, who decades later retired as assistant director of the Chaplain Service with the Veterans Health Administration; Wayne Hunter, who went on to serve as director of the U.S. Army Chaplain School; and Francis McPeek, who embarked on an unorthodox and visionary path in race relations most significantly in his role as executive director of the

Commission on Human Relations for the City of Chicago.[95] Seward Hiltner, one of Boisen's first students at Elgin, taught at the University of Chicago and at Princeton and stoutly defended his former teacher as the chaplaincy profession increasingly ostracized him.

The support of his students became even more critical in his last hospitalization for acute psychosis in 1935. Promptly upon departure from Worcester Hospital, Boisen found new employment at Elgin State Hospital near Chicago. Elgin had been envisioned as a potential, and prominent, site for expansion of the clinical program, but there was no candidate to take the position as supervisor and educator—until Boisen became available. Boisen's position became untenable at Worcester as he refused to relinquish work with students and Cabot's opposition hardened. Elgin emerged as a landing spot. Elgin had the added appeal of proximity to Boisen's professional friends and academic affiliation, Arthur Holt and Arthur C. "Cush" McGiffert, Jr., who were both professors at Chicago Theological Seminary.

McGiffert was professor at Chicago Theological Seminary from 1926 to 1939. He served as president of Pacific School of Religion in Berkeley, California, from 1939 to 1945 and returned to Chicago Theological as its president, serving from 1946 to 1958.[96] Boisen, with McGiffert's support, had a long-standing relationship with Chicago Theological Seminary. McGiffert also invited Boisen to teach as guest faculty at Pacific. Personal friends and allies, such as Holt and McGiffert, and institutional allies, such as the seminary in which they taught, facilitated Boisen's move to Elgin. Boisen gave these friends credit for "back[ing] this project of mine . . . upon a clinical foundation instead of upon a foundation of textbooks." Boisen ruminated that taking up work in Elgin freed him from Cabot and Guiles' control: "The work which I have started will probably go along just as well without me along the lines which Dr. Cabot and Guiles will determine whether I stay or not. It will not be the development which I shall want to see, and in the new field [Elgin] I shall then be free to do what is not being done elsewhere and to give what cannot be obtained elsewhere. I foresee no difficulty in getting students." And, as was the case with Eastman and Holt, Boisen's relationship with "Cush" McGiffert was more than professional, in response to McGiffert's inquiry about Boisen's latest bout,

> You asked yesterday what the recent illness had taught me in regard to the nature of such experiences. That is a big question. . . . I have come out of that experience still convinced of their purposive character. They are not due to the operation of blind forces but are intended to accomplish something, to solve some problem. And in them there is manifest an Intelligence which is beyond our own. Now just what the purpose is in this case I do not yet see clearly. . . . I am hoping that the Seminary which had faith enough in me seven years ago

when everything was still untried will have faith enough in me now to give me a chance to put over this plan which I have suggested and accomplish what will I think prove to be a very important pioneer undertaking.[97]

Boisen's friendships with Eastman, Holt, and McGiffert—all associated at one time or another with Chicago Theological Seminary—transcended the professional. Boisen's communications with McGiffert, as with Eastman, combined the professional and pragmatic with the compassion and patience required to draw out and develop this peculiar man's vision. Additionally, Alice Batchelder, the not-entirely-requited love of his life, lived and worked in Chicago.[98]

A fraught triangle between Boisen, Batchelder, and Dunbar emotionally overwhelmed Boisen in 1930. Batchelder's terminal cancer diagnosis and death undisputedly ignited Boisen's final hospitalization in 1935. Boisen grieved and obsessed over Batchelder's imminent death: "Again I had the idea that this earth should have become a brilliant star, but something had gone wrong and instead it would become only a Milky Way. I recall identifying with my father and feeling that he was getting old and would be unable to carry on much longer."

As Boisen tailspined into "an abnormal condition," he had colleagues and students who were critical to his emotional and professional survival and functioning.

> Fortunately, Beatty, and McPeek and Hunter were quick to recognize the signs of trouble and there was no disruption of the social situation. They guided me carefully, and on November 11 they spirited me away to the Sheppard and Enoch Pratt Hospital in Baltimore so quietly that scarcely anyone in Elgin knew about it. I was there on December 2, at the time of Alice's death. About two weeks later I was able to return and resume my teaching at the Seminary before the end of the quarter. Once more the disturbance had cleared up within four weeks. I look upon this episode as another problem-solving experience.[99]

In August, Boisen had "received a note from Alice, saying that she was going into retirement for an operation and that the edict had gone forth, 'No callers, no flowers.'"[100] As Boisen gathered the terminal nature of the illness and quickly spiraled downward emotionally, Beatty reached out to Catherine Wilson, who shared an apartment with Batchelder and Batchelder's sister, Anne. Wilson filled Beatty in on Batchelder's decline and death. Wilson explained that she was "an invalid confined to the house" and that she and Batchelder's sister were consumed in care for the dying Batchelder—on the one hand wanting to respect her privacy and on the other uncertain how much to tell the hospitalized Boisen. He said, "I leave to your discretion, Mr.

Beatty, how much of this is wise to pass on to Mr. Boisen. Even under normal conditions her death would prove a tragic loss to him but now—what will it mean! I'm so sorry for him!"[101]

Beatty took point for Boisen's personal concerns during his hospitalization in Baltimore. Ross Chapman, superintendent of Sheppard, and Enoch Pratt wrote Beatty on Boisen's progress. He noted the rapid improvement of Boisen's symptoms warranting release and return to work only several weeks after his attack but suggesting that Boisen "get in touch with you [Beatty] and Professor Eastman after his arrival." Chapman also noted Boisen's difficult relationship with his sister "because of the fact that the patient's relatives in Boston have a marked horror of mental illness, and following the patient's last illness refused to have him in the house for a period of seven years because of their belief that all mentally ill patients are homicidal."[102]

During Boisen's illness, Beatty served as de facto trustee and steward of Boisen's care, finances, and reputation,

> In conference with Dr. Eastman at the seminary concerning the financial arrangements for Mr. Boisen, . . . A.T. [Anton Theophilus] has enough money to take care of reimbursing you for the first month. . . . For the second month . . . McPeek and Hunter together owe Boisen enough so that they can take care of that bill. Hunter can get the cash (we hope) from his father. . . . Eastman suggests that, for the third and final month, he is willing to be responsible for collecting the necessary amount from Boisen's friends as the seminary.[103]

While Beatty coordinated collecting funds for Boisen's treatment, he also pondered the risk they assumed with Boisen's employers at the Seminary and the State of Illinois,

> There is a question of whether the Board of Directors, if they find out that AT is having another upset, will not rule him out entirely as a teacher. If they do, blooey!!! . . . For the present, we are getting along. One of these days, however, things are going to blow up. We feel all the time that we're sitting on a nice little keg o' dynamite. If the Board of Directors at the School and the Welfare Department at Springfield begin asking questions about Mr. Boisen's "illness" at the same time, we'll be out on a limb.[104]

Likewise, Eastman managed Boisen's affairs at Chicago Theological Seminary, where both Boisen and Eastman taught: "We [Eastman and Beatty] have simply announced that you were ill and in the East. We have said nothing about the nature of the illness. If you do not return this term, we shall probably have to inform the students of the exact situation, but we shall delay this as long as possible. . . . Your close friends here think of you daily, and you can always be sure of our help in any way we can give it."[105]

Those who helped Boisen during this last major crisis had a relationship that combined aspects of the professional and the personal. These were colleagues and students who had a professional interest and stake in their teacher's (and seer's) professional functioning and well-being. On the one hand, they frankly admitted Boisen's illness for what it was and insisted that he receive treatment when they manifested. On the other hand, they demonstrated patience and compassion to draw out and implement a vision even if it manifested along with some madness. They also demonstrated personal concern and compassion in becoming an impromptu surrogate family for a lifelong bachelor in crisis and assumed significant personal and professional risk in defending their, sometimes ill, friend.

NOTES

1. Boisen, *Out of the Depths*, 89.

2. Carroll Wise, one of Boisen's early students at Worcester Hospital, alluded to his talent for drawing people from different disciplines and contradictory philosophies to work together. Wise alludes to Richard Cabot and Helen Flanders Dunbar (whatever their other professional and personal differences were) working together as one such collaboration that Boisen facilitated. Interview with John Thomas, Carroll Wise, and Al Shervy, no date, Audio Recording, ACPE Papers, Emory University, Decatur, GA.

3. Vacek, *Madness*, 6; Christopher E. DeBono, *An Exploration and Adaption of Anton T. Boisen's Notion of the Psychiatric Chaplain in Responding to Current Issues in Clinical Chaplaincy* (Ph.D. Diss., University of Toronto, 2012), 247–48.

4. Edward E. Thornton, *Professional Education for Ministry: A History of Clinical Pastoral Education* (Nashville, TN: Abingdon Press, 1970), 58–59.

5. Henri Nouwen, "Anton T. Boisen and the Study of Theology Through 'Living Human Documents'" (Unpublished Manuscript, no date), 7, Box 1, File 4, Henri Nouwen Papers, John M. Kelly Library, University of St. Michael's College, Toronto, ON.

6. Nouwen, "Anton T. Boisen and the Study of Theology," 29.

7. Henri Nouwen, "Pastoral Supervision in Historical Perspective," 42–43 (Unpublished Manuscript, no date), Box 287, File 306, Henri Nouwen Papers, John M. Kelly Library, University of St. Michael's College, Toronto, ON.

8. Nouwen, "Anton T. Boisen and the Study of Theology," 154–55.

9. Glenn H. Asquith, Jr., ed., *Vision from a Little Known Country: A Boisen Reader* (Macon, GA: Journal of Pastoral Care Publications, Inc., 1991), 113.

10. Boisen, "Inspiration in the Light of Psychopathology," 18.

11. Boisen, "Inspiration in the Light of Psychopathology," 10.

12. Boisen, "Inspiration in the Light of Psychopathology," 18.

13. Boisen, "Inspiration in the Light of Psychopathology," 14.
14. David A. Steere, "Anton Boisen: Figure of the Future?," *Journal of Religion and Health* 7, no. 4 (1968): 370.
15. Ronald L. Numbers, "The Fall and Rise of the American Medical Profession," in *The Professions in American History*, ed. Nathan O. Hatch (South Bend, IN: University of Notre Dame Press, 1985), 57–67.
16. Nouwen, "Anton T. Boisen and the Study of Theology," 66.
17. Thornton, *Professional Education for Ministry*, 33.
18. Richard C. Cabot, "Adventures on the Borderland of Ethics: A Plea for a Clinical Year in the Course of Theological Study," *Survey Graphic* 8, no. 3 (1925): 275–76. In this article, Cabot cites his collaborative relationship with Dr. Alfred Worcester, a medical colleague. Alfred Worcester was the Rev. Ellwood Worcester's cousin, a critical figure in securing Boisen's release from custodial care, providing him with early training in the craft of clinical pastoral education and provided Boisen professional support and personal friendship through the remainder of his life.
19. Anton T. Boisen, "Concerning the Relationship Between Religious Experience and Mental Disorders," *Mental Hygiene* 7, no. 2 (1923): 311.
20. Christopher E. DeBono, *An Exploration and Adaptation of Anton T. Boisen's Notion of the Psychiatric Chaplain in Responding to Current Issues in Clinical Chaplaincy* (Ph.D. Diss., University of St. Michael's College, 2012), 38.
21. Gerald N. Grob, *Mental Illness and American Society 1875–1940* (Princeton, NJ: Princeton University Press, 1983), 178.
22. Grob, *Mental Illness and American Society*, 147.
23. Grob, *Mental Illness and American Society*, 147.
24. Clifford Whittingham Beers, *A Mind That Found Itself: An Autobiography* (New York, NY: Longmans, Green, and Co., 1912).
25. Grob, *Mental Illness and American Society*, 148–49.
26. Grob, *Mental Illness and American Society*, 148.
27. Thornton, *Professional Education for Ministry*, 67. Boisen and Bryan's meeting at Worcester State Hospital was fortuitous. Fred Eastman, gathering information to aid Boisen in his search for chaplaincy employment at a Hospital, surmised,

> there was practically no chance to enter a state institution with the sort of work you want to do because most of such institutions are so limited in budget that they cannot engage enough doctors for their patients, and therefore would be unwilling to engage a minister or other worker for experimental purposes. . . . There is some chance, however, that you could enter some institution as Bloomingdales at White Plains, the McLean Hospital in Boston, . . . These private and semi-private institutions are better equipped financially and as a rule are more forward looking.

Fred Eastman to Boisen, March 21, 1923, Series 2, Box 3, Folder 27, Boisen Papers, Chicago Theological Seminary.
28. Grob, *Mental Illness and American Society*, 232.
29. Seward Hiltner, "The Debt of Clinical Pastoral Education to Anton T. Boisen," *The Journal of Pastoral Care* 20, no. 3 (1966): 130.
30. Stokes, *Ministry After Freud*, 42.

31. Powell, *Healing and Wholeness*, 140–41. Boisen received absolute discharge from custodial care on February 7, 1923, almost a year after leaving Westboro Hospital. Robert Charles Powell, *Anton T. Boisen (1876–1965): "Breaking an Opening in the Wall Between Religion and Medicine"* (Buffalo, NY: Mental Health Chaplains, 1974), 8–10.

32. Nouwen, "Anton T. Boisen and the Study of Theology," 57.

33. Raphael Zon to Boisen, March 10, 1941, Series 2, Box 7, Folder 67, Boisen Papers, Chicago Theological Seminary.

34. Raphael Zon to Boisen, March 10, 1941, Series 2, Box 7, Folder 67, Boisen Papers, Chicago Theological Seminary.

35. Robert David Leas, *Anton Theophilus Boisen: His Life, Work, Impact, and Theological Legacy* (Macon, GA: Journal of Pastoral Care Publications, Inc., 2009), 91.

36. Powell, *Anton T. Boisen*, 12.

37. Powell, *Anton T. Boisen*, 31, fn. 79.

38. Crenner, *Private Practice*, x.

39. Crenner, *Private Practice*, 14.

40. Crenner, *Private Practice*, 14.

41. Crenner, *Private Practice*, 74.

42. Crenner, *Private Practice*, 232–33.

43. Powell, *Anton T. Boisen*, 10. Whether Campbell accepted Boisen in order to give him a chance at rehabilitation or through Cabot's influence, or a combination of both motives, is unclear. However, Powell implies that Boisen and Campbell's reunion was fortuitous: "No doubt he found Campbell's views congenial for Campbell defined mental illness as the product of maladjustment to the total life situation, . . . Campbell emphasized 'the meaning of the whole reaction in the light of the situation out of which the attack developed,' and respectfully recognized the religious aspects of Boisen's case." Also indicative of Campbells sympathetic attitude was his own work: *Delusion and Belief* (Cambridge, MA: Harvard University Press, 1926).

44. Glenn H. Asquith, Jr., *The Clinical Method of Theological Inquiry of Anton T. Boisen* (Ph.D. Diss., Southern Baptist Theological Seminary-Louisville, 1976), 68–69; Asquith, "The Case Study Method of Anton T. Boisen," 85–86. During his work with Lyons, Boisen transitioned his experience in surveying trees—a craft he learned from Zon—to surveying people. As individual trees live within a larger context, "by applying case study principles and going into a home as a social worker to help a person in need, he found that he could study 'the entire person in his social setting.'"

45. Charles E. Hall, *Head and Heart: The Story of the Clinical Pastoral Education Movement* (Macon, GA: Journal of Pastoral Care Publications, Inc., 1992), 9.

46. Powell, *Anton T. Boisen*, 29, fn. 64.

47. Powell, *Anton T. Boisen*, 25, fn. 24.

48. Alice Batchelder to Boisen, July 30, 1920; Alice Batchelder to Boisen, November 29, 1930, Box 1a, Folder 4, Boisen Papers, Chicago Theological Seminary.

49. Nouwen, "Anton T. Boisen and the Study of Theology," 43.

50. Nouwen, "Anton T. Boisen and the Study of Theology," 44.

51. Nouwen, "Anton T. Boisen and the Study of Theology," 45.
52. Nouwen, "Anton T. Boisen and the Study of Theology," 42; Boisen, *Out of the Depths*, 45–46.
53. Boisen to Macfie Campbell, Series 2, Box 3, Folder 15, Boisen Papers, Chicago Theological Seminary.
54. Boisen to Thomas Klink, January 1, 1964, Boisen Papers, Kansas Historical Society, Topeka, KS.
55. Anton T. Boisen, "Clinical Pastoral Training in Retrospect and Prospect: Remarks at Faculty Luncheon—Union Theological Seminary" (*Lecture*, Union Seminary, New York, NY, October 30, 1957), Series 2, Box 2, Folder 6, Boisen Papers, Chicago Theological Seminary. In 1947, then ensconced at Elgin State Hospital in Illinois, Boisen credited Chicago Theological Seminary's influential role as "the institution from which my chief support was derived" in gaining employment, both, at Worcester State Hospital and in 1932 at Elgin. Anton T. Boisen, "Chaplain's Department: Sixteenth Annual Report" (Unpublished Manuscript, 1947), Series 2, Box 2, Folder 6, Boisen Papers, Chicago Theological Seminary.
56. Boisen to Thomas Klink, January 1, 1964, Boisen Papers, Kansas Historical Society.
57. Anton T. Boisen, "Clinical Pastoral Training in Retrospect and Prospect," Series 2, Box 2, Folder 6, Boisen Papers, Chicago Theological Seminary.
58. DeBono, *An Exploration and Adaptation*, 43.
59. Boisen to Fred Eastman, November 12, 1922, Box 1a, Folder 9, Boisen Papers, Chicago Theological Seminary.
60. Boisen, *Out of the Depths*, 151.
61. Boisen, *Out of the Depths*, 152; Interview with John Thomas, Carroll Wise, and Al Shervy, no date, Audio Recording, ACPE Papers, Emory University, Decatur, GA.
62. Vacek, *Madness*, 116.
63. Interview with John Thomas, Carroll Wise, and Al Sherve, no date, Audio Recording, ACPE Papers, Emory University, Decatur, GA.
64. Powell, *Anton T. Boisen*, 31, fn. 81.
65. Thornton, *Professional Education for Ministry*, 56.
66. Boisen, *Out of the Depths*, 122.
67. Nouwen, "Anton T. Boisen and the Study of Theology," 71–72. Carroll Wise estimated a twelve-hour workday for Boisen's early clinical students at Worcester Hospital working the wards. Again, seminars and case work were to be done outside those twelve hours on students' own time. Interview with John Thomas, Carroll Wise, and Al Shervy, no date, Audio Recording, ACPE Papers, Emory University, Decatur, GA.
68. Thornton, *Professional Education for Ministry*, 200–1.
69. Fred Eastman, "Father of the Clinical Pastoral Movement," in "Anton T. Boisen and the Origin of the Movement for the Clinical Training of Theological Students, Three Articles," *The Chicago Theological Seminary Register* 41, no. 1 (1951): 15.

70. Leas, *Anton Theophilus Boisen*, 115. Boisen recalled that he invested virtually his entire discretionary income (he received room and board from Elgin Hospital) into his clinical training project from 1932 to 1938. Anton T. Boisen, Interview by Francis McPeek, 1952, Audio Recording, ACPE Papers, Emory University, Decatur, GA.

71. Hiltner, "The Heritage of Anton T. Boisen," 9–10.

72. Grob, *Mental Illness and American Society*, 263.

73. Hall, *Head and Heart*, 10.

74. Hall, *Head and Heart*, 27–28.

75. Thornton, *Professional Education for Ministry*, 76. The Guiles-Dunbar feud eventually blossomed into a full-blown "schism" splintering of the clinical pastoral education movement between the New York-based Council for Clinical Training, led by Dunbar, and the Boston-centered Institute for Pastoral Care, led by Guiles and Cabot. Upon Boisen's ouster from Worcester in 1930, he moved on to Elgin State Hospital in Illinois and founded the Chicago Council for the Training of Theological Students, which cooperated with, but was autonomous from, the New York group. Additionally, Guiles, according to Robert Leas, "not more than a month into the program [in 1928] . . . took a violent dislike to Reverend Donald Beatty, Boisen's very capable assistant. Boisen opined that Guiles 'was dominated all too often by a will-to-power that makes it difficult for him to do teamwork. He is apt to be particularly antagonistic to all those who are in any rivals and who thus threaten his security.'" Leas, *Anton Theophilus Boisen*, 141–42.

76. Thornton, *Professional Education for Ministry*, 76–77.

77. Powell, *Healing and Wholeness*, 272. Powell reports in footnote, "For fiscal year 1932–33, the Council's total receipts were $14,325; by 1934–35, $22,701; by 1936–37, $33,124; by 1938–39, $45,609. Dunbar began courting the William C. Whitney Foundation in late 1934 and obtained $13,250 from this foundation alone over a five-year period."

78. Nouwen, "Anton T. Boisen and the Study of Theology," 92.

79. Nouwen, "Anton T. Boisen and the Study of Theology," 93.

80. Fred Eastman to Boisen, January 1, 1921, Box 2, Folder 1, Boisen Papers, Chicago Theological Seminary.

81. Fred Eastman to Boisen, August 20, 1921, Box 2, Folder 1, Boisen Papers, Chicago Theological Seminary.

82. Alice Batchelder to Boisen, July 17, 1920, July 29, 1920, October 22, 1930, November 24, 1030, Box 1a, Folder 4, Boisen Papers, Chicago Theological Seminary.

83. Alice Batchelder to Boisen, July 29, 1920, Box 1a, Folder 4, Boisen Papers, Chicago Theological Seminary.

84. Alice Batchelder to Boisen, November 24, 1930, Box 1a, Folder 4, Boisen Papers, Chicago Theological Seminary.

85. Boisen, *Out of the Depths*, 170.

86. Powell, *Healing and Wholeness*, 214. According to Powell "Boisen's disturbed condition cleared within three weeks."

87. Boisen to A. C. McGiffert Jr., August 7, 1931, Series 2, Box 5, Folder 49, Boisen Papers, Chicago Theological Seminary.

88. Boisen, *Out of the Depths*, 171. Leas elaborates that Boisen "accused" Guiles of raising money to send him to Europe for a year following the end of his hospitalization. While Boisen was in hospital, Guiles took charge of the educational program at Worcester. While neither Guiles nor Cabot wanted Boisen to return to educational activities, Superintendent Bryan supported Boisen's return as clinical educator. Upon Boisen's move to Elgin in 1932, Bryan appointed Carroll Wise, not Guiles, as Boisen's successor. Leas, *Anton Theophilus Boisen*, 142.

89. Powell, *Healing and Wholeness*, 121.

90. Boisen to Donald Beatty, October 17, 1956, Box 1, Folders 29, 30, Boisen Papers, Chicago Theological Seminary. While Dunbar was legendarily circumspect about documenting her personal feelings, Boisen recorded the following, demonstrating a combination of self-reproach, conflicted loyalties, professional esteem, and personal affection for Dunbar:

> Looking back after nearly thirty years I still see Helen Dunbar as an instrument of the finest precision sent to help in the launching of our project. I still believe that I was right in so recognizing her and loving her. But I was tragically wrong in not obeying absolutely the prompting which bade me give her up. If only I had done so, keeping her love and her respect, what might have happened? It was through her that Alice Batchelder consented to see me, and it seems not beyond the realm of possibility that something resembling the "family-of-four" might have resulted. As it was, I was stricken down and Helen's subsequent career was filled with tragedy and her splendid talents largely lost to the field of religion.

Anton T. Boisen, Untitled Memorandum, September 16, 1959, Box 1a, Folder 7, Boisen Papers, Chicago Theological Seminary.

91. Anton T. Boisen, "Out of the Depths" (Unpublished Manuscript, no date), 135d, Box 1a, Folder 13, Boisen Papers, Chicago Theological Seminary.

92. Robert C. Powell, "Emotionally, Soulfully, Spiritually 'Free to Think and Act': The Helen Flanders Dunbar (1902–1959)," *Journal of Religion and Health* 40, no. 1 (2001): 108.

93. Powell, *Healing and Wholeness*, 215.

94. Powell, *Healing and Wholeness*, 215, fn. 2.

95. Hiltner, "The Heritage of Anton T. Boisen," 5; Anton T. Boisen, "In Memoriam Francis W. McPeek (1911–1958)," Series 2, Box 5, Folder 52, Boisen Papers, Chicago Theological Seminary.

96. Bruce Lambert, "A. C. McGiffert Jr. A Seminary Leader and Educator," *The New York Times* (April 14, 1993): 100.

97. Boisen to A. C. McGiffert, Jr., August 7, 1931, Series 2, Box 5, Folder 49, Boisen Papers, Chicago Theological Seminary; A. C. McGiffert, Jr. to Boisen, July 19, 1942, Series 2, Box 5, Folder 49, Boisen Papers, Chicago Theological Seminary.

98. Glenn H. Asquith, Jr., "Introduction," in *Vision from a Little Known Country: A Boisen Reader*, ed. Glenn H. Asquith, Jr. (Macon, GA: Journal of Pastoral Care Publications, Inc., 1992), 8.

99. Boisen, *Out of the Depths*, 176–77.

100. Boisen, *Out of the Depths*, 176.

101. Catherine Wilson to Donald Beatty, December 16, 1935, Box 1a, Folder 8, Boisen Papers, Chicago Theological Seminary; Catherine Wilson to Donald Beatty, November 27, 1935, Box 1a, Folders, Boisen Papers, Chicago Theological Seminary.

102. Ross Chapman to Donald Beatty, December 16, 1935, Box 1a, Folder 8, Boisen Papers, Chicago Theological Seminary.

103. Donald Beatty to Lewis Brown Hill, December 5, 1935, Box 1a, Folder 8, Boisen Papers, Chicago Theological Seminary.

104. Donald Beatty to Lewis Brown Hill, December 5, 1935, Box 1a Folder 8, Boisen Papers, Chicago Theological Seminary.

105. Fred Eastman to Boisen, December 4, 1935, Series 2, Box 3, Folder 29, Boisen Papers, Chicago Theological Seminary.

Chapter 5

Boisen's Productive "Retirement"

RESEARCHER AND CRITICAL RECEPTION

The mid-1930s mark the apogee of Boisen's career and a major turning point. His clinical movement was reasonably well established but started to move in directions different from what he had envisioned. The main philosophical difference witnessed in the growing influence of Wilhelm Reich's ideas and methods upon the clinical movement as it gravitated toward student-centered therapeutics as against Boisen's patient-centered focus. Boisen's interest in research also failed to resonate in the chaplaincy profession. Boisen officially retired as Elgin's chaplain in 1938 to work full time at Chicago Theological Seminary—he, however, returned to Elgin in 1942 due to lack of chaplain availability during the War. While Boisen continued to teach and supervise, his attention turned preponderantly toward research and writing for publication. Boisen's work and ambitious research and publication agenda made him too prominent to be ignored entirely in both pastoral care and psychology.

Henri Nouwen implies that "retirement" in 1938 was, indeed, a euphemism and perhaps, more aptly, a "time of fulfillment" for Boisen in his efforts to publish what he discovered "around the relationship between mental illness and religious experience." Nouwen continues that he "show[ed] an astonishing vitality and creativity in the last 25 years of his life. Boisen always considered training and research two essentially related aspects of his concern." And as advancing age and health difficulties "caused him to put less emphasis on training he gave free rein to his desire to do more research" and publish his insights.[1]

Boisen's most intellectually significant work, *The Exploration of the Inner World: A Study of Mental Disorder and Religious Experience*, appeared in 1936.[2] This work of 316 pages sets forth the results of many of his case studies, historical examples—such as George Fox, and, in conclusion, his own personal "journey into the lower regions."[3] Boisen's work flowed from his effort to synthesize objective study with his own personal, driving, experience: "All this I see not as a mere intellectual proposition. I feel it as a grim and awful reality." A reality, at least for the author, that was sustained and supported by his unconventional love, Alice Batchelder, memorialized, albeit cryptically, in initials "A.L.B." in the book's preface.[4]

Exploration of the Inner World is the most fully developed iteration of Boisen's synthesis of the scientific with personal experience. It was generally received with cautious, provisional, approval from scholarly and clinical critics of the time. However, even they admitted that Boisen's approach and use of language were unusual and somewhat alien to an audience largely composed of scholars and clinicians. Edmund Conklin, psychology professor at Indiana University, noted Boisen's "combination of fields of knowledge not ordinarily brought together within the comprehension of one person." In this case these fields included not only scholarly psychopathology and religion but also personal experience of "the confusion and excitement of a catatonic dementia praecox." Conklin notes, "This is the magnum opus of a devoted life. Its earnestness, its almost tearful sincerity, appears on every page. It is a profoundly personal book. Many will doubtless find its weakness in this very personal nature of the work, but the reviewer, who has read it carefully twice and is familiar with scientific techniques as well as psychopathology and to some extent with the literature of religion, does not yet feel inclined to condemn because of this freely admitted personal bias." Conklin rhetorically asked Boisen, "The reviewer would still like to know why the author had the second attack, why the majority of catatonic dementia praecox cases fail . . . . Perhaps the author may yet give us another volume in which some of these possibilities are worked out. And, if he does, it should have a title less dramatic but more likely to attract the scholar than the one placed on this book."[5]

Charles Patterson, professor of the philosophy of religion, at the University of Nebraska, commended Boisen's synthesis for the aid it promised in the practice of religious ministry with the mentally ill: "Fully aware of the power of religion for the accomplishment of good in some lives he [speaking of religious professionals generally] has tried to make this power available for the individual whom he is trying to help. But lacking the scientific information the psychologist and psychiatrist possess, he has been unable to use religious power to any good advantage. It is the genius of Dr. Boisen's book that he shows how these two methods of approach can be used together."[6]

Boisen's 1960 autobiography *Out of the Depths: An Autobiographical Study of Mental Disorder and Religious Experience* may be the book for which he is best known. As he states in his foreword, the intent of his "own case record" was to put forth "firsthand evidence which is the basis of any authority I may claim as an explorer in this field."⁷ Thomas Klink, one of Boisen's former students, granted that "it would be easy to dismiss this book as the ruminations of a now aged Victorian." Yet, he tended to view it as a personal story of spiritual struggle and overcoming, "There is the timeless human dilemma of the reconciliation of flesh and spirit. . . . Boisen has written another companion volume to the gospels in which the Answer is to be found."⁸

Richard Jenkins' review likened Boisen's book to Clifford Beers' *A Mind That Found Itself*, and said it is "one of the most significant personal documents in the field of psychiatry to come to light in the present century." While Jenkins admires and appreciates Boisen's case record as an effort to gain greater understanding in psychopathology and religious experience, he repeats Boisen's criticism "of theological seminaries for failing to make use of scientific method in the study of present-day religious experience." He, implicitly, deplores the specialization of his time that may have forwarded understanding in some areas, yet hindered it in others in ignoring connections between discrete phenomena. As ever narrowing specialization became the order of the day during Boisen's lifetime, Boisen "found himself working in a no man's land between religion, psychiatry and sociology." Jenkins feared that excess specialization could lead to counterproductive "dogmatic rigidities"; by not dialoging with other disciplines and perspectives, he commended Boisen's work of "original synthesis" as offering insights others may be prone to ignore.⁹

Clyde Steckel, of Illinois College, offered sharper appraisal of Boisen's penultimate work. Accusing him of "refus[ing] to analyze the dynamics of his own case record," he states that Boisen's work displays the "reluctance [that] also has something of the flavor of the mystic's unwillingness to analyze an experience that is essentially ineffable." Likewise, Steckel indicates that Boisen "has [not] modified or extended his general thesis as it was first advanced in 1936 in *The Exploration of the Inner World*" besides uncritically asserting that "certain forms of mental disturbance are similar to religious experience" without doing more than to "repeat and illustrate it." Close to Steckel's main criticism is Boisen's intense relationship to his own experience. While this fault may not have been laid as strongly against William James in 1890, it excludes Boisen as a true scientist in 1960: "giv[ing] no indication that he is aware of this change in mood, and this is why he gives the impression of answering questions no longer being asked and of avoiding crucial issues currently raised." For Steckel, as well as for the clinical pastoral education movement of the 1960s, Boisen was, at best, a relic of a bygone era doggedly pursuing, and consistently failing, to answer questions that nobody is asking.¹⁰

Paul Pruyser, psychologist at the Menninger Clinic, and a contributor to the work on psychology and religion and to chaplaincy as a profession, provides a more developed example of critical engagement with Boisen.[11] Pruyser, along with Nouwen and Hiltner, may represent the most nuanced, informed, and searching critics of Boisen and his work during his later years. Publicly, Pruyser was collegial and supportive toward Boisen; his private thoughts suggested a more ambivalent attitude.

In 1960, Pruyser approvingly quoted Gordon Allport: "A narrowly conceived science can never do business with a narrowly conceived religion. Only when both parties broaden their perspective will the way to understanding and cooperation open."[12] As academic and professional specialization carried the day, Boisen, like Pruyser, practiced an interdisciplinary approach. Building upon, perhaps moving a step beyond, William James, he stated, "The old question was: Which are the significant data of religious experience? The new question is: Which data of experience are of religious significance?" Pruyser suggests the more controversial, repetitive, and self-absorbed aspects of Boisen's work: "Whatever one may think of Boisen's propositions in detail." Yet, in Pruyser's estimation, Boisen's project recast "religion" in a broader and more inclusive light, "I think that this is a position which places religious experience functionally and experientially most clearly at the nexus of holistic, integrating tendencies of the organism. In this theoretical framework religion is not an adjutant to integration; it *is* integration."[13] Boisen's larger, more inclusive, view of the phenomena and experiences that constitute religion provided a central core of Boisen's work and contribution not only to religion but to psychology as well.

Like Hiltner, Pruyser felt Boisen's life and contribution merited reflection upon his death. In 1967, Pruyser noted that Boisen's "writings are intensely autobiographical, and his vocational choice was profoundly personal." He considered that the overtly and intensely personal nature of his work yielded questions, impatience, at times scorn, for Boisen's work and whether it possessed any ongoing significance. For Pruyser, "history will answer these questions and give its verdict."[14] In Boisen, Pruyser saw an ally in "that the mentally ill are not hopelessly fixed in their miserable condition. They can be helped when one realizes that in their symptoms they are already trying to help themselves."[15] His work was, for Pruyser, especially significant in its probing and in-depth examination of specific patients: "he used first-hand observations instead of second-hand reports which most of his predecessors relied on." Boisen had a penchant for study of the larger context of the individual that "comes through with great force to anyone who has had the opportunity to read the unpublished case studies he collected about his hospital patients. These show that he was not easily fooled by one-shot impressions."[16]

A multidisciplinary approach fueled Boisen's method. Alluding to Boisen's sociological works and early training in forestry; Pruyser opined that Boisen "had a penchant for a simultaneous vision of the trees as well as the forest.

As a clinical worker and while focusing on the individual, he placed great emphasis on social roles and social learning" and considered wellness and illness as socially and historically conditioned situations and experiences.[17] Additionally, Boisen's work as a promoter and administrator not only expanded "James' brilliant vignettes into full-fledged case studies" but also "created a drastic change in the psychology of religion by his organizational work. Largely due to his pioneering efforts and his work as a teacher and supervisor we can see the laboratory of our discipline shift from the university campus, with students as the typical subjects, to the hospital, with patients as the sources of observation."[18]

For Pruyser, Boisen's work was not without problematic elements. Boisen cited resources "monotonously for only one or two phrases which he repeated over and over, while others he cited polemically, with protests."[19] Of possibly greater concern, "he divided the mentally ill into two rigorously distinct groups: the organic and the functional disorders." The "organic" quickly falling from Boisen's attention as he focused on "functional" illness, preferably those most resembling Boisen's own case. Functional illnesses as falling into "positive," or "valid," experiences and outcomes that lead to resolution as compared to "negative, or "invalid," experiences and outcomes that resulted in ongoing illness and disintegration.[20] Boisen's, at times rigid, dichotomies threatened his ability to conduct objective observation of the phenomena of experience and illness. For Pruyser, however, both Boisen's insights and limitations were reflective of his "profoundly personal" quest, which culminated in the publication of *Out of the Depths*, which is Boisen's own case study, "one of the varieties of religious experience." "Of all the case studies he assembled, this is the richest and the most purposive: to show the dynamics of faith at work in the nooks and crannies of one lonely man's productive existence."[21]

Pruyser was personally acquainted with Boisen. His recollections, mediated through Henri Nouwen, reveal a somewhat conflicted combination of respect, impatience, awe, and detachment toward the, then, aged and infirm patriarch of the chaplaincy movement. Pruyser privately wrote Nouwen:

> The most outstanding feature of the man at the time I knew him was his flat affect. There is an awful psychiatric expression referring to chronic schizophrenic patients, who have made a good hospital adjustment, or sometimes have been discharged and live on the outside. The expression is "burned out case." This phrase came into my mind time and time again when I talked with him and saw him act. He was not without humor and delicacy, but something had happened to his feelings and their expression.
>
> He was very courteous to me, interested in some of my thoughts, and whether he himself talked about pleasant or unpleasant things in his life, it was all stated

in the same monotonous, deliberately affect-free language. He also had a faraway look. Yet I must say that there was something very likeable about the man, perhaps in part because of the tragic stamp on his life. I have always felt that his *Out of the Depths*, which came out a year or so later, conveys in its tone and selection of topics exactly the impression I gained in my personal confrontation with him. The language is beautiful, topics are moving, but there is something utterly pathetic about it all. There is something of homesickness in it, ennobled by a sense of suffering. In his presence I felt respect towards him for there was an odd distance between himself and the rest of the world. I also felt at that time that he knew he was dying slowly and with several ups and downs physically, so that one felt somehow in the presence of a man preparing himself for death. This certainly augmented by sense of reverence toward him, but again, made it difficult for me to invest myself in him.[22]

Nouwen also kept notes of his personal interviews with Pruyser. These reveal a sharper attitude, indicating a man who respected and valued Boisen's work—but found Boisen, personally, disagreeable. While Pruyser attributes "humor and delicacy," Nouwen's notes recall Pruyser saying Boisen "had absolutely no sense of humor—it just sort of passed him by in other people, he didn't understand it. . . . He was evidently quite autistic; he was capable of sitting for an entire evening in a corner. Unless someone spoke to him, he very rarely spoke to anyone else, unless he happened to like that person particularly. The result was very stark conversations." In private, Pruyser dismissed Boisen as a serious scholar: "Dr. P gave us the very strong impression that in dealing with Boisen's work . . . [when he cited scholarly sources such as Mead, Freud, Jung, etc.] . . . he picked out the things that seemed to pertain to his case, and these were the things that came out later as part of his ideas part of his theories. Sometimes he quoted other people. He was not a scholarly man. . . . once he read them, they seemed to stick, and he put them in."[23]

Pruyser also vividly recalled that Boisen would have been adamant about his illness as a critical part of triggering his life's work. Nouwen recalled Pruyser asking "what my interest in Boisen was, and I mentioned that I was fascinated by the work he had accomplished in spite of being a schizophrenic, and Dr. P. pointed out that Boisen, if he'd heard that, would have been very quick to correct me, and to say that is was not in spite of being a schizophrenic, but because of his being a schizophrenic, his viewing the entire schizophrenic breakdown in many people as a constructive process."[24]

Pruyser's critique of Boisen's work and life reveals an insightful, nuanced, and at times contradictory portrait of a man who in the minds of many had been defined by his mental illness.[25] While Pruyser applied terms such as "schizophrenic," "autistic," "burnt-out case" to Boisen, it is also important to recall—as Pruyser acknowledges—that Boisen was elderly, and often physically infirm, during the time he knew him. Furthermore, while Boisen's work could be tedious, repetitive, and it may be fair to question his use of sources, it is difficult to credibly dismiss someone with over eighty published academic writings as "not a scholarly man." Pruyser, however, publicly affirmed Boisen as an ally in a new and more hopeful approach to mental illness and a more scientific approach to pastoral care. Regardless, however, of Pruyser's—or anybody else's—critiques or personal opinions of Boisen, from 1936 onward, he was an established clinician, educator, and researcher who spanned the fields of pastoral care, psychology, and sociology. Boisen's work could be critiqued, or even panned outright, but by this time, his contributions were too big to be ignored.

THE EXILED PATRIARCH

Boisen's "retirement" also witnessed growing alienation between him and the movement he started. The estrangement between the movement and its patriarch had multiple causal factors. Among them were Boisen's geographic isolation from the clinical movement's early centers in New England and New York. Boisen's interest in research and writing found few takers among the theologs who followed after him. Boisen's geographic and intellectual alienation from what would become mainstream clinical pastoral education culminated in the, often clandestine and uncredited, rise of Wilhelm Reich's teachings as the core philosophy behind clinical pastoral education. In many ways, Reich, not Boisen, is CPE's true father. The rise of Reich emanated from Boisen's isolation from the movement, exemplified clinical pastoral education's shift from patient care to student therapeutics, and personified its suspicion toward intellectual pursuits and nonemotive practices, such as reading, research and writing.[26]

Boisen and clinical pastoral education's early centers were literally, geographically, distant from each other. Following Boisen's 1930 hospitalization—which made his position on the East Coast at Worcester State Hospital untenable—he found new employment in the Midwest at Elgin State Hospital in Illinois. Elgin's superintendent, Charles Read, was enthusiastic about Boisen's program and had long awaited appointment of a supervisor to Elgin. He had been forced to wait due to lack of candidates. Elgin's clinical program, under Boisen's direction, welcomed nine students in its first session in summer 1932.[27] While clinical training grew quickly in the Chicago area after Boisen's arrival—he worked in circumstantial isolation. In 1932, the closest clinical program was located in Pittsburg led by Boisen's once and, soon to be, future assistant Donald Beatty.[28] As Boisen worked tirelessly at building a future both for himself and for his clinical training and research, his movement carried on without him and moved in directions of which he would not always approve.

Nouwen argued that Boisen's students tended to be independent, unruly, nonconformists who did not immediately gravitate to parish church assignments that church organizations had in mind for them. Boisen's students were unlikely to follow his lead simply because he told them to: "They were angry men, and most of their students were too. . . .they were ready to doubt the relevance of their theological education. They were uncertain, puzzled men who were anxiously looking for a way to make their vocation more meaningful." Nouwen quoted Beatty at length:

> Most of us, I suspect, were not conformists. Less than now, if reports are accurate, we were encouraged in our questioning of concepts and beliefs we could not in conscience accept. Our schools were not, in most instances, ready to let us openly express our doubts about some of the aspects of our religious traditions. Moving into the area of the physician we were often stimulated by the very intentness with which dedicated men tried out and tested and often rejected old methods and old concepts while they worked at new hypotheses. The basis of their "authority" was not tradition but verified judgement based on careful investigation. We liked that! And within our lights we wanted to use that approach to our own distinctive function.[29]

After Boisen left for Elgin, Dunbar rose to leadership within the New York–centered Council for Clinical Training.[30] While Boisen retained high regard, and personal affection, for Dunbar throughout her life, the two diverged in areas that moved Boisen and what would become mainstream clinical pastoral education in different directions. While Dunbar was theologically trained—she was firstly a psychiatrist and a medical doctor—and these priorities manifested in the New York organization. For Boisen, clinical training was first and last a theological endeavor. While he enthusiastically welcomed and actively promoted an interdisciplinary approach, and welcomed non-pastors as students, clinical training, first and last, was theology.

Dunbar envisioned clinical training in less theology-centered ways. Charles Hall notes that Dunbar's secularized vision (or perhaps *differently* secular vision) would have "physicians participating in the clinical training movement, and she hoped that law students and medical students, as well as theological students would be included in clinical training programs." He also detects a subtle distinction between the New York Council for Clinical Training vision of the pastor as "physician of the soul" and the Boston-based Institute for Pastoral Care vision of the pastor as "shepherd of the soul."[31]

Dunbar's professional interests and aspirations also propelled her vision for clinical training. Dunbar was interested, as a physician, in the relationship of body, mind, spirituality, and emotion in health and wellness. She sought laboratories to test her ideas and to provide practical skills and training for future practitioners—and likely had her fellow physicians and psychiatrists in mind. Robert Powell examines Dunbar's critical role in "psychosomatic" medicine: "Two interrelated aspects of psychosomatic medicine that receive great emphasis in Dunbar's writings, but little attention elsewhere, are concern for the prevention of disease, and recognition that most chronic illnesses have a significant emotional component. In fact, this public health standpoint was among the major reasons for encouraging cooperation between religion and medicine. Clergymen, Dunbar noted, visit freely with parishioners in their homes and can be encouraged to send parishioners 'to a general physician or psychiatrist at a time when relatively simple treatment can cure them.'"[32] Dunbar was, perhaps, born at an inopportune time: "By the late 1930s, however, public health and preventative medicine seemed to have become passé, and Dunbar found little moral support from within either medicine or psychiatry. . . . it became ever more obvious that work with the Council would be detrimental to her medical career"; she pared down her participation in the late 1930s and early 1940s—leaving the Council to others.[33]

Edward Thornton speaks of the clinical training movement having "right-wing" and "left-wing" traditions in the 1930s and 1940s. The "right wing" associated with the theological approach of Boisen and especially his protégé Seward Hiltner, while the "left wing" associated with the psychoanalytic, specifically Reichian, approach of Robert Brinkman.[34] By 1938, Hiltner, Dunbar's onetime assistant, had left for new employment with the Federal Council of Churches to be succeeded by Brinkman. By 1941, as Dunbar cut, at least overt, participation in the clinical training movement, leaving Brinkman, and the Reichians, firmly in charge.[35]

Boisen, as well as his protégés Beatty and Wayne Oates,[36] fiercely opposed Wilhelm Reich's growing influence within the clinical training movement. The ascendancy of Reichian therapeutics was the main, and immutable, philosophical wedge between Boisen and what would become the ruling philosophy behind clinical pastoral education.

However, before turning to Reich, let us examine other circumstantial aspects that contributed to Boisen's alienation from the movement he founded. He was a very busy man. Shortly upon arrival at Elgin, Boisen's attention increasingly turned toward publishing the results of his work. This comprised a massive research, writing, and editing agenda, which resulted in five books and over forty published articles. Four years after arrival in Illinois, Boisen published *Exploration of the Inner World*, his most prominent work. In 1946, he published a brief and practically oriented manual for parish pastors, *Problems in Religion and Life*.[37] The year 1950 witnessed the publication of fourth, revised and enlarged, edition of his hymnal dedicated for use in mental hospitals, *Hymns of Hope and Courage*.[38] He returned to his interests in sociology and psychology in *Religion in Crisis and Custom*, which was printed in 1945 and republished in 1955.[39] Finally, 1960 witnessed his last and most remarkable book, his autobiography and personal case study, *Out of the Depths*.[40]

Other circumstantial factors contributed to Boisen's marginalization besides his publishing concern. World War II, and the decades to follow, turned attention away from the state hospital, its long-term patients, and the associated market for in-depth, longitudinal, case studies of the type Boisen invented under Cabot and Zon's direction and influence. During World War II many of Boisen's students entered service as military chaplains. During and after the war, many of these chaplains, went on to work in acute care general hospital settings where visits with people in trouble would be brief, often one-shot affairs. Nouwen points out that for military (and often acute care chaplaincy) patients, "the safe structure of the church and the community, the organized forms of ministry were gone" and the chaplain would not have the ongoing structural support and context of the hospital to support and facilitate an ongoing pastoral or therapeutic relationship. As Boisen's students, particularly Hiltner, noted this change in circumstance—clinical training moved away from the deep, rich, broad, intensive—and lengthy and time-intensive - Boisen case study for brief "verbatims" that attempted to capture brief interactions between patient and chaplain for classroom discussion and critique.[41]

Boisen's later years at Elgin were filled with much writing, editing, haggling with publishers, as well as a gradual physical decline—all from a man who officially "retired" in 1938. As of his 1952 interview with Francis McPeek, Boisen alluded to several months' recent hospitalization due to a prostatectomy and ensuing complications. He had recently endured bouts of bronchitis, had three surgeries for hernia since the mid-1930s, and walked with increasing pain and difficulty due to arthritis in a hip.[42]

While Boisen showed the, often unacknowledged, limits imposed by declining health and intensive focus on getting his insights into print, he undoubtedly had significant limitations as a teacher. Lennart Cedarleaf recalled clinical education with Boisen in 1943. He "was a single issue, research-oriented theological scientist. His primary focus was his 'case.' His case was his John 3:16, by which he understood and interpreted the inner world of the deeply disturbed. He had no pastoral curiosity about people whose character was shaped by forces dissimilar from those forces which shaped his own person." Cedarleaf wondered: "His cane was his constant companion. He leaned on it. It steadied his gait. It often thumped to give emphasis to a Boisen point. We sometimes suspected he may have been tempted to use it to tap our heads when we questioned or resisted his 'wisdom.'"[43] Nouwen notes, "Boisen himself was not a great group leader. He was often too preoccupied by his own view on the matter to freely acknowledge and utilize the ideas which came up in the discussion. He often left group members free for twenty or thirty minutes without interruption. If he felt that the discussion had moved too far away from his own ideas, he delivered a short monologue and let it go on from there. And after the discussion was over, Boisen gave a straight lecture, with a few questions. He hardly paid attention to what the students had said."[44]

Many factors contributed to Boisen's alienation and exile from the clinical training mainstream, some of which were circumstantial. Ensconced in the Midwest, Boisen toiled far from the early centers of clinical pastoral education in New York and Boston. He was engrossed in a massive publishing project as his physical health declined as decades passed. While Boisen's research agenda, and coping with advancing age and chronic physical (and likely subclinical mental) illnesses, gave reason enough for him to be "preoccupied," his noted lack of interest in ideas and agendas that diverged from his own provides insight on why many of his "angry" and restless understudies "moved in directions which he did not want to follow."[45]

1) *Nuttier than a Fruitcake*: the rise of Wilhelm Reich in Clinical Pastoral Education.

One direction in which Boisen did not want to follow, and viewed with horror and disgust, was Reichian psychotherapy. Austrian psychiatrist Wilhelm Reich's overarching, underground, and often unacknowledged influence on clinical pastoral education reached its maturity with Robert Brinkman's ascendancy in the New York group in the late 1930s and the early 1940s. Reich's association with Brinkman and the clinical movement filtered through Dunbar—and especially Theodore Wolfe—the man she married shortly after distancing herself from Boisen in 1930. Wolfe translated many of Reich's works from German into English and facilitated his emigration to the United States, on literally the last ship leaving Norway prior to Nazi invasion.[46]

Wolfe brokered Reich's indirect influence on Brinkman and the clinical training movement. Wolfe had little use for Boisen's, or his own wife's, theologs, dismissing them as "cockroaches."[47] Wolfe left Dunbar and the two divorced in 1939.[48] Wolfe, apparently, had a positive relationship with Brinkman, whom he encouraged to leave chaplaincy and take up practice as a psychotherapist—this Brinkman did upon resigning directorship of the New York-based Council for Clinical Training.[49]

Theodore Wolfe's last spouse, Gladys Meyer, gave an insight into Reich's odd charisma and beguiling hold:

"Real" life began for Dr. Wolfe with his work with Dr. Reich. He would describe how everything he read, saw, heard, and felt changed in quality; and the vague, impatient emptiness began, with great anxiety to be filled up. A bond of gratefulness to Reich stemmed from that deepest core of himself which Reich had made accessible to him. And he loved Reich.[50]

Myron Sharaf, Reich biographer and one-time student, attests to Reich's charisma as well. "[T]he standard psychiatric opinion of Reich was well reflected by the title of Martin Grotjahn's review in 1943 of *The Function [of the Orgasm]*: 'Nuttier Than a Fruitcake.'" Sharaf recalled his first meeting with Reich in 1944:

> His whole syndrome of ideas appealed strongly to me: the concept of a deeper, more joyous sensuality; the affirmation of adolescent love life; the linking of sexual freedom with a nonauthoritarian social order; the relationship between emotional suppression and economic exploitation of submissive, "unalive" workers; the sense that "unarmored" man could experience a more vital existence; a psychiatric therapy that dealt not only with psychological complexes but also with bodily rigidities; even the notion of a universal energy identical to the energy that moved in sexual excitation. I found it all intoxicating.[51]

The great man inquired of his potential student:

> "Are you healthy?" . . . I was familiar enough with his writings to know that he was not referring to my everyday health, but was talking about my "genital health," my "orgastic potency." Being fairly inexperienced at the time (as well as inhibited), I replied in an embarrassed way that I didn't know whether I was healthy or not. He tactfully dropped the subject. . . . Perhaps he would permit me after all to enter this "dangerous" field. I remember staring full of admiration, as he stood in the doorway. He noticed my stare, then assumed a "back to work" expression and returned to the basement. Later he commented that he had recognized the mystical, religious look in my eyes, the "burning eyes" he had seen so many times when people first made contact with him and his work. That same adoration, he was to say later, would often turn to hatred when the longing to be "saved" by Reich was disappointed.[52]

Who was Reich? His career had a most auspicious beginning. From 1924 through 1930, he was director of Sigmund Freud's training seminar and widely considered Freud's heir apparent,[53] enviously called "Freud's pet" by many of Reich's peers.[54] Reich metaphorically referred to himself as "a shark in a pond of carps" in comparison to his fellow Freudians.[55] Controversy over his methods and aggressive personality—combined with the rise of Hitler and Fascism—saw him expelled from Freud's circle and eventually led to his meeting with Wolfe and flight to the United States.

Reich's ideas, occasionally brilliant, deeply influenced clinical pastoral education, especially the exhortation "relax, express, let go" Nouwen attributed to him.[56] As Freud's seminar leader, Reich focused on "resistances." Sharaf asserts that as a patient proceeded in psychoanalysis,

> "defensive character traits" . . . rigid politeness, evasiveness, apprehensiveness, and arrogance had originally developed in childhood as a way of warding off strong emotional stimuli from within or without . . . . In analysis, they continued to function as a way of blocking strong emotional experiences, now provoked by the unsettling process of analysis itself. The defensive character traits which in their totality Reich termed "character armor," served to protect the individual against pain, but also served to restrict severely the capacity for pleasure.[57]

For Reich, the way to break through "character armor" and "character resistance" was to "make the unconscious conscious" in provoking strong emotional experiences from his patients.[58] "Needless to say, a repeated pointing out of the patient's defensive character traits does not endear the analyst to the patient. On the contrary, it usually arouses considerable anger." Still, such provocation served the greater good; "the patient learn[s] that the consequences of anger need not be so terrible; the patient need not hold on to his controlled politeness." Sharaf points out that many in the psychological community disagreed with aspects of Reich's methods in that it failed to truly prioritize the patient, "'resistance analysis'—or 'character analysis'" encouraged therapist "personal biases and interests to override the patient's needs" treatment goals and priorities.[59]

Reich promised answers for people pining for them in the aftermath of the horrific irrationality of the Holocaust, World War II, and Hitlerism. Those answers lie in addressing what Reich considered the basic and fundamental truth underlying all things: "Since the life process and the sexual process are one and the same, it goes without saying that *sexual, vegetative energy is active in everything that lives* [italics are Reich's]. This statement is very dangerous precisely because it is simple and absolutely correct."[60] For Reich, neither Hitler's charisma nor his promises could explain his rise to absolute power. Rather, the Hitler conundrum was based in "the psychic structures of the people who make up the society."[61] Obedience to absolute authority is nurtured from childhood: "the family is the authoritarian state in miniature, to which the child must learn to adapt." However, the way to maturity and liberation, for Reich, is found, basically, in sex, and fascist structures depend on inventing "substitute gratifications" to preserve childlike dependence. "Militarism is based essentially on a libidinous mechanism. The sexual effect of a uniform the erotically provocative effect of rhythmically executed goose-stepping . . . consciously exploits these sexual interests. It not only designs flashy uniforms for the men, it puts the recruiting into the hands of attractive women." At last, "The sexual morality that inhibits the will to freedom, as well as those forces that comply with authoritarian interests, derive their energy from repressed sexuality."[62] Breaking through, by force if necessary, accumulated repressions, resistances, and armoring in order to provoke emotional and affective release was necessary to free people and peoples. The ultimate example was "the satisfactory orgasm [which] made the difference between sickness and health."[63]

But, how to achieve "the satisfactory orgasm"? Upon arrival in the United States, Reich proposed machines and therapies promising to facilitate this august goal. One of Reich's most famed devices, the one that landed him in jail, the "orgone energy accumulator," was typically, as Christopher Turner explains,

> a wooden cupboard about the size of a telephone booth, lined with metal and insulated with steel wool—a box ... He claimed could charge up the body with the life force that circulated in the atmosphere (a force which he christened "orgone energy")—mysterious currents that in concentrated form could not only help dissolve repressions but also treat cancer, radiation sickness, and a host of minor ailments. As he saw it, the box's organic material absorbed orgone energy, and the metal lining stopped it from escaping, so the box acted as a greenhouse; and, supposedly, there was a noticeable rise in temperature in the box.[64]

Often "vegetotherapy," later rechristened "orgone therapy," followed a session in the box.[65] Turner records, "Reich's third wife, Ilse, described it as 'doing away with the psychoanalytic taboo of never touching a patient,' and replacing it with 'a physical attack by the therapist.' Reich would relax the patient's taut muscles with deep breathing exercises and painful massage, until he or she broke down in involuntary convulsions, which Reich called the 'orgasm reflex.'"[66]

Reich, however, was not finished inventing. By the 1950s, "he had now built a 'cloudbuster,' an orgone gun that was designed not only to influence the weather—diverting hurricanes and making it rain in the desert—but to be the first line of defense against an alien invasion. It was a kind of orgone box turned inside out, so that it could work its therapeutic magic on the cosmos."[67] Reich convinced acclaimed scientist Albert Einstein to study his orgone box; after two weeks of tests, Einstein, unsurprisingly, refuted Reich's claims.[68]

Why would Reich's teachings and methods resonate with aspiring ministers undergoing clinical training, and how far did his influence reach? Reichianism ascended within the Council for Clinical Training with Brinkman, whom Thornton describes as "something of a devotee of Reichian psychoanalysis," and through Brinkman's influence, Reichian methods gained influence within the early clinical training program.[69] Charles Hall explicates further on Reich's appeal within the New York cohort: "(clinical pastoral education) Supervisors tended to be persons who, in part thorough a moralistic religious heritage, had developed patterns of denial and repression of feelings. Reich encouraged sexual expression and sexual freedom. Reichian therapy was liberating to them. They saw Reich's focus on the interrelationship of mind and body and his emphasis on getting in touch with one's feelings as supporting their search for clinical theology."[70]

In 1955 Psychiatrist Leon Salzman suggested: "His religious zeal and high moral and ethical principle and his fanatical concern for the welfare of all people have stirred up many people with similar ideals'" as well as "the torments of a hounded, lonely, self-glorified exile—not acceptable in academic circles and involved in many skirmishes with the law. . . . It is this martyr quality, which has attracted many sensitive moralists, writers, and clergymen."[71] While Charles Hall gives a plausible explanation of Reich's appeal, he cryptically adds: "In the process of getting in touch with emotions and with unconscious conflicts, there was some 'acting out' on the part of a few New York group supervisors, although not the leaders, and on part of some of the students in clinical training."[72] Henri Nouwen's unpublished study, and critique, of clinical pastoral education suggests a naive second generation to emerge after Boisen: "A second danger was the anti-intellectual attitude of many supervisors which made them uncritical admirers of the new theories which entered the psychiatric milieu. They were fed up with the long irrelevant papers they had to write in their seminaries; they wanted to work and see results. And the doctors had results, visible and concrete. Their theories at least worked!"[73]

Hall equivocates on the spread of Reichianism within the clinical movement, suggesting it was limited to "a few" supervisors and "some" students in New York who were "acting out." By the mid-1950s, Reich's ideas and techniques were readily found at the State Hospital in Norristown, Pennsylvania. Newly retired superintendent Arthur Noyes recalled he "initiated a (clinical pastoral education) similar program at Norristown soon after I came here, but some of those concerned with sending students to the hospital were interested in Reich's "box." I found that the hospital chaplain possessed one and had great confidence in its efficacy. As you probably know, this 'box' was finally debarred from interstate commerce."[74] Reich's methods spread at least as far as North Dakota and Iowa. Al Sherve recalled his first unit of clinical education at Jamestown State Hospital in North Dakota in summer 1955, mentioning that his supervisor

> Came to Jamestown with an Orgone Box, which was sort of a hush-hush business . . . he didn't want anyone to know about it because he was afraid of being

kicked out of the hospital, at this time Reich had lost his status, he was in prison. . . . he [his clinical supervisor Bjorn Nielsen] used the orgone box with some of us . . . one is supposed to relax in these boxes, it never worked with me and I never saw the purple sparks jumping around. Bjorn willed that box to me and I still have it and I plan to donate it to ACPE for the 50th Anniversary!

Sherve went on to further clinical training at Independence State Hospital in Iowa. He recalled:

[I] sat in the orgone box on the third floor of another building for 45 minutes, usually taking Reich's book *The Function of the Orgasm* and reading that while sitting there waiting for something to happen, but nothing ever happened! After sitting in the orgone box, I would move out of that and Walter [Bell, his supervisor] had a little room where I would come in, undress, lay down on the bed and do deep breathing therapy with him for 45 minutes . . . then we had our seminars from ten until noon, talking about Reich, occasionally a verbatim . . . but not too much of that.[75]

Sharaf's first meeting with Reich had the air of the forbidden. Reich advised him "'not to go into the work, it is too dangerous, there is too much opposition, the work is very difficult.' Of course, this kind of warning only increased my zeal."[76] Sherve's comments also hint at the clandestine, cutting-edge, patina Reichianism carried for some in the clinical training movement. Reich was a hero martyred to the cause of liberation that the "little man" (another term Reich used) did not, and perhaps could not, understand.[77] It offered a new and vaguely dangerous way of being and acting that had to be carefully stewarded. It was esoteric gnosis for the initiated to be carefully guarded from the "carps" who were not ready for the unarmored life of the properly predisposed.

THE DISSENTERS

Boisen's marginalization was partially due to circumstance, personality, and his teaching limitations. It was also due to the emergence of Reichian orthodoxy within the movement, which demanded a shift from patient-centered care to student-centered therapeutics at the cost of Boisen's fact, knowledge, and research-driven approach.[78] Boisen, and his fellow dissenters, were not pleased with clinical education's change in course—especially its uncritical acceptance of Reichian ideas and techniques. Boisen offered:

There was a tendency to accept Freudian doctrine on authority without scrutinizing it closely . . . I was especially troubled by a tendency to accept the easy solutions to some of the perennial problems of sin and salvation. Take, for example, a patient who is torn with conflict between the demands of conscience and his erotic desires and impulses. The solution offered by some of our chaplain-supervisors was that of getting rid of the conflict by lowering the conscience threshold. There were even those who accepted the later teachings of Wilhelm Reich, advocating a freedom quite at variance with the basic insights of the Hebrew-Christian religion.[79]

The patriarch of clinical education, now dissenter, like his early protégé Helen Dunbar, was in the words of Robert Powell a staunch "facts first" person who insisted "that the novice needed to gain a knowledge base, needed to learn something, specifically, about a few specific human beings—that the novice had to do some original 'research,' so to speak, and be 'trained' before he or she could move on to the more interactive processes of education and supervision."[80]

Allison Stokes related her interview with Wayne Oates, a Boisen protégé and fellow dissenter, amid the emerging Reichianism: "When Oates surveyed his roomful of books, Boisen indicated that 'these over here are the trash and the hay. Those over here are the finest of wheat.' The latter, said Oates, were Freud, Adler, Jung, etc." When Oates returned to Louisville, he told Gaines Dobbins, his Ph.D. committee chair at Southern Baptist Seminary:

> You know nobody has really read Freud; that's what bothers me. I learned at Wake Forest that before you can critique a person you have to have read the primary sources. I learned at Duke, in church history with Ray Petrie, that you *dare* not quote a secondary source without getting *killed*.[81]

Following this observation, Oates dutifully set about correcting his deficit via "a classic approach, which insists on an analysis of the text." In the mid-1940s he scoured universities across the South and the East coast to read what Freud actually wrote—texts he found surprisingly hard to find for someone referenced by so many. Freud's primary texts became the basis of his doctoral dissertation in psychology.[82]

Wayne Oates, the founder of an independent tradition of clinical pastoral education with a Southern accent, went into revolt against the New York-based Council for Clinical Training for reasons of conviction, temperament, and practical need. Oates made common cause with Boisen partially out of political commonality, partially out of standing contacts and philosophical agreement with Boisen, and partially out of affection toward his mentor.

Nouwen, who knew Oates personally, attested to his strong personality that not everyone found agreeable: "He is somewhat of an angry old man who had a lot of conflicts in this life but for no price would have liked to miss them . . .

his aggressive personality, accentuated by his stick which he carries around him since his back troubles, make students fear and respect him." In spite of his combative nature, "he is able to tolerate strong personalities besides his own."[83] Beginning with Oates' high school experience as a page in the U.S. Senate, he was accustomed to politics, the adversarial process, and conflict as unavoidable parts of the human experience—and even appeared to enjoy them. Recalling conflicts with fellow Southern Baptists and a failed attempt to start a clinical training program in a local hospital, the happy warrior recalled, "we did get our tails kicked around a lot. Both within the denomination and those outside. . . . but it was fun because I saw it as essentially a political process, and to me politics are fun."[84]

Oates' connection with Boisen started in 1943, when Boisen visited one of Oates' classes at Southern Baptist Seminary in Louisville.[85] Oates arranged to travel to Elgin to study with Boisen for the summer of 1945. To his dismay, he learned that "Dr. Boisen had been unseated from his position as chaplain and teacher at Elgin in a power struggle with Fred Kuether and other persons in the Council for Clinical Training and Bill Andrews had been put in his place, unknown to us before we arrived." Oates encountered a program very different from the theologically centered program he expected; he described a syllabus "largely that of an exploration of the psychoanalytic interpretation of cases. We were not permitted to study or discuss the 'theological implications' of a case until the last week of the twelve-week unit of CPE. . . . discussion of pastoral possibility and theological meanings were strictly off-limits." As Oates vigorously objected: "Kuether and Andrews were considerably angry at me because I was super aggressive in challenging their lack of pastoral concern, Biblical information, and theological perspective. . . . Let's face it, I thought they meant it when they said they thought that a student should express his hostility."[86] Many years later, in 1970 as Glenn Asquith, Jr. undertook his first unit of clinical training, he echoed Oates' sentiments regarding the "emphasis on psychology at the expense of theology. We would give theology an obligatory nod as we discussed cases, but then we would quickly turn to psychology to answer the question of 'what's *really* going on.'"[87]

Clinical pastoral education's march toward Reich alienated the movement from the seminaries to whom Boisen wanted to sell his new kind of theological education.[88] Nouwen recalls that "around 1950 the Episcopal seminaries became more and more concerned about the therapeutic approach in clinical training. . . . with the many confused and disturbed students they saw return to the seminary from training."[89] Clinical trainings' emphasis on psychoanalytics, to the short shrift, if not outright exclusion of theology, let alone orgone boxes and vegetotherapy, may explain some of the growing mistrust and suspicion. Seward Hiltner, professor at the University of Chicago School of Divinity, offered on the doubling up of psychoanalytics with an ardently Reichian bent; "with the Reichian content that eventually emerged, it was double dangerous. Indeed, I sometimes think it was almost a miracle that clinical training survived this combination."[90]

Hiltner's approach at the University of Chicago and Princeton tended to be more conciliatory, seeking to use his position and institutional standing to conciliate between the clinical organizations and the seminaries in essential accord with Boisen's model. He strove for reconciliation of academics with practical application, in Thornton's words, "a model that equips seminarians for effective pastoral work and creates a research community dedicated to empirical inquiry into the religious dimension of life."[91]

Oates, partly by circumstance, partly by need, partly by his own personality, pursued a more aggressive dissent in implementing his mentor's idea of a new kind of theological education based in his seminary in Louisville. Aggressive confrontation between Oates and his clinical supervisors at Elgin in Summer 1945 had ramifications that lasted decades. Oates planned to implement a clinical training program in Louisville. In order to do this under Council auspices, he needed to interview with, and gain endorsement from, Fred Kuether, the secretary of the Council and Oates' old supervisor from Elgin. Oates recalled, "I went to Chicago to ask Fred Kuether as the Executive Secretary for the Council of Clinical Training to include the plan I just described as a bona fide part of the Council of Clinical Training's work. I met him at Elgin State Hospital, I explained the plan, he said that I was a Southern Baptist who was so opposed to the use of alcohol that I could never fit in with the other supervisors of the Council."[92] While Oates provides the only witness to this interaction, Edward Thornton affirms that upon rejection, Kuether offered "no alternatives for developing an indigenous program under adequate supervision. Oates was thrown back on his own resources at this point."[93]

Oates returned to Kentucky with "my mind made up. I simply returned to Louisville and set up the program without the supervision of Bonacker," and hence renegade from the Council for Clinical Training. Oates' program developed "clinical facilities and supervision that would be wholly responsible to seminary educational policies"; thus the seminary became his de facto accrediting organization. Oates proceeded to establish clinical training in acute care and state hospitals predominantly in the South. Unlike other clinical pastoral education programs, clinical education became closely intertwined with the seminary curriculum, through the doctoral level, at the Louisville Seminary, guided by Oates and his students.[94]

Kuether and the New York organization were not pleased with Oates' sense of initiative. Oates was "shocked to have, first, the superintendent of the Baptist Hospital and the President of the Baptist Seminary to call me in and tell me that Fred Kuether had written them letters, air mailed special delivery, seeking to negate and sabotage the program. They were both angry at his doing this and the end result was that I had to tell them the whole story I just told you. They closed ranks behind me and wrote him letters to that effect." Oates, orphaned, without the support of either the New York or the Boston clinical training organizations "made my own way with my senior support system [the seminary faculty] and with the continuing comradeship with Dr. Boisen."

Oates' political, administrative, and clinical talent succeeded in spite of his pariah standing within mainstream clinical pastoral education of the time. The wounds of this political fight, and also his gratitude for Boisen's support, remained decades later. Oates reminisced: "He [Boisen] and I have much in common, not the least of which was the fact neither of us was a certified supervisor, he died! [Oates' drawl rising in emphasis] uncertified, except for the fact he was certified as being dead." While Oates was "grandfathered" into supervisor certification upon the merger of several clinical bodies—including Oates Southern Baptist group—into ACPE in 1968, Oates opined, "I am confident that if I were to come up now for advanced standing as a student I probably would be told that I was not affirmed . . . after all, it is not a matter of life and death."[95]

Oates, and Boisen's, common cause rooted in several factors. Both had practical need for each other amid geographic, professional, and social exclusion from the emerging mainstream. Oates, and his Louisville contingent, offered fellowship, welcome, and warmth to a man increasingly stigmatized and excluded. Boisen, in turn, offered mentorship, training, and the founder's credibility to Oates' upstarts. Oates, like Boisen, was a rigorous "facts first" scholar as well as clinician, insisting, first to himself, that he actually read Freud in order to be able to critically apply his work. Finally, for Oates, as well as Boisen, clinical pastoral education was first, last, and always a *theological* endeavor—stating in words welcome to his Southern Baptist base of clinical, and political, support, "we are committed to the clinical pastoral methodology of teaching, but we are not remotely interested in the use of the method in such a way as to make the substance of the Christian faith incidental or irrelevant."[96]

LETTERS FROM THE VOID

One of Boisen's most deeply held insights was the interconnection of the individual and community in building wellness or illness, in E. Brooks Holifields's words, "the social formation of self."[97] That mental illness, or wellness, was not the result of personal virtue nor personal failing but, at least in part, resulted from, and depended upon, relationship with those around us, our "fellowship of the best." Like contemporary psychiatrists, C. F., Karl, and Will Menninger (as well as their associate Pruyser), Boisen "believed that persons with mental illnesses could be treated and helped at a time when custodial care or lifetime exile were the only alternatives."[98]

Writing to a former parishioner of Boisen, Karl Menninger noted "Boisen was one of the first clergymen who took any interest in the research problems of religion in a psychiatric hospital, he is a kind of hero of ours."[99] The files from Boisen's "retirement" include caches of letters written him by obscure persons whose lives had been shrouded in shame and stigma—in Boisen, they found someone whose experience mirrored their own and offered hope for better days.

Boisen's correspondents, mostly through reading *Exploration of the Inner World* and Boisen's explicit reference to his own experiences of mental illness and perseverance, wrote about their own experiences of illness, caring for ill family members, and hope that better times may await them as well. J. C. Pipes, a Baptist missionary living in North Carolina, wrote, "I have had a similar experience to that which you have had, and have largely overcome and have come back to a life of service which could never have come to me had I not gone through this experience." He recalled, "At about the age of nineteen. . . Blackness and darkness enveloped me, and my experience for the next six years is similar to that of John Bunyan. I never ceased to try to pray, and I would have moments when all this hell would pass and the light would shine, but soon I would plunge again into this condition." Pipes continued, "while working in a field preparing to put out a crop of corn, I had another religious experience that lifted the shadows and brought light to my troubled soul. I saw myself crucified with Christ. All my life of sin was blotted out. I was dead and from the standpoint of my sins they existed no more, I was clean before God and before my fellow man." Pipes confided to Boisen a life of ups-and-downs, including the sudden death of his first wife, a happy second marriage along with significant fluctuations in his physical and mental health, which included "a struggle of depression for the next two years, but I have pondered it, and read every book I could get my hands on, and have reconstructed my religious conviction anew and I believe in a more real, vital and intelligent reality. Previous to this experience I was classed as an extreme fundamentalist. Now I believe that all light should be sought that will bless and save humanity from any source."[100]

Florence Lerrigo recalled: "a veritable light in the darkness to me, as its revelation of the constructive use of mental illness came to me at the close of a ten year period during which. . . I had struggled in the quiet interludes between four mental depressions to find my way to a balanced, stable life." For Lerrigo, Boisen's works encouraged the mentally ill to "own their own self-respect" in "a full share in the work of the world, . . . My work which began twelve years ago as an office secretary at Pilgrim Place in Claremont the community of retired Christian workers here, has grown in the past eight years to include responsibility for the promotional and publicity writing for this organization. I have increased in stability and strength, and to some degree, in writing skill too."[101] An elderly Boisen responded, using the formulaic, at times monotonous, language he often used when asked about mental illness: "I like to think of mental illness as the price we have to pay for being men and having the power of choice and the capacity for growth. In some of its forms I see manifestations of the power to heal which are closely related to certain forms of religious experience. This is especially true of those periods of darkness which the mediaeval mystics called 'the dark night of the soul.' The important question is always the direction in which we are moving."[102]

Boisen also heard from caretakers for mentally ill spouses and siblings. W. E. Jenkins confided: "My wife has had five serious breaks or mental conflicts. She is now in a county retreat waiting for the court to carry out its adjudication. She has been pronounced dementia praecox . . . . We have had her in private institutions in Ohio and Georgia each time. Insulin has been used during this last spell, but she has skipped again on arriving home. Our money is all gone now." In spite of the pain and helpless desperation that underlie his words, he states, "I will never give up hope, . . . my wife, with God's healing grace, . . .will be well someday to be of real service in this world with the mentally ill. My wife has been a writer, a teacher, and an all "A" student through college." Reflecting on his experience and his encountering Boisen's books, Jenkins imagined new paths for his own life, even amid catastrophe: "Since my wife has been ill, I have prayed that I might become more able to help mankind in preventative measures of mental troubles. . . . I really feel that there is work for me in this field, I see the need and should serve. Only I need training."[103]

Thomas McDill brought Boisen the ordeal of escorting his brother from Mississippi to a hospital in Grand Rapids, Michigan. "I followed this with a call to Joe's wife in Mississippi and she urged me to try to get Joe to accept treatment at Grand Rapids. She had received favorable reports of the medical staff there and the financial burden would be a serious problem at $32.00 per day." McDill drove his brother north and

> Everything had a special meaning to him, e.g. a sign indicating the direction to Dyer meant that we were on our way to see a dying man. He expressed considerable anxiety at a number of points, and wanted to stop, spend the night and continue the trip the following day. More and more, I felt I was losing control of the situation, and I was seriously questioning my ability to keep him in a state of mind that would enable him to hold on to reality. Chicago symbolized

Jerusalem, Lake Michigan was the Sea of Galilee, and we were going northward into Galilee. Highway repairmen were "paviours," preparing the highway for the king. With these assertions, there was renewed anxiety of being vulnerable to the attacks of Satan. [104]

Upon arriving at the hospital,

> fortunately Dr. Mulder was still there. . . . He stated quite emphatically at the beginning that Joe needed hospitalization and produced the papers for his signature. Joe then turned on me and said I had deceived him and led him into a trap. All of this, I might say at this point, had made me feel more and more that Joe was slipping into a full-blown paranoid state. He refused to sign the papers, and Dr. Mulder dismissed us saying that we could see him the next morning . . . But the shock of this approach was so sobering to Joe, that he was in a very stable state all evening.

As the evening progressed the brothers "discussed possibilities for the future, going over your (Boisen's) thesis on Schizophrenic studies rather thoroughly. Everything worked out all right the next morning. He signed the papers." McDill's progress—ending the Chicago area—appears to have been aided by Boisen's direct intervention. He continued, "and your time with Joe turned out to be his greatest incentive to hold on to reality and to give full cooperation in treatment."[105]

Lu Lu Wendel viewed Boisen as a hero and an inspiration in her own life: "His books describe the inner process the way I experienced it myself, except, after recovery my work has been in action and service and not in research and writing." In his elderly years, the once hospitalized Wendel befriended Boisen and provided aid with his personal affairs and provided a remembrance of Boisen in his final months. Wendel recalled "His last communication had been 'But of how much good would I be to you?' and my reply was 'This is not the question. Rather, would you welcome my visit?'" Wendel arrived at Elgin following her pilgrimage from California:

> "Where am I?" and my clear explanation settled his doubt. The next day he knew where he was. Had no-one previously taken time to explain, or was it his lack of memory? . . . I went to the fountain on the ward and brought back a cup of fresh water. He drank it eagerly. . . . I could not help but think of all the fine thoughts that in 88 years of his life had gone through this head; of all the suffering that this man had gone through was described in his books. Here he lay, his face hollowed out, his eyes sunk back deeply; his hands shaking slightly, his body weak and helpless. "Are you comfortable?" I asked and he replied with a clear "NO!" but smiling.[106]

Boisen clearly appreciated Wendel's visit, friendship, and her efforts to publicize Boisen's works. In 1963, a few years prior to Wendel's visit and when Boisen had somewhat greater strength, he wrote Victor Obenhaus, the dean of Chicago Theological Seminary: "I have known Mrs. W[endel] thru correspondence for about three years as a one-time patient who is tremendously enthusiastic for the cause of mental hygiene. She is a woman of energy and ability who makes a good first impression but has been something of a problem to the clinical training fraternity in the San Francisco area by reason of her too great zeal." While wanting to encourage Wendel's sense of service and the purpose she gained from advocacy for the mentally ill, Boisen also implied that Wendell needed supervision: "I do have serious misgivings about turning her loose as our representative so far away. . ., but I do believe she will [not] do any harm if she is content to operate in a small way."[107]

Of Boisen's mentees in navigating mental illness, perhaps the most surprising is the coming of full circle in his relationship with Fred Eastman. Eastman was a seminary classmate of Boisen and an early partner with Boisen in church work following graduation. He was a steadfast and candid friend throughout Boisen's initial hospitalization at Westboro and features prominently in Boisen's personal papers and in Boisen's *Out of the Depths*. In the mid-1950s Eastman described age-related physical illnesses that compounded "under mental or nervous strain. Which leads me to think that the effects of the nervous condition which first floored me in March 1951 are still operative. Now, Anton, I've told you more than I've told anyone else only because you are such a good friend and you may have from your long experience with patients some counsel for me. Please do not reveal any of this to anyone else." As the emotional side of infirmity mystified Eastman, he "found more help in prayer and hard work . . . than in all the doctors."[108] In the late 1950s, Eastman described fluctuating symptoms: "I continued to show improvement up to a few days ago. I gave credit to the Electric Shock Treatments I had been Nov. 20 and Dec. 8. . . . But a few days ago, I felt as though I were slipping back into the old groove of nervousness, sleeplessness and a bit of melancholy. . . . Is this normal for EST?" Eastman also asked Boisen's opinion on the relative value of in-hospital treatment as compared to the use of tranquilizers and rest at home.[109]

Boisen promptly responded, "If you think you have to have medication of some sort, I would prefer the drugs to EST. I don't see what earthly good the shock treatment is going to do for you beyond what may be derived from your faith in it, and the further fact that it may satisfy your need for punishment." As for Boisen's view on early antipsychotic medications of the 1950s, "They do seem to allay anxiety. I doubt if they do more. I would therefore give my vote for Lilla [Eastman's wife] and the tranquilizers and more occupational therapy. I don't think you need any more punishment. You're one of the finest persons I know and one of the best disciplined and most orderly."[110]

Without the aid of friends and allies, Boisen may have never left custodial care let alone been able to embark on a course that led to clinical training for pastors and theologians as well as establish a profession of health-care institutional chaplaincy distinct from the parish. Boisen's friends were critical in providing the training, vocational, financial, and personal support he needed in order to function adequately, and even brilliantly, in the world. Boisen's need for help and support in no way diminishes his accomplishments. Without his single-minded, bordering on obsessive, vision of traversing the chasm between science and religion and his perseverance amid adversity, the support of his friends and allies would have availed nothing. As Boisen progressed in his euphemistic "retirement," he increasingly stood as a mentor and a source of hope to those who had traversed "little-known countries" of their own.

NOTES

1. Henri Nouwen, "Anton T. Boisen and the Study of Theology Through 'Living Human Documents'" (Unpublished Manuscript, no date), 146–47, Box 1, File 4, Henri Nouwen Papers, Special Collections, John M. Kelly Library, University of St. Michael's College, Toronto, ON.

2. Boisen, *The Exploration of the Inner World.*

3. Boisen, *Exploration of the Inner World*, 295.

4. Boisen, floridly, dedicated the book "To the memory of A.L.B. For her sake I undertook the adventure out of which this book has grown. Her compassion upon a wretch in direst need, her wisdom and courage and unswerving fidelity have made possible the measure of success which may have been achieved. To her I dedicate it in the name of the Love which would surmount every barrier, and bridge every chasm and make sure the foundations of the universe." Boisen notes in his autobiography that he wrote this dedication 1935 after receiving news of Batchelder's terminal illness and "wholly absorbed in the task of writing this dedication" triggered his last hospitalization. Boisen, *Out of the Depths*, 176.

5. Edmund S. Conklin, "Book Review: The Exploration of the Inner World," *The Journal of Religion* 17, no. 3 (1937): 296–98.

6. Charles H. Patterson, "Book Review: The Exploration of the Inner World," *Journal of Bible and Religion* 5, no. 3 (1937): 146–147.

7. Boisen, *Out of the Depths*, 9.

8. Thomas W. Klink, "Book Review: Out of the Depths," *Christian Advocate* (January 5, 1961).

9. Richard L. Jenkins, "Book Review: Out of the Depths," *American Journal of Orthopsychiatry* 31 (1961): 649–50.

10. Clyde J. Steckel, "Book Review: Out of the Depths," *Journal of Bible and Religion* 9 (1961): 263–64.

11. Among Pruyser's interests in common with Boisen was chaplain and pastor as diagnostician of personal and spiritual problems. Paul W. Pruyser, *The Minister as Diagnostician: Personal Problems in Pastoral Perspective* (Philadelphia, PA: Westminster Press, 1976).

12. Paul W. Pruyser, "Some Trends in the Psychology of Religion," *The Journal of Religion* 40, no. 2 (1960): 113.

13. Pruyser, "Some Trends in the Psychology of Religion," 121.

14. Pruyser, "Anton T. Boisen and the Psychology of Religion," 209–10.

15. Pruyser, "Anton T. Boisen and the Psychology of Religion," 212.

16. Pruyser, "Anton T. Boisen and the Psychology of Religion," 215.

17. Pruyser, "Anton T. Boisen and the Psychology of Religion," 216.

18. Pruyser, "Anton T. Boisen and the Psychology of Religion," 218.

19. Pruyser, "Anton T. Boisen and the Psychology of Religion," 211.

20. Pruyser, "Anton T. Boisen and the Psychology of Religion," 213.

21. Pruyser, "Anton T. Boisen and the Psychology of Religion," 219.

22. Paul W. Pruyser quoted in Nouwen, "Anton T. Boisen and Theology Through Living Human Documents," 49–50; Pruyser to Nouwen, August 15, 1967, Box 290, File 333, Henri Nouwen Papers, Special Collections, John M. Kelly Library, University of St. Michael's College, Toronto, ON.

23. Paul Pruyser Interview, June 14, 1967, Box 290, File 333, Henri Nouwen Papers, John M. Kelly Library, University of St. Michael's College, Toronto, ON.

24. Paul Pruyser Interview, June 14, 1967, Box 290, File 333, Henri Nouwen Papers, John M. Kelly Library, University of St. Michael's College, Toronto, ON.

25. In 1952 Francis McPeek, one of Boisen's early students, made over two hours of audio-recorded interviews with Boisen in anticipation of his autobiography that would eventually become *Out of the Depths*. McPeek's audio recordings give a flavor of Boisen's personality and character in his early seventies. At times, Boisen engaged in animated conversation. McPeek asked Boisen about his 1920 hospitalization in which an attendant "gave you a working over," Boisen responded calling it an "ancient form of shock treatment . . . not quite the prestige shock treatment has today" as Boisen audibly chuckled in the background. During significant portions McPeek patiently mines for responses amid many one-word answers, such as "right," and "yes." McPeek, at times, solicited Boisen on his well-being and focus. McPeek's interviews help elucidate Pruyser's contradictory assessment of Boisen as having "humor," and "no sense of humor . . . he didn't understand it" and gives a portrait of how the same person can demonstrate starkly different facets of character, even during the same extended conversation. McPeek also demonstrates patience and solicitude to draw out and develop his, at times odd, teachers' insights. Anton T. Boisen, Interview by Francis McPeek, 1952, Audio Recording, ACPE Papers, Special Collections, Emory University, Decatur, GA.

26. Powell, *Healing and Wholeness*, 74. Powell, in his dissertation on Helen Dunbar, writes, "Another 'bioanalytically' oriented and somewhat forgotten—or denied, or repressed—figure in the history of the psychosomatic medicine is Wilhelm Reich, director of Freud's training seminar from 1924 to 1930 . . . . Somewhat analogous to Freud's notion of character as a 'precipitate,' Reich conceived of character as

a kind of 'armoring,' a ridged outer shell protecting the individual from reality but at the same time limiting his capacity to experience life."

27. Boisen, *Out of the Depths*, 171–73.

28. Interview with John Thomas, Carroll Wise, and Al Sherve, no date, Audio Recording, ACPE Papers, Special Collections, Emory University, Decatur, GA. The panelists, especially Wise, pointed out Boisen's circumstantial isolation following 1932. Wise also mentioned Helen Dunbar's proficiency in courting hospitals to her cause of clinical training with demand for supervisors quickly outstripping supply.

29. Henri Nouwen, "Anton T. Boisen and the Study of Theology Through Living Human Documents" (Unpublished Manuscript, no date), Box 1, File 4, Henri Nouwen Papers, Special Collections, John M. Kelly Library, University of St. Michael's College, Toronto, ON.

30. By 1935, she "wrested the Council for Clinical Training out of the hands of Cabot and Guiles." Powell, *Healing and Wholeness*, 272.

31. Hall, *Head and Heart*, 42–43.

32. Powell, *Healing and Wholeness*, 260.

33. Powell, *Healing and Wholeness*, 272.

34. Thornton, *Professional Education for Ministry*, 83.

35. Thornton, *Professional Education for Ministry*, 83–84; Henri J. M. Nouwen, "Pastoral Supervision in Historical Perspective" (Unpublished Manuscript, no date), 52–53, Box 287, File 306, Henri Nouwen Papers, Special Collections, John M. Kelly Library, University of St. Michael's College, Toronto, ON.

36. Wayne Oates started an independent CPE movement at Southern Baptist Seminary in Louisville, Kentucky, associated with the Southern Baptist Convention.

37. Boisen, *Problems in Religion and Life*.

38. Anton T. Boisen, *Hymns of Hope and Courage*, 4th Revised and Enlarged edition (Chicago, IL: Chicago Theological Seminary, 1950).

39. Boisen, *Religion in Crisis and Custom*.

40. Boisen, *Out of the Depths*.

41. Nouwen, "Anton T. Boisen and the Study of Theology," 134–35.

42. Anton T. Boisen, Interview by Francis McPeek, 1952, Audio Recording, ACPE Papers, Special Collections, Emory University, Decatur, GA.

43. Lennart Cedarleaf, "Anton Boisen—A Memoir," May 13, 1987, Box 4, Folder 13, ACPE Papers, Special Collections, Emory University, Decatur, GA.

44. Nouwen, "Anton T. Boisen and Theology Through Living Human Documents," 59–60.

45. Nouwen, "Anton T. Boisen and the Study of Theology," (Unpublished Manuscript), 143.

46. Myron Sharaf, *Fury on Earth: A Biography of Wilhelm Reich* (New York, NY: St. Martin's Press/Marek, 1983), 257–59.

47. Nouwen, "Anton T. Boisen and the Study of Theology," (Unpublished Manuscript), 119.

48. Powell, *Healing and Wholeness*, 273.

49. Thornton, *Professional Education for Ministry*, 91–92.

50. Sharaf, *Fury on Earth*, 258.

51. Sharaf, *Fury on Earth*, 15; Martin Grotjahn, "Book Review: Recent Psychoanalytic Literature," *Psychosomatic Medicine: Experimental and Clinical Studies* 5, no. 3 (1943): 309–11. Grotjahn continues, "It is intended as a scientific contribution to psychosomatic medicine. Actually, it is a surrealistic creation. . . . It is not the translation of the German book which W. Reich published in 1927 under the same title and which became a landmark in psychoanalysis as a therapeutic and scientific technique, deeply influencing almost the entire generation of younger psychoanalysists. Now W. Reich is beyond reason and has peculiar dreams about 'bions' which are primitive living organisms created in a test tube."

52. Sharaf, *Fury on Earth*, 17.

53. Christopher Turner, *Adventures in the Orgasmatron: How the Sexual Revolution Came to America* (New York, NY: Farrar, Straus and Giroux, 2011), 8–9.

54. Sharaf, *Fury on Earth*, 5.

55. Sharaf, *Fury on Earth*, 81.

56. Nouwen, "Anton T. Boisen and the Study of Theology," (Unpublished Manuscript), 122.

57. Sharaf, *Fury on Earth*, 75.

58. Wilhelm Reich, *Character Analysis*, 3rd edition (New York, NY: Orgone Institute Press, 1949), 39–40.

59. Sharaf, *Fury on Earth*, 76.

60. Wilhelm Reich, *The Function of the Orgasm: Sex-Economic Problems of Biological Energy* (New York, NY: Farrar, Straus and Giroux, 1973), 116.

61. Wilhelm Reich, *The Mass Psychology of Fascism* (New York, NY: Farrar, Straus & Giroux, 1970), 17–18.

62. Reich, *The Mass Psychology of Fascism*, 30–32.

63. Turner, *Adventures in the Orgasmatron*, 5.

64. Turner, *Adventures in the Orgasmatron*, 5.

65. Reich, *Character Analysis*, xi.

66. Turner, *Adventures in the Orgasmatron*, 9; Reich, *The Function of the Orgasm*, 330.

67. Turner, *Adventures in the Orgasmatron*, 12.

68. Turner, *Adventures in the Orgasmatron*, 5–6.

69. Thornton, *Professional Education for Ministry*, 92.

70. Hall, *Head and Heart*, 44.

71. Leon Salzman, "A Critique of Wilhelm Reich's Psychoanalytic Theories," *The Journal of Pastoral Care* 9, no. 3 (1955): 153–61. Salzman offers a balanced overview and critique of Reich's life and work. Salzman offers, "In his voluminous writings—over 120 articles and books—it is frequently impossible to separate the valid from the fantastic, the work of the genius from that of the misguided scientist." Salzman, like Boisen, distinguished between Reich's early work and his later work: "the pre-orgone, and the orgone phase. In the pre-orgone phase, Reich was a brilliant traditional Freudian psychoanalyst. . . . His *Character Analysis*, published in 1933, was a milestone in psychoanalytic theory and practice." Reich took a turn in his later work: "disowned by Freud, [Reich] took the libido theory literally and began to search for the energy which heretofore was considered a theoretical conception." "Reich claims to have isolated it and demonstrated it visually, chemically, and

electroscopically. The flickerings (blue) in the sky are expressions of atmospheric orgone, as are bions, which are microscopic vesicles charged with orgone, . . . which is recharged in the breathing process. . . . It has become increasingly difficult to accept Reich's observations about orgone energy, particularly since his experiments have not been duplicated except in his laboratories and he will not allow outsiders to check his experiments except under his own auspices." While Reich's early work exhibited brilliant insight, he warns against the devotion he sees in some to Reich's post-orgone work: "Perhaps his followers have also confused scientific theory and practice with moral principles. They confuse devotion with truth, isolation and unacceptance with sainthood, profundity with fact, and polemic with scientific evidence. . . . Reich's scientific formulations lead us only to a dead-end psychologically, philosophically, and scientifically."

72. Hall, *Head and Heart*, 44.

73. Henri J. M. Nouwen, "Pastoral Supervision in Historical Perspective" (Unpublished Manuscript, no date), 51, Box 287, File 306, Special Collections, John M. Kelly Library, University of St. Michael's College, Toronto, ON.

74. Arthur P. Noyes to Boisen, October 5, 1960, Series 8, Box 2, Folder 61, Boisen Papers, Chicago Theological Seminary.

75. Interview with John Thomas, Carroll Wise, and Al Sherve, no date, Audio Recording, ACPE Papers, Special Collections, Emory University, Decatur, GA. Thomas and Wise can be heard laughing in the background at Sherve's hapless adventures in the orgone box.

76. Sharaf, *Fury on Earth*, 17.

77. Sharaf, *Fury on Earth*, 13.

78. Nouwen, "Anton T. Boisen and the Study of Theology," (Unpublished Manuscript), 120–21.

79. Boisen, *Out of the Depths*, 186. Note, Boisen does not dismiss Reich entirely, distinguishing Reich's "later teachings" as the focus of his objection. Anton T. Boisen, "Book Review: Wilhelm Reich *Character Analysis, The Sexual Revolution*," *Psychiatry* 8, no. 4 (1945): 505–6. Boisen explicates further on Reich: "These two books make an attack so fundamental upon the established mores that it would require more space than I am allotted to do justice to the authors reasoning. . . . he is aggressively mechanistic and hedonistic in his point of view. The chief end of life is for him the attainment of pleasure and the escape from unpleasure and the aim of all psychotherapy is the establishment of orgiastic potency." While Boisen's asceticism clashed viscerally with Reich's "hedonism," he also objects to unsupported assertion, "annoyingly deficient in reference footnotes. . . . wholly lacking in sociological and anthropological perspective." Even, Reich, however, was not without value, having "some gleams of insight. A real contribution, in my mind, is the discussion of the masochistic character and of the Freudian concept of the "death instinct." . . .There is, he says, no such thing as a wish to experience unpleasure or annihilation. Any such tendency is only apparent. Actually, the masochist is striving for a pleasurable goal hidden behind that frustration and his suffering is objectively given, not subjectively desired. And suicide in a melancholic may be only the last possible means of release from painful tension." Boisen appreciates Reich's sympathy toward suffering and his intent to provide relief.

80. Powell, "Whatever Happened to 'CPE,'" March 18, 1999, accessed July 7, 2019, www.pastoralreport.com/pastoralreportarticles/3778818.

81. Wayne Oates, Interviewed by Allison Stokes. In Stokes, *Ministry After Freud*, 176.

82. Stokes, *Ministry After Freud*, 176; Wayne Oates, *The Significance of the Work of Sigmund Freud for the Christian Faith* (Ph.D. Diss., Southern Baptist Theological Seminary, Louisville, KY, 1947).

83. Nouwen, "Pastoral Supervision in Historical Perspective," 57.

84. Wayne Oates, no date, Audio Recording, ACPE Papers, Special Collections, Emory University, Decatur, GA. Allison Stokes recalls Oates correcting her impression that Southern Baptists are "narrowly conservative," Oates representing, albeit a minority, tradition "of vigorous, nonconformist, dissent: 'a zestful lot of people who are creative and curious and imaginative: kicking the slats out of this, kicking the slats out of that, and polemically related to establishmentarianism. This is not what gets in the popular press.'" Stokes, *Ministry after Freud*, 177.

85. Oates, Audio Recording, ACPE Papers.

86. Oates, Audio Recording, ACPE Papers.

87. Glenn H. Asquith, Jr., "Anton T. Boisen: A Vision for All Age" (*Lecture*, College of Pastoral Supervision and Psychotherapy Plenary Session, March 15, 2015).

88. Boisen, *Out of the Depths*, 149–50. Boisen's early deliberations, in conjunction with a job offer from Worcester Hospital, occurred in dialogue Arthur Holt—lifelong friend and colleague from Chicago Theological Seminary: "We had become convinced that the strategic point of attack lay in the theological schools. We were convinced that these schools themselves needed overhauling." Theological education needed to "make use of scientific method[s] in the study of present-day religious experience," including psychology, sociology, and field observation.

89. Nouwen, "Pastoral Supervision in Historical Perspective," 53.

90. Nouwen, "Anton T. Boisen and the Study of Theology," (Unpublished Manuscript), 122.

91. Thornton, *Professional Education for Ministry*, 90.

92. Oates, Audio Recording, ACPE Papers. According to Oates, cultural differences regarding alcohol factored into their disagreement—but for different reasons. Upon rejection from Kuether—and hence the CCT, "I then recall that I had lambasted a supervisor at Elgin for being drunk the morning he was supposed to preach. Fred hung the whole issue on alcohol. He refused to approve my program." Andrews and Kuether were the only two persons to whom Oates' allegation of workplace intoxication could have applied.

93. Thornton, *Professional Education for Ministry*, 154. Oates acknowledged his need for ongoing mentorship and training, implicitly acknowledging his fiery temperament exemplified in his interactions with Kuether. He admitted, "I realized that I needed supervision." Oates proposed with Kuether that a Louisville CCT supervisor, Ralph Bonacker, was able and willing to provide supervision. Due to his relationship with CCT, and Oates' now renegade status, Bonacker was forbidden to provide the, at least formal, supervision and mentorship Oates sought in spite of Bonacker and Oates' apparent mutual esteem and positive working relationship. Oates, Audio Recording, ACPE Papers.

94. Thornton, *Professional Education for Ministry*, 155.
95. Oates, Audio Recording, ACPE Papers.
96. Oates, Audio Recording, ACPE Papers.
97. E. Brooks Holifield, *A History of Pastoral Care in America: From Salvation to Self-Realization* (Nashville, TN: Abingdon Press, 1983), 316.
98. DeBono, *An Exploration and Adaptation*, 69; Menninger Clinic, "The Menninger Website," http://www.menningerclinic.com/about/Menninger-history.htm.
99. Karl Menninger to Roberta Smith Cagle, December 19, 1963, Anton T. Boisen Papers, Kansas Historical Society, Topeka, KS. Cagle wrote to Menninger, offering to donate memorabilia to Menninger's foundation relating to one of Boisen's early, and brief, pastorates at Beecher, Bible and Rifle Church in Wabaunsee, Kansas. Cagle noted, "There [at Wabaunsee] he tried experiments in community work that made him many enemies, but my mother and father remained his staunch friends and defenders, . . . he always wrote to them at Christmas, sent them reprints of his articles, and his autographed book." Of particular interest was "a notebook that Doctor Boisen wrote about his community projects at Wabaunsee, illustrated with snap-shots he took. I was eight years old at the time and I remember that he always had his camera with him." Cagle to Menninger, December 16, 1963, Boisen Papers, Kansas Historical Society, Topeka, KS.
100. J. C. Pipes to Boisen, April 28, 1937, Box 1, Folder 16, Boisen Papers, Chicago Theological Seminary.
101. Florence Lerrigo to Boisen, May 20, 1959, Box 1, Folder 14, Boisen Papers, Chicago Theological Seminary.
102. Boisen to Florence Lerrigo, May 25, 1959, Box 1, Folder 14, Boisen Papers, Chicago Theological Seminary.
103. W. E. Jenkins to Boisen, February 5, 1939, Box 1, Folder 12, Boisen Papers, Chicago Theological Seminary.
104. Thomas McDill to Boisen, April 18, 1953, Series 2, Box 1, Folder 15, Boisen Papers, Chicago Theological Seminary.
105. Thomas McDill to Boisen, April 18, 1953, Series 2, Box 1, Folder 15, Boisen Papers, Chicago Theological Seminary.
106. Lulu Wendel, "A Visit" (Unpublished Manuscript, September 1965), Box 1, Folder 19, Boisen Papers, Chicago Theological Seminary.
107. Boisen to Victor Obenhaus, June 25, 1963, Box 1, Folder 1, Boisen Papers, Chicago Theological Seminary.
108. Fred Eastman to Boisen, April 21, 1954, Series 2, Box 3, Folder 29, Boisen Papers, Chicago Theological Seminary.
109. Fred Eastman to Boisen, March 24, 1957, Series 2, Box 3, Folder 29, Boisen Papers, Chicago Theological Seminary.
110. Boisen to Fred Eastman, March 26, 1957, Series 2, Box 3, Folder 29, Boisen Papers, Chicago Theological Seminary. Eastman mentioned "Serpasil" (Reserpine)—used in treatment for high blood pressure and as an antipsychotic, and "Thorazine" (Chlorpromazine) the first of the antipsychotic medications.

Chapter 6

The Scientific Seer

Boisen envisioned himself working in a "no man's land" between science and religion. The profession and clinical education he envisioned would populate that land and bridge the tribes: "theological schools. . . . had been failing to make use of the scientific method in the study of present-day religious experience. We were also impressed by the failure of the psychologists and sociologists and psychiatrists to carry their inquiries to the level of the religious. Here then was a great no man's land which needed to be explored."[1] Boisen's signature vilusion envisioned dialogue between medicine and religion. He was an enthusiastic advocate of the tools of science to better understand religious experience as well as psychosis. Glenn Asquith points out that Boisen fell in the tradition of William Adams Brown, his professor of systematic theology at Union Seminary. Brown, an "evangelical liberal" closely akin to William James in his pragmatism, taught that "science is not to be considered the enemy of theology" and for theology, and theologians, to truly thrive in the modern era, they must find ways to use the tools of science to better understand the workings of the theological in a scientific era.[2]

Was Boisen a scientist? Did he practice "science"? Paul Pruyser asked rhetorically, "Where his observations objective? Are they repeatable? Did he have hypotheses, or were his leading thoughts only pet peeves or exalted hunches? Did he use respectable methods of sampling, data gathering and statistical analysis? Was he not, after all, a somewhat odd or sick clergyman? Would it not be safer to describe him as a crusader, an enthusiastic organizer or a dedicated and intelligent missionary? Or, for dignity's sake, as a religionist?"[3]

Pruyser, making conscious play on Boisen's forestry background, noted "a penchant for a simultaneous vision of the trees as well as the forest. As a clinical worker and while focusing on the individual, he placed great emphasis on social roles and social learning." Boisen's deep and broad case studies "turned [William] James' brilliant vignettes into full-fledged case studies with a longitudinal perspective."[4] Pruyser criticized Boisen's use of sources, "monotonously for one or two phrases which he repeated over and over, while others were cited polemically, with protests." Adding he did not have a firm understanding of psychoanalytics, he said, "He used from Freud mainly the general tenor of the libido theory, and the notion of intrapsychic conflict, and had only a vague appreciation for the dynamic unconscious, . . . despite his references to both Freud and Alexander."[5] Privately with Henri Nouwen, Pruyser dismissed him as "not a scholar." Pruyser's, at times contradictory, public and private comments show his uncertainty, and some frustration, on how to classify Boisen the professional, the person, and whether he qualified as a scientist. Finally, "History will answer these questions and give its verdict."[6]

Pruyser moderated less patient and less generous views on Boisen's work, such as those elicited in Clyde Steckel's dismissive review of Boisen's autobiography.

> He is disappointed that students have not tested his hypothesis clinically, but the truth is that thorough the years Boisen has himself done little more than repeat and illustrate it. He has not formulated specific questions as a basis for investigation, nor has he proposed detailed methods of research. . . . He stands within the tradition of the "religious experience school" of several decades ago, variously exemplified by Edwin Starbuck, William James, . . . The mood today is one of grave skepticism regarding the possibility of discovering general categories of religious experience, since it is no longer assumed that the requisite stance of detached objectivity is possible.[7]

Thomas Klink, one of Boisen's former students, warmly digressed with gratitude toward his former teacher, whose case study he was reviewing: "As a war-time seminary student, to be lent, for purposes of courting, his 'A-ration' bearing Ford." While lauding his teacher's pioneering role and aid in a personal time of need, he suggests that Boisen reflected "human understanding of another time" and "It would be easy to dismiss this book as the ruminations of a now aged Victorian."[8]

Klink provided a key, but probably unintentional, insight on Boisen as scientist as well as seer by referencing Boisen's "Victorian" upbringing.[9] Boisen's active intellectual life spanned over seventy years from college in the 1890s through his final published works in the early 1960s. Boisen lived to witness a sea change in how science and medicine were conceptualized and practiced. As the more holistic, contextual, and, also, idiosyncratic—less focused and far less technically advanced—science of Boisen's youth gave way to specialization and standardization, Boisen's approach and methods reflected an earlier era. Boisen's grand hypotheses, his in-depth inquiry into specific cases, his comfort with cross-disciplinary work, and his holistic vision and practice based in a more communitarian form of life (witness Bloomington, Indiana, of Boisen's childhood and the State Hospitals where he was, as Pruyser rightly observed, a "participant observer") were thoroughly formed by Victorian science and religion.[10] His approach became glaring unfashionable as mobility and individualism increased and as the scientific and academic disciplines became increasingly specialized, more intently focused on discrete questions, and suspicious of disciplinary border transgressors.

VICTORIAN SCIENCE

Victorian experiences and assumptions formed Boisen both as a minister and as a scientist. Nineteenth-century positivism framed Boisen's scientific vision via faith in a mechanistic universe governed by law—laws presumably applicable to the mind and soul, as well, and discoverable by patient and thorough observation and survey. Bold conclusory statements often drove this science, conclusions that could be confirmed, amended, altered, or perhaps even discarded as fact accumulated.

Pierre Laplace (1749–1827) apocryphally asserted "that he had no use for God in his system of the world. 'I have no need for that hypothesis.'" Laplace likely had no particular beef with God so much as he based his cosmology on other evidence. Roger Hahn, rather, explains that Laplace's "system" was informed "by direct participation in the progress of Newtonian science... He based his understanding on palpable evidence and calculation rather than metaphysical systems of thought of either a Christian or a pagan variety."[11]

Newton's, and Laplace's, mechanistic approach inevitably influenced investigation of the human mind as well. Sigmund Freud, an early inspiration and source of hope for Boisen during his 1920 hospitalization, "continued to think of himself as a man of science, ... in keeping with the goals of nineteenth-century positivism, he remained committed to providing a naturalistic account of mental processes.... as subject to lawlike behavior as was the physical universe."[12] Jonathan Simon hints that the practice of Victorian science seemed to indicate that Boisen would not have been the first to start his research with a conclusion: "an enduring characteristic of [Louis] Pasteur's scientific approach was his tendency to jump to bold general conclusions based on relatively little evidence and then to work in a thorough and persistent manner to demonstrate the correctness of his intuitions. Often his initial ideas failed to pan out, but he found no difficulty in refining them or simply changing his position in light of the accumulating evidence."[13]

Victorian scientists, like Pasteur, armed with the emerging methods of Newtonian science, delivered stunning results and new possibilities to the stagnant practice of medicine in discovery of the germ theory and in vaccination to treat or prevent infection. Likewise, Freud and Boisen witnessed new hope and possibility in the application of scientific observation and survey aimed at discovering the mysterious laws they imagined must govern mind and soul, as well as body.

THE EDUCATION OF A VICTORIAN SCIENTIST IN CHANGING TIMES.

Positivist scientists, like Newton, Laplace, Pasteur, and certainly Freud, defined science in the Victorian era and established the assumptions and parameters underlying Boisen's scientific chaplaincy. As scientists like Pasteur broadened therapeutic hopes, scientists responded to growing hopes and expectations regarding sciences' promise to resolve practical human problems in a wide range of fields. Boisen's personal background and training in science and scientific methods relate to two prominent, and pragmatic, scientists of the Victorian Era who came of age amid American Progressive reform: Raphael Zon and Richard Cabot.[14]

Ask Zon
Ask Zon, Zon, Zon, Zon, Zon
Ask Zon!
Ask him by the telephone,
Ask with laughter or with a moan,
But for heaven's sake
Ask Zon!
What a pattern of lucidity that sesame drives home!
Ask Zon!
Do you want to know the scientific title of a tree?
Or is it parlor forestry as done in District Three?
Or is it Bolsheviki, or the crops at Saloniki,
Or the natives of Tahiti who are honing to be free?
Ask Zon!
(Refrain)
Ask Zon, Ask Zon,
Ask him by the telephone,
Yell or whisper, type or scribble,

But for heaven's sake,
Ask Zon!
(Refrain)
Ask Zon, Ask Zon
Don't neglect to put in writing
What you get him to reciting,
It may save pain or fighting;
But for heaven's sake,
Ask Zon!
If he doesn't know the answer, no one does; you're safe,
My boy;
But to save yourself a sorrow and your enemies a joy,
Ask Zon![15]

This ditty's unidentified author witnesses to the breadth and depth (with perhaps a tinge of envy and annoyance) at the Russia native's knowledge not only of forestry but of global events and affairs generally. Raphael Zon, a Victorian "renaissance" figure of broad and deep knowledge, interests, and learning, was born in Simbirsk (present-day Ulyanovsk), Russia, in 1874—making him two years older than Boisen. Lenin[16] happened to be one of Zon's older school classmates, and a one-time personal acquaintance, whom Zon recalled as "rather bashful." Young Zon's own political radicalism in Tsarist Russia earned him an eleven-year jail sentence. Having escaped prison in 1894, he wound his way through Europe and arrived in the United States in 1897.[17]

Zon was a foundational figure in the establishment of the U.S. Forest Service and his influence on American forestry cannot be overstated. Gifford Pinchot, a leading figure in American Progressive Era reform, was a leading adviser to Theodore Roosevelt, and chief of the U.S. Bureau of Forestry, referred to Zon, a younger colleague, as his "advisor and . . . guide" and called Zon's office "the first cradle and treasure house of forest research in America."[18]

Zon's ardent advocacy of forestry research led to the establishment of the first forest experiment station in 1908. Stations, such as those Zon advocated for and established, did surveys on forests and their composition, did research and experimentation on forest management and stewardship, and experimented in production and use of forest commercial products.[19] While, in Norman Schmaltz's words, Zon was "an ardent supporter of forest research, Zon never advocated 'science for science's sake,' considering such a slogan an alibi for incompetence. Research must be geared to practical problems."[20]

Zon, in turn, learned his craft from his studies at New York State College of Forestry at Cornell University. The Forestry School's "learn-by-doing methodology" assigned its students "a project of surveying a forty-acre wooded lot, making a map of the plot, estimating the timber on it, calipering the trees, and calculating the real value of the stand."[21] Zon's philosophy of practical, "learn-by-doing," empirical research he would pass on to his students and subordinates, including Boisen. Zon, however, was more than a teacher in research methods. Zon provided mentorship and sympathetic friendship from their first meeting in 1906 until Zon's death in 1956.

Boisen gave a sense of his initial, animated, meeting with Zon:

> He is a Russian Exile and has a lot to tell when you can succeed in drawing him out. He has been in this country 6 years now and received his degree in forestry from Cornell. . . . He is a modest quiet fellow and dresses rather shabbily, but he is a very keen thinker and a very efficient man. He thinks conditions are indeed black in Russia. The universities have all been closed by the government and the reports which are sent from there are not exaggerated. He is a great admirer of the Japs [sic] and is exceedingly sorry that they did not succeed in imposing an indemnity upon Russia because then the defeat of the government would have been brought home to the people.[22]

Zon's practice of a practical, observation-based science linked to providing practical results lay close to the center of Boisen's scientific chaplaincy. Personal friendship further enlivened Zon's provision of research and analytical methods. Zon was Boisen's first teacher and preceptor in the practice of the scientific method and served as his supervisor in the Office of Silvics within the Forest Service. Zon assigned his assistant the task of producing a survey on "commercial hickories."[23] Boisen's survey classified "hickories" into broad categories of different types of hickory: the trees' range and distribution, reproduction, longevity, susceptibility to disease and injury, the properties, and potential economic utility of the lumbers produced from the various trees. Boisen's survey is larded with photographs, drawings, maps, graphs, and statistics illustrating his observations.[24] Boisen, under Zon's direction, intended to provide a reasonably thorough survey of the various forms of hickory trees, their properties, and general, but practical, advice regarding the commercial and economic utility of the trees, and lumber, being surveyed. More specific, detailed, topics for scientific study, such as treatment and cure of tree disease, for example, lay outside the scope of his survey, better addressed by research, and researchers, to come.[25]

Boisen's practice of science, following Zon's lead, centered on survey. Apparently, the two colleagues and friends speculated on the possible utility of the survey for more than just trees. Shortly after starting work at Worcester State Hospital, Boisen wrote his former boss: "many times I have heard you say that you would like to work out a book on sociology on the basis of plant societies. And now this very thing is being attempted and it seems to be a really fruitful approach." While Boisen wrote, ostensibly, on the utility of forestry methods for studying people, he added "while this letter is addressed to Raphael Zon it is also intended for Frau Anna who seems to be much better in keeping up personal correspondence than her husband. Her letter was received last summer and very much appreciated."[26]

Boisen's correspondence, visits, and personal contacts with Zon included candid conversation on the relationship between science and religion. Zon remained deeply skeptical that the two could be reconciled fruitfully:

> I am, I am afraid, too much steeped in the scientific approach to give much weight to faith as a prophylactic and therapeutic measure. I do not deny the value of faith any more than I could deny the effect of a sedative to quieten the patient and make him reconciled to the world he lives in. A hypodermic, however, gives only temporary relief. It numbs the nerves where a keen analysis is needed to uncover the cause and devise a remedy. Religion and science seem to me incompatible. They operate with two entirely different methods. One is based on faith, the other on knowledge of facts that can be visualized in one form or another tested and experimented with.

Ever the advocate of science over and against religion, Zon could also cast a critical eye toward science as well, admitting the need for caution and a healthy skepticism: "Science, operating even with an exact method, is still full of fantasies and unproved theories."[27]

Zon's critique elicited a vigorous response:

> Now about those objections, I am wondering just where you got the impression that I said anything about faith healing except to dismiss it. All the way thru what I have been trying to do is to examine the beliefs and attitudes of men objectively and as to psychotherapy, that begins with the beliefs or faith of the other fellow and the things that are on <u>his</u> mind. I grant that ideas and attitudes are elusive. Nevertheless, I am ready to go to the mat with you anytime on the proposition that they are tremendously important and unless we take them into account, we shall never understand mankind, either individually or collectively. It's precisely at this point that so many medically trained men fall down when it comes to dealing with mental patients. Their training has blinded them to the terrific reality of ideas and emotions to the patients with whom they are dealing. Now I have learned to expect that from some of these dumb medical men, but hardly of Raphael Zon.

Boisen needled further:

> Doesn't the physicist have to learn to measure gases as well as solids? Doesn't he have to learn to deal with light and heat as well as with iron and granite.

Maybe my metaphors are somewhat mixed, but any way you see what I mean, the great driving forces of love and hate and fear and anger must be taken into account, and it may be that you can't reduce them to physiology. Isn't that perhaps the fallacy which has driven so much of present-day academic psychology into a blind alley?[28]

Boisen's relationship with Zon (and his family) spanned several decades and—similar to his relationship with Fred Eastman—was characterized by candid, even blunt, conversation, belying not only professional interaction but the give-and-take of real friendship. Boisen regularly updated Zon on his work and life in Elgin—including sharing photos of himself with his students.[29] Included with a desk copy of *Exploration of the Inner World*, Boisen wrote: "I am however guided by the consideration that among those whom I have known you stand out by reason of the breadth of your interests and the sureness of your understanding. I am also guided by the fact that if there is in this volume anything of value, your patience and kindness toward the author at the time he was pretty sick had a good deal to do with it."[30]

Boisen's interactions with Zon, as scientist and friend, left him with his core takeaway of what an enlightened scientific chaplaincy should try to uncover via survey—"that any person and any nation should be judged by what it is in process of *becoming*, rather than by what it *now* is."[31]

Boisen needed to adapt the science of surveying trees and forests to surveying people and peoples. Prominent Boston physician Richard Clarke Cabot was already pioneering similar work and was critical in Boisen's transformation. By 1922, the time of Boisen and Cabot's first meeting, Cabot's interests were migrating away from the clinical practice of medicine toward ethics and medical humanities. Cabot's youthful musings pondered a possible midlife career shift, "practice[ing] medicine till 45 or till I can live on my income, then I will cultivate other fields." Cabot biographer Christopher Crenner suggests an additional motive. Cabot was passed over for an anticipated promotion at Harvard Medical School. While the stoic "Cabot's public good sportsmanship on this occasion drew general praise; but his later private notes suggest a very real disappointment." His patient load decreased from the triple digits to forty and he withdrew from the medical school to establish a new base in "social ethics" within the main Harvard campus.[32]

Cabot's reinvention as medical outsider focused on the development of the physician-patient therapeutic relationship, which he thought was being lost amid a narrowing focus on technical proficiency. Central to Cabot's methods and teaching were diagnostics and the case study. While the therapeutic relationship was critical to the direction in which Cabot wanted to move, he pled for clinical training along objective lines of what a minister or "the doctor actually does (not what he is supposed to do) when he visits a patient." Cabot incredulously wrote: "the theological schools provide no training and no practice. It has been assumed apparently that skill and ability to help people in trouble could not be learned by practice while in seminary—that men either had it by nature and instinct or lacked it—but that in any case it *could not be taught.*" His proposed clinical year would do what Cabot's teaching intended to do for "medical practitioners, most of whom can testify that during their medical course they learned this unlearnable art not, of course, as they would like to, not in that perfection which they could wish for, but vastly better than their own stumbling hesitating attempts when first they began."[33]

Cabot's plan for clinical teaching was based in observation and work with specific cases. As Boisen placed heavy emphasis on diagnosing spiritual maladies, he based this in Cabot's attempt to balance the therapeutic relationship with technical, scientific, and especially diagnostic skill.[34] Cabot's Clinicopathological Conferences, dedicated to the science and art of diagnosis, had a flair for drama,

> the featured physician, often Cabot himself in the beginning, listening to a summary of diagnostic information collected from a single hospitalized patient, a boy with severe backache in the first published case in 1924. Following a description of the patient's history of symptoms were observations from the physical examination and the results of laboratory and radiological testing. . . . The outcome of an autopsy or a surgery that had identified the active disease was kept hidden. . . . The featured physician then completed the first part of the exercise by venturing a definitive diagnosis. In the dramatic conclusion, the examining pathologist stepped forward and announced the actual microscopic and physical findings on autopsy, identifying the hidden disease.[35]

While Cabot's Clinicopathological Conferences sought to teach medical students the art of sifting through "distracting secondary" symptoms to drive toward the underlying pathology, his conferences, perhaps unintentionally, impressed humility upon its observers and participants. An observing social worker noted, "to see the doctors accept the fact that they were wrong was a deeply humbling experience for the audience," and Crenner, himself a medical doctor, added, "and for the doctors too, no doubt."[36] Many years later, Seward Hiltner witnessed Cabot's conferences in which "three defending physicians in succession went down in defeat." Henri Nouwen noted that not everyone appreciated Cabot's approach: "Especially European doctors who visited the conferences were flabbergasted. In Europe, they felt, this would be impossible. The doctor would lose all his respect if he were confronted in front of all his students with his own weaknesses and mistakes."[37]

Boisen, along with many social workers, attended Cabot's courses with rapt attention, recalling his offering "on the preparation of case records for teaching purposes . . . as one of the best courses I have ever had."[38] Boisen's encounter with Cabot helps explain Paul Pruyser's admiration for an aspect of Boisen's "uniqueness" in that his case studies examined "longitudinally and was fully aware of the ups and downs, the contradictions and inconsistencies, the morbid fantasies or the healthy reality testing which one patient would manifest over a stretch of time." Thus, Boisen's case studies "show he was not easily fooled by one-shot impressions."[39]

Cabot's case studies were not dissimilar to the methods Boisen learned from Zon and forestry school. As Boisen's *Commercial Hickories* studied and catalogued varieties of hickories, their uses, their limitations, and diseases, so also Cabot's *Differential Diagnosis* catalogued all sorts of aches, pains, and complaints patients would one day present to his aspiring physicians and surgeons. Cabot's *Differential Diagnosis* was familiar to, and deeply influential upon, Boisen's own practice of scientific chaplaincy, and case study method.

Getting to the heart of a physical malady, for Cabot, required a more thorough examination than depending solely on the most prominent symptom. Cabot explained, "Cases of disease present, as we say, certain leading symptoms as pain, cough, or 'nervousness,' so that it occupies the foreground of the clinical picture. Such a *"presenting symptom,"* (italics original) . . . may turn out to be of minor importance when we have studied the whole case." While warning that a first look may be deceiving, Cabot proceeded to lay out his plan for differential diagnosis:

(a) To present a list of the common causes of the symptoms most often complained of by patients, e.g. the causes of pain in the back, of vomiting, or of hematuria.
(b) To classify these causes in the order of their frequency, so far as this is possible.
(c) To illustrate them by case-histories in which the presenting symptom is followed home until a diagnostic problem and its solution are presented.[40]

Cabot's discussion of "Epigastric Pain" illustrates how he indexed symptoms, illustrated them through his cases, and showed that the most obvious symptom or solution to an illness may mislead as much as illumine. Cabot's cases also demonstrated that apparent strictly somatic illnesses may be psychological or even spiritual in their root cause. The cases also show limitations in Cabot's objectivity. In a style that would be typical of Boisen later on, Cabot indexed and categorized "causes" of "epigastric pain." Some prime suspects included, "constipation," "appendicitis," "lead-poisoning," "intestinal obstruction," and even non-physical causes such as "neuroses."[41]

In "Case 76," "A salesman of forty-nine came to the hospital on December 10, 1907, complaining of pain, constipation, and vomiting. He is in the habit of taking several drinks of whisky a day, but has never been sick until the present illness, and his family history is good." Cabot, at times, jumbled objective fact of reciting patient symptoms with subjective judgments. What constitutes a "good" family history? Cabot's "first impression [is] naturally that 'rum done it.'"[42] Upon more probing inquiry, it was found that the patient "for three years used drinking-water coming through 30 feet of lead pipe," ultimately revealing lead poisoning to be the culprit: "a well-marked lead line was found on the gums, visible *only on the inner side of the teeth of the lower jaw*." (italics original)[43]

Even Cabot's seemly somatic category of "epigastric pain" could reveal, apparently, non-somatic causes—or causes Cabot could not readily identify. In Case 92, "A teamster of forty-eight . . . began to have steady epigastric pain, usually dull, sometimes sharp." Physical examination revealed nothing out of the ordinary. However, "the patient was depressed, seemed very apathetic, and at times refused nourishment." Cabot puzzled: "We cannot afford to leave out of consideration the psychic symptoms in this case. A middle-aged laboring-man does not begin to be sleepless and nervous without obvious cause. The ordinary cause for such symptoms is alcoholism, which could be definitely excluded here. In view of the patient's [physical] depression, his persistent headaches, his nervousness, insomnia, and apathy, a mild type of insanity (depressive maniac psychosis) seems probable, especially since no cause for his depression can be found in any of the recent events of his life." Cabot yielded the diagnosis as "Melancholia" as "the patient became more and more depressed. Two special consultants pronounced the case simple melancholia, and he was removed to an asylum."[44]

Cabot and Boisen's practice of science showed marked similarities. Both attempt to identify and categorize general types of illness: physical, mental, and spiritual. Both also plumb nuanced causes of the malady and how the most prominent symptoms may mislead and distract from the underlying cause. Cabot and Boisen both focus on diagnosis and in categorizing individual and social illnesses—Boisen, like Cabot, offered less guidance on how to treat and resolve illness once it had been identified.

BOISEN'S SCIENTIFIC CHAPLAINCY

Boisen, during the mature phase of his practice of chaplaincy, was explicit by what he meant by "science." His course materials at Elgin State Hospital posit: "What we mean by 'science.'" Boisen's science of chaplaincy was based in the following "Scientific Principles":

1. <u>Empiricism</u>—the raw material of experience in all its complexity is taken as the starting point. Scientific reasoning proceeds from the concrete to

the abstract, from the immediate to the remote, form the particular to the general. The scientist may be guided by generalizations and "hunches," but actual experience gives him his primary sources and his final authority.
2. Objectivity—the personal equation is so far as possible eliminated in that facts and conditions are so described that others may repeat the experiment or observe for themselves and draw their own conclusions. Reliance is placed upon such tests rather than upon persuasion or argument.
3. Continuity—new phenomena are explained in terms of previous observation and generalization, the unknown in terms of the known. No explanations are accepted except in terms of tested and ordered experience.
4. Particularity—the field of inquiry must be limited and the problem clearly defined. It is necessary for the time being to devote oneself to some small portion of the universe and to neglect the rest.
5. Universality—the particular can be understood only in the light of the general and the aim of all scientific work is to discover relationships that are universally valid.
6. Provisionality—the true scientist is careful to recognize that all his findings are tentative and subject to revision.
7. Economy—"Neither more nor more onerous causes must be assumed than are necessary to account for the phenomena." Corollaries:
    a) Between two theories, each of which accounts for a given set of facts, that one is to be accepted which brings them into unity with the wider field of experience.
    b) As between two explanations, a multiple simple hypothesis is more apt to be true than a single recondite explanation.
    c) The scale of accuracy in any bit of investigation must be exactly suited to the end in view, to the yardstick used and to the material under investigation. It may be as much an error to use to fine a scale as one that is too coarse.
8. Disinterestedness—the desire to find the truth must be supreme. Rigid honesty and accuracy and the ability to recognize and discount personal bias must characterize the good scientific worker.

Boisen's "principles" fueled his notion of how to test "suggested explanations (hypotheses)":
1. Controlled experimentation designed to measure the influence of a given variable by excluding all external stimuli so as to determine the exact functional relationship.
2. Naturalistic observation—exact description together with explanation in terms of relationships.
3. Statistical studies designed for the evaluation of variables where controlled experimentation is not possible.

Finally, Boisen pointed to the "science" he expected his students to perform in their work at Elgin:

> "According to standard practice in clinical training three types of records have been developed: 1) ward observation, 2) records of interview, and 3) case studies."[45]

Boisen's collection of data started with "ward observation." During this phase, Boisen or his students were to collect a broad and deep survey of patient affect, attitudes, work and employment, marriage and family life, leisure activities, interactions with others, childhood, schooling, maturity, sexuality, opinions and attitudes especially toward religion, and, in language showing Helen Dunbar's indelible influence, "Sense of the Mysterious and Uncanny," to provide a broad and deep portrait of the person.[46]

Even as Boisen's detailed and lengthy case studies gave way to variants of Russell Dicks' brief verbatims in the clinical pastoral education world, Boisen showed himself capable of incorporating other viewpoints and experiences. In Boisen's "Beginning Course," he cited Dicks' (as well as Carl Rogers') material and incorporated the verbatim—a student retelling of a critical, brief, contact with a patient word for word as best the student could remember to illustrate the patient and his presenting problem and how the student chaplain attempted to address it.[47]

Boisen's scientific chaplaincy collated a broad and deep survey on the patient as well as the record of interactions and encounters, providing the basis for Boisen's case studies. As Zon's "silvics" divided trees into myriad categories with uses, characteristics, and illness and as Cabot's *Differential Diagnosis* examined classes of patient complaints and their sources (and potential distractors), so also Boisen focused on intensive observation and diagnosis. Boisen's cases started with an intensive examination of a specific patient: "The diagnostic impression is a consideration of the patient's problem in the light of his previous history and of our knowledge of other causes of mental disorder. It is directed specifically toward the problems of classification, prognosis and treatment." Boisen intended his specific, and exhaustive, studies of specific people as a basis to do for mental health and spirituality what Cabot's *Differential Diagnosis* had done in medicine: "What is there in this man's peculiar experience which becomes intelligible when we consider it in the light of certain leads or theories? What light does this case throw upon the laws of the spiritual life with which we are all concerned?"[48] While Boisen sought to contribute to the science of chaplaincy, spirituality, and the treatment of mental illness, he did not see himself as one person acting alone who would pose and resolve all questions but as member of a larger scientific community in which others would build upon and, when necessary, correct and supersede his work.

Boisen's *Exploration of the Inner World*[49] is his most complete and advanced contribution and best exemplifies his effort at scientific chaplaincy. He sets forth his "hypothesis that there is an important relationship between acute mental illness of the functional type and those of sudden transformations of character so prominent in the history of the Christian church since the days of Saul of Tarsus" and "that certain types of mental disorder and certain types of religious experience are alike attempts at reorganization."[50] He is limited in his claims regarding what kinds of mental illness fit his examination. By "functional" mental illness, he means "peculiarities of belief and conduct" that "are without demonstrable disease of brain or nervous tissue." These "functional" illness he opposes to "organic" mental illnesses resulting from some observable "disease of the brain," such as that caused by "syphilis, and the structural changes, such as hardening of the arteries."[51]

From his case studies, Boisen proposes three general "reaction patterns" to functional mental illnesses: (1) "Drifting": "they reach the point where the dream world has become the real world. The drive for self-realization is thus short-circuited and the individual becomes more and more listless and ineffective and unable to take care of himself." (2) "Delusional Misinterpretation": "They refuse to admit defeat or error and resort to distortion of belief in order to escape the sense of failure and guilt." While Boisen implies that this category of his system implies a deepening illness and a poor attempt at the "reorganization" he hopes to promote, it also "serves to keep him from going to pieces and enables him to maintain a certain degree of integration and poise." For Boisen, the final, and most hopeful, category was (3) "Panic": "few individuals can drift down to destruction or succeed in building up an effective system of delusional misinterpretation without at some time becoming aware of their danger." Boisen's "panic" reaction most closely reflected a mystical, religious experience that he equated with a successful recovery from a bout of "acute" mental illness. While exhibiting "emotional disturbance," and "feels himself to be as one dead," "Such disturbances, whether of the stuporous or agitated type, are not in themselves evils, but are analogous to fever or inflammation in the body. They are attempts at cure and reorganization which are closely related to certain reorganized types of religious experience."[52]

Boisen culls his examples from extensive case studies of patients conducted by him and his students at Worcester and Elgin State Hospitals. He statistically categorized his cases by "reaction pattern" according to these three types.[53] An obvious question resides in subjectivity of such terms as "panic," "self-deception," and "drifting." At this point, Boisen's science shows confusion between objective and subjective categories that can also be observed in his teacher's, Cabot, *Differential Diagnosis* cases. However, Boisen, "In accordance with scientific procedure," sought "to discover relationships within experiences which any qualified investigator may observe and to make no claims beyond those which he should be able to verify and accept." Boisen realized the unverifiability of theological beliefs and doctrines and "as a rule, avoided the word 'God.' I have referred instead to the 'Greater-than-self,' to 'that which is supreme in our hierarchy of loyalties,' . . . Such terms are neutral. They point to social facts which no competent and fair-minded man can deny and they suggest certain significant relationships."[54]

While Boisen's categories can be criticized as, in themselves, vague and subjective, he essayed a provisional effort in scientific survey and categorization and invited investigators to confirm (or disconfirm) his findings and correct or build upon them. As some of Boisen's critical reviewers suggest, Boisen's impassioned and explicit personal investment in his topic, along with his tendency for grandiose, hyperbolic (mystical?) language, was likely alienating to audiences accustomed to the staid style typical of science and the academy. In *Exploration of the Inner World*, he concludes in expansive language: "my mind goes back to the beginning of my journey into the lower regions. Once more I am standing on the threshold of the limitless unknown, face to face with death and life. It is not merely my personal fate that is at stake. I see unfolding before me the great drama of the ages."[55] Such operatic language is not typically found in scientific journals and peer-reviewed monographs.

Did Boisen practice science? He did not "cure" mental illness as the antimicrobial revolution of his age provided miracle cures to once fatal diseases. His passion, personal involvement, and mix of the mystical and the scientific puzzled and alienated many of his interlocutors. Some of the criticism directed toward Boisen's work, his "science," reflected his sometimes expansive and, often, tedious and repetitive writing style. Some criticism reflected annoyance with an odd and driven man who had worn out the welcome of his chaplain audience. Boisen in many ways was an old Victorian who practiced science in the Victorian style. He was broadly knowledgeable and unafraid of crossing disciplinary boundaries if he thought his inquiry demanded it. His works featured broad and often bold statements, reflecting his personal experience and effort to use patient observation to uncover the grand laws that must govern the human mind and soul. Boisen made a pioneer effort to do for his newfound field what he did for hickories and what Richard Cabot did in his *Differential Diagnosis*. Boisen's provisional work was to survey and catalogue types of mental illness in relation to spiritual experience to better facilitate diagnosis and as a means to identify persons who may most benefit from his new type of scientific chaplaincy. He saw his work as a provisional effort to be followed by scientific chaplain researchers to come who would confirm or disconfirm his work and correct or build upon it.[56]

Chapter 6
CONCLUSION

The puzzle and paradox of Anton Boisen shows him relevant and instructive beyond the narrow scope of origins of the clinical pastoral education movement. Seward Hiltner pointed to some of the significant paradoxes that eluded and frustrated Boisen's critics and interlocutors. His professional corpus transgressed disciplinary boundaries between pastoral care, theology, psychology, psychiatry, sociology, social work, even forestry in pursuit of his driving ambition. That driving ambition was to gain understanding of and mastery over what happened to him in 1920 in his psychosis that also yielded his signature vilusion of breaking an opening between medicine (science in the larger sense) and religion. The aging Victorian navigated an era of ever-increasing specialization and ever-narrowing interest. His broad intellectual interests, even more so his openness about his own intense personal experiences, rendered him a closer of unclosable paradoxes: the dualities of disciplinary specialization, the growing enmity between science and religion, the duality of madness and mysticism, religious experience, in his own life.

The overarching dualities of Boisen's life were between mysticism and mental illness, science and religion. He sought to overcome these dualities as a spiritual and professional task with profoundly personal import. Boisen's professional/personal task, however, he envisioned as a quest that may light the path of others to follow. His hopeful assessment of "functional" mental illnesses—those that drove him to psychosis and hospitalization as efforts in problem solving—as much the workings of a creative mind as the afflictions of a sick man. But how to tell the difference between creative vision and malignant delusion? Boisen fashioned a pragmatic mysticism to aid in telling which was which. Williams James, Boisen's intellectual, and spiritual, predecessor, advised distinguishing "snake" from "seraph" through the practical result of religious experience. Boisen had the practical help of fellow experiencers and friends to keep him on task and in reality, as most people experience it.

Boisen's pragmatic mysticism drove his life work of addressing the divide between science and religion. His creation of clinical pastoral education envisioned using the practical, but even mystical, experience of crisis as a means of learning about the human condition and finding new ways of bringing healing and resolution to it. Boisen's clinical pastoral education, and his new profession of institutional chaplaincy, bore no enmity toward the role of the traditional church pastor—it simply envisioned its role elsewhere. Boisen's clinical training and institutional chaplains were to be fully engaged in the clinical work and educational programs of the institutions, usually medical, in which they resided. They were to be engaged in research, teaching, and treating patients making use of scientific methods—alongside their colleagues in medicine, nursing, social work, and psychology.

Boisen's call to adventure that led to his life vision and work started with his experience of psychological collapse. Boisen's clinical diagnosis has been, and remains, controverted—some describing it as schizophrenia, or some species of schizoaffective or schizotypal disorder, some describing it as bipolar disorder with psychotic features. A definite diagnosis is difficult and contingent. Boisen lived a long life and had a variety of witnesses who had interests and agendas of their own regarding how he should be remembered. Finally, wellness, illness, and psychiatric diagnosis are socially and historically conditioned categories further complicated by the fact that the patient is now long dead and no longer available for examination. Boisen's exact diagnosis, however interesting a topic of discussion that may be, is finally beside the point. What is undeniable was that he intermittently exhibited symptoms of severe mental illness and likely exhibited subclinical symptoms at other times as well.

Many of Boisen's experiences while ill, his "vilusions," are often dismissed as the flotsam of psychotic delusion, meriting no further comment. Boisen's experiences of "special things," to borrow Ann Taves's term, of voices, visions, dreams, serve as an invitation to delve further, and more seriously, into how these "special things" may be indicative of creativity and perhaps not psychotic delusion alone. Boisen dedicated much of his professional and personal endeavor into separating the vision from delusion in his experience of the special and the inexplicable.

Boisen did not hail from, nor affiliate with, a school or tradition of mysticism or mystical experience as may be found in some aspects of Roman Catholicism or Eastern Orthodoxy. Boisen's liberal rationalist variant of evangelical Protestantism viewed "visions" and "voices" with anything from puzzlement to derision. Boisen had neither road map nor template for mystical or religious experience that evaded rational explanation. For Boisen to transform madness to mysticism, he had to rely on the resources at hand. He looked to Williams James' and Raphael Zon's fact-driven, pragmatic, objectivity as well as his own "fellowship of the best," his friends and colleagues for guidance.

Boisen as "mystic" experienced on a plane that transcends reason and logic while not abandoning reason or logic. Boisen's predecessor, in experience as well as intellect, William James, lectured and wrote on "visions, voices, rapt conditions, guiding impressions, and 'openings'" that relate the individual experiencer to what that person considers "divine." While these experiences may indicate mental disorder, they may also indicate sanctity or inspiration or all these states simultaneously. However, for Boisen and James, not all of these experiences had equal value or were to be necessarily encouraged.

Boisen followed James in traversing regions where "snake" and "seraph" abide side by side and where it can be difficult to readily distinguish between the two. Forester Raphael Zon inspired Boisen to assess people and peoples by what they were becoming and not by what they necessarily were at present. James, a founder of pragmatism as a philosophy, judged phenomena by their practical results. For Boisen, help in determining the practical fruits of ineffable experience, were they illness or inspiration, lies not only in individual judgment but in his "fellowship of the best," trusted others with whom the experiencer could entrust her or his experiences. While Boisen tended to offer few definitive answers to his questions, his lifetime projects of clinical education and institutional chaplaincy offer some practical hints toward how he envisioned building his "fellowship of the best."

Boisen's quest to separate the mystical from the mad, the wheat from the chaff, the inspired from the flotsam, and then to find ways to implement his insights in practical and socially useful ways depended on the help of others. Boisen's acclaimed "loneliness" is often a judgment imposed upon him—in pejorative ways by those quick to condemn a man they did not understand and did not like. Boisen did have friends—many of his friendships may have been unconventional in lacking the warmth and outward emotive forms associated with conventional "friendship." Nevertheless, Boisen maintained friendships that spanned decades—these friends were critical in anchoring Boisen to reality as most people understand it. They were critical to aiding him in separating delusion from vision and in helping their odd and visionary friend in transforming his vilusions into something socially useful. Many of Boisen's friends, his first chaplaincy employer William Bryan at Worcester State Hospital, his associate Donald Beatty, and his colleagues at Chicago Theological Seminary in particular courageously assumed serious professional and reputational risk on behalf of their sometimes mad, and institutionalized, friend.

Boisen fortuned upon a mix of friends, possessing different personalities and aptitudes, who brought a combination of patience, firmness, and compassion critical for Boisen to separate vision from delusion. They encouraged him in operationalizing a complex vision for a new kind of pastoral care and a new kind of theological education. Boisen's unconventional friends acted with the patience to separate vision from delusion in dialoging with him on his ideas, experiences, and "vilusions." For example, Ellwood Worcester—a kindred mystic and visionary himself, blessed (and plagued) with visions and dreams—believed in Boisen when nobody else would. Fred Eastman, who eventually suffered clinical depression himself, was instrumental in helping Boisen put his fractured soul back together amid his first hospitalization and set him on track to a new and functional future of offering socially useful and usable work and insight. Worcester and Eastman were examples of friends who understood Boisen's visions, his "automatisms," and were ready and willing to help him tame, or at least exercise greater control, over his mystical experiences so he could have a better chance at using his experiences fruitfully and so they would afflict him less painfully. They helped him channel and control his experiences so he could better interact with, and function within, reality as most people experience it. The fact that Boisen needed help, sometimes lots of it, does not detract from his vision and accomplishment but rather points up the visionaries whom he inspired and who surrounded him.

Boisen's central and driving vilusion was of uniting science and religion in amicable dialogue in service of truth, learning, and human well-being. While recognizing the fact of specialization by discipline, he was also the product of a more unitary experience of knowledge as was current in his Victorian youth and upbringing. For Boisen, theology and medicine (and science in the larger sense) were distinct fields—yet all fields and all knowledge and experience had irrevocably theological charge. Theologians who ignore or distain science are not truly theologians because they ignore the totality of God-given knowledge.

Boisen envisioned closing the duality between medicine (science in the larger sense) and religion in his scientific chaplaincy. Part of closing this duality included using the tools and methods of science in gaining greater understanding of the workings of the human soul and mind. Boisen used survey tools provided by Richard Cabot in the medical case study and Raphael Zon in forestry survey methods to study individuals suffering crisis. Boisen's case studies provided broad and deep biographical information and progress notes regarding individuals in crisis—studies that typically spanned twenty to forty pages. Boisen's cases specialized in broad and deep survey—observing and describing experiences and phenomena in religious experience, mysticism, and mental illness in specific individuals. He used his case studies as a contingent effort to provide a taxonomy of mystical experience and mental illness that other chaplain researchers could follow. In accord with the science in which he had been trained, he expected, and earnestly hoped, that others would follow in his footsteps to confirm, amend, or overturn his findings. Boisen, at least implicitly, foresaw successor scientific chaplains who would strive for deeper understanding and more effective treatments for people in crisis.

Boisen's autobiography provides his longest and most complete case study. He viewed his painful and jarring voyage to a "little-known country" of mental illness and mystical experience as an effort in problem solving analogous to an inflamed reaction to infection. While Boisen remained tenaciously, for some aggravatingly, fixated on cases similar to his own, Boisen's method inspired others to use crisis as a means of learning and education. Working with actual people facing crises in real time is foundational to clinical education in many disciplines and was foundational to clinical pastoral education in all its forms post-1925. Clinical education melded scientific observation and documentation with, what was for him, an irreducibly theological endeavor. Clinical pastoral education was first, last, and always theological education intended to study the workings of religious experience in the real lives of real people facing real crisis. Boisen and other early clinical pastoral education dissenters such as Wayne Oates were implacable foes of any effort to turn this new kind of clinical education into anything but theological education. While Boisen and Oates appreciated and welcomed psychology's insights, they vigorously and uncompromisingly protested the often-clandestine influence of Wilhelm Reich's ideas and methods within the clinical education community that distracted clinical pastoral education from its pastoral and theological *raison d'etre*.

Boisen's scientific chaplaincy envisioned spirituality care geared specifically to the needs of the institutions in which these chaplains served. They were not just church pastors who worked at, or "visited," the hospital, jail, or did a "hitch" in the military. Boisen's scientific chaplains were trained to work as an integrated part of the treatment and care teams found in these institutions. Boisen expected his students to become professionals fully conversant with the needs and aspirations of the hospitals and health-care institutions, the armed forces, prisons, schools as well as those operating within these highly complex settings.

While Boisen's scientific chaplains were usually ordained or recommended by a specific religious body, conversant with the ritual and community needs of that community, sectarian concerns were secondary to the scientific chaplain's task. Serving the spiritual need of people in need or crisis, regardless of faith or lack thereof, was the scientific chaplain's primary task. Professionals engaged in Boisen's task were to engage in counseling with people undergoing crisis to try to discern the, often nebulous, category of spirituality need—close to emotional need and psychological need, but not the same thing—and to engage the patient toward amelioration or resolution of the crisis. Boisen's primary area of interest was, of course, individuals suffering from mental illness.

Perhaps the greatest divergence between clinical training as Boisen envisioned it and as it actually developed lies in Boisen's interest in research. As the influence of Wilhelm Reich's emotive, feelings first, methodology rose to prominence in clinical pastoral education, along with it came suspicion toward more cerebral enterprises. Research was essential to Boisen's project, but hardly at all taken up by his successors. Boisen's case studies formed significant source material for his roughly eighty scholarly writings. While recent years have witnessed some glimmers of newfound interest in chaplaincy and spirituality care research, for the most part, the Reichian chaplaincy mainstream demonstrated little interest in Boisen's and Dunbar's bookish pursuits.

Clinical pastoral training from Boisen's era to the present has been predominantly, but not exclusively, comprised of freestanding training centers typically residing in the chaplaincy departments of acute care hospitals. Boisen initially wanted his new kind of clinical training to revolutionize seminary curricula in bringing together learning from textbooks with learning from living human documents. While his academic affiliation at Chicago Theological Seminary seemed inclined toward Boisen's ideas, Boisen's notion of melding seminary curricula with clinical training gained its greatest traction at Wayne Oates' seminary in Louisville. In the case of Oates' Southern Baptist Seminary, the melding of clinical training with the seminary institution was a creation of need. As the clinical training mainstream within the Council for Clinical Training (an ACPE predecessor) rejected Oates' application, Oates, in the alternative, found a receptive sponsor in his hometown seminary.

While many of Boisen's ideas for clinical training and institutional chaplaincy have been taken into the chaplaincy mainstream, it has also diverged from Boisen's original ideas in significant ways. Recalling the loneness and lack of therapeutic interaction he suffered as an institutionalized person, Boisen uncompromisingly viewed his chaplaincy profession and training programs as patient centered. Chaplains, clinical education supervisors, and even those in training were to focus their attention on people in need, especially his "theologs" working with the state hospital residents who were close to Boisen's heart. As clinical training moved increasingly toward Reich, and psychodynamics, the goal and focus of clinical training increasingly centered on the needs, priorities, and psychotherapeutic aims of the clinical students themselves. While Boisen did not dismiss the developmental psychological and spiritual needs of clinical students, these were not his priority and he disagreed with the clinical training communities increasing prioritization of student psychodynamics at the expense of work with patients.

Boisen's intellectual and scholarly vision for clinical training also differed significantly from what became the clinical training mainstream. His (and Helen Dunbar's) intellectual "facts first" approach differed philosophically and temperamentally from clinical training's emerging emotive "feelings first" Reichian bent. For Boisen, clinical training began, and continued, alongside a deep and robust theological education. For Boisen, theology was a much broader matter than religion alone. For Boisen, a "theolog" properly prepared for clinical training needed a solid background in psychology, sociology, and science—areas he viewed as having as much theological import as scripture, church history, and homiletics. Ministers of religion and his own institutional chaplains needed to be prepared to assess and promote individual and social well-being that far transcended the parochial.

Anton Boisen's life and mystical experience were of closing unclosable dualities: inspiration and illness, sacred and secular, science and religion. Friends who possessed patience, firmness, and compassion were critical in sluicing out the vision from the madness and in helping him structure and operationalize his visions, which definitively changed his profession and how people are trained and educated for it. Boisen's experiences of the special, his hybrid of the scientific and the mystical, his ability to close unclosable paradoxes, as well the friends who helped him offer clues on relating to mysticism and mental illness offer clues on how to interact with mysticism and mental illness in our present time as well.

NOTES

1. Boisen, *Out of the Depths*, 149–50. Boisen's "we" refers to himself and Arthur Holt, with whom Boisen engaged church work in Kansas and who was instrumental in Boisen's affiliation with Chicago Theological Seminary.

2. Asquith, *The Clinical Method of Theological Inquiry of Anton T. Boisen*, 108–9.

3. Pruyser, "Anton T. Boisen and the Psychology of Religion," 210.

4. Pruyser, "Anton T. Boisen and the Psychology of Religion," 216, 218.

5. Pruyser, "Anton T. Boisen and the Psychology of Religion," 211.

6. Pruyser, "Anton T. Boisen and the Psychology of Religion," 210. Boisen's critics, at least implicitly, raise the issue of researcher bias—that Boisen was using his "research" to beg affirmation of his claim to have gotten "well." Health and spirituality researcher Harold Koenig points out that present-day research is often driven by a "passion [that] comes from a personal experience the researcher has had in the past. The experience is usually, but not always, a negative one." Koenig cites medical and pharmaceutical research where "millions of dollars" and "sometimes entire research programs and even academic careers rest on confirming" a researcher's hypotheses are commonplace. For Koenig, asking if a researcher is biased or has a stake in a certain outcome is the wrong question to ask. Rather, "bias is everywhere in scientific research. The code of scientific ethics, however, requires that researchers design studies so that their own biases do not enter into the way the study is run, the data is analyzed, or how the results are interpreted." Harold G. Koenig, *Spirituality & Health Research: Methods, Measurements, Statistics, and Resources* (West Conshohocken, PA: Templeton Press, 2011), 76, 41.

7. Steckel, "Book Review: Out of the Depths," 264.

8. Klink, "Book Review: Out of the Depths." Klink, a former student of Boisen, moved on to become a colleague of Pruyser as coordinator of graduate studies in religion and psychiatry at the Menninger Foundation.

9. It is more likely Klink is hinting to (1) Boisen's objective age, and (2) Boisen's material asceticism. Boisen's asceticism was underlined in the 1940s and 1950s by his staunch opposition to the growing influence of Wilhelm Reich upon the clinical pastoral education movement. "I was especially troubled by a tendency to accept the easy solutions. . . . Take, for example, a patient who is torn with conflict between the demands of conscience and his erotic desires and impulses. The solution offered by some of our chaplain-supervisors was that of getting rid of the conflict by lowering the conscience threshold." Boisen, *Out of the Depths*, 186.

10. Pruyser, "Anton T. Boisen and the Psychology of Religion," 212.

11. Roger Hahn, "Laplace and the Mechanistic Universe," in *God and Nature: Historical Essays on the Encounter between Christianity and Science*, eds. David C. Lindberg and Ronald L. Numbers (Berkeley, CA: University of California Press, 1986), 256, 273.

12. Jon H. Roberts, "Psychoanalysis and American Christianity, 1900–1945," in *When Science & Christianity Meet*, eds. David C. Lindberg and Ronald L. Numbers (Chicago, IL: The University of Chicago Press, 2003), 228–29.

13. Johnathan Simon, "Louis Pasteur: The Chemist in the Clinic," in *Outsider Scientists: Routes to Innovation in Biology*, eds. Oren Harman and Michael R. Dietrich (Chicago, IL: The University of Chicago Press, 2013), 46–47. Pasteur's scientific practice and career crashed through disciplinary borders, starting in chemistry, then veterinary medicine before graduating to practicing medicine on people.

14. Paul Pruyser, in Nouwen's interview notes, expressed puzzlement at why Boisen "though so much of" Zon besides that he "had taught him statistics." Boisen's correspondence with Zon provides evidence of their friendship as well as professional relationship that transcended utilitarian ends. Paul Pruyser Interview, June 14, 1967, Box 290, File 333, Nouwen Papers, Special Collections, John M. Kelly Library, University of St. Michael's College, Toronto, ON. Boisen explicitly mentioned Cabot and singled out his book *Differential Diagnosis* (which appeared in many editions and reprints) as foundational to developing his own case study and teaching method. Henri Nouwen, BOISEN, August 1964, Nouwen Papers, Special Collections, John M. Kelly Library, University of St. Michael's College, Toronto, ON.

15. Norman J. Schmaltz, "Forest Researcher: Raphael Zon," *Journal of Forest History* 24 (1980): 38.

16. Born Vladimir Ilych Ulyanov. Simbirsk was later renamed in honor of the city's prominent son. Timing and circumstance placed young Zon at the crossroads of momentous events in Russian and world history. Simbirsk was also home for Alexander Kerensky, leader of the ill-fated Provisional Government that briefly held power in Russia in 1917 in the months between Tsar Nicholas II Romanov's abdication and Lenin's coup in the fall of the same year. Kerensky's father was principal of the school both young Lenin and Zon attended.

17. Schmaltz, "Forest Researcher," 25.

18. Schmaltz, "Forest Researcher," 26.

19. Schmaltz, "Forest Researcher," 27–28.

20. Schmaltz, "Forest Researcher," 31–32.

21. Schmaltz, "Forest Researcher," 25.
22. Anton T. Boisen to Louise Boisen, September 16, 1905, Theophilus A. Wylie Papers, Special Collections, Wylie House, Indiana University, Bloomington, IN.
23. Boisen, *Out of the Depths*, 57.
24. Anton T. Boisen and J. A. Newlin, *The Commercial Hickories* (Washington, DC: Government Printing Office, 1910).
25. Boisen and Newlin, *Commercial Hickories*, 32–33.
26. Boisen to Raphael Zon, December 1, 1926, Raphael Zon Papers, Minnesota State Historical Society, St. Paul, MN.
27. Raphael Zon to Boisen, April 6, 1937, Zon Papers, Minnesota State Historical Society.
28. Boisen to Raphael Zon, May 12, 1937, Zon Papers, Minnesota State Historical Society.
29. Boisen to Raphael Zon, December 16, 1944, Zon Papers, Minnesota State Historical Society.
30. Boisen to Raphael Zon, March 21, 1937, Zon Papers, Minnesota State Historical Society.
31. Boisen, *Out of the Depths*, 180.
32. Crenner, *Private Practice*, 14.
33. Cabot, "Adventures on the Borderland of Ethics," 275.
34. Crenner, *Private Practice*, 72.
35. Crenner, *Private Practice*, 79–80.
36. Crenner, *Private Practice*, 80–81.
37. Henri Nouwen, "Anton T. Boisen and the Study of Theology and the Study of Theology Through 'Living Human Documents,'" 61, (Unpublished Manuscript, no date), Box 1, File 4, Henri Nouwen Papers, Special Collections, John M. Kelly Library, University of St. Michael's College, Toronto, ON.
38. Boisen, *Out of the Depths*, 147.
39. Pruyser, "Anton T. Boisen and the Psychology of Religion," 215.
40. Richard C. Cabot, *Differential Diagnosis, Vol. I: Presented Through an Analysis of 385 Cases* (Philadelphia, PA: W. B. Saunders Company, 1916), 17.
41. Cabot, *Differential Diagnosis*, 155.
42. Cabot, *Differential Diagnosis*, 169–70.
43. Cabot, *Differential Diagnosis*, 170–71.
44. Cabot, *Differential Diagnosis*, 194–95.
45. Anton T. Boisen, "Types of Mental Illness, A Beginning Course: For Use in the Training Centers of the Council for the Clinical Training of Theological Students. Part I. Outlines and Records" (Unpublished Manuscript, 1946), Series 7, Box 2, Folder 40, Boisen Papers, Chicago Theological Seminary. This typewritten manuscript used for clinical teaching purposes at Elgin State Hospital marks Boisen's maturity as a researcher and teacher.
46. Boisen, "Types of Mental Illness, A Beginning Course," Series 7, Box 2, Folder 40, Boisen Papers, Chicago Theological Seminary.
47. Boisen, "Types of Mental Illness, A Beginning Course," Series 7, Box 2, Folder 40, Boisen Papers, Chicago Theological Seminary.

48. Boisen, "Types of Mental Illness, A Beginning Course," Series 7, Box 2, Folder 40, Boisen Papers, Chicago Theological Seminary.
49. Boisen, *Exploration of the Inner World*.
50. Boisen, *Exploration of the Inner World*, ix.
51. Boisen, *Exploration of the Inner World*, 313.
52. Boisen, *Exploration of the Inner World*, 28–30.
53. Boisen, *Exploration of the Inner World*, 40–41.
54. Boisen, *Exploration of the Inner World*, 298–99.
55. Boisen, *Exploration of the Inner World*, 295.
56. Present-day "scientific chaplaincy" may be seeing a modest reemergence of the kind of case studies and research toward which Boisen pointed. Chaplaincy researcher George Fitchett offers regarding "a growing consensus about the importance of research for the future of health care chaplaincy." He notes that not all research-oriented and research-informed chaplains need to conduct "RCT's [Random Controlled Trials] or other quantitative research, but by writing case studies about the work they do every day." He specifically cites Boisen, and his deep, broad, longitudinal case studies as offering hints from a forgotten past that can inform the present. George Fitchett, "Making Our Case(s)," *Journal of Health Care Chaplaincy* 17 (2011): 3, 15–16.

Bibliography

Alighieri, Dante. *Dante: The Divine Comedy, A New Verse Translation by Clive James*. Edited and translated by C. James. New York, NY: Liveright Publishing Company (2013).

Asquith, Jr. Glenn H. "Anton T. Boisen: A Vision for All Ages," *Lecture*, College of Pastoral Supervision and Psychotherapy, Plenary Session (March 15, 2015).

———. "The Case Study Method of Anton T. Boisen," *The Journal of Pastoral Care* 34 (1980): 94.

———. *The Clinical Method of Theological Inquiry of Anton T. Boisen*. PhD Diss., Southern Baptist Theological Seminary, Louisville, KY (1976).

———. *Vision from a Little-Known Country: A Boisen Reader*. Macon, GA: Journal of Pastoral Care Publications, Inc. (1992).

Beers, Clifford Whittingham. *A Mind That Found Itself: An Autobiography*. New York, NY: Longmans, Green, and Co. (1912).

Boisen, Anton T. "Book Review: Wilhelm Reich's *Character Analysis, The Sexual Revolution*," *Psychiatry* 8 (1945): 505–506.

———, and J. A. Newlin. *The Commercial Hickories*. Washington, DC: Government Printing Office (1910).

———. "Concerning the Relationship Between Religious Experience and Mental Disorders," *Mental Hygiene* 7 (1923): 311.

———. "Conscientious Objectors: Their Morale in Church Operated Service Units," *Psychiatry: Journal of the Biology and Pathology of Interpersonal Relations* 7 (1944): 215–224.

———. "In Defense of Mr. Bryan: A Personal Confession by a Liberal Clergyman," *American Review* 5 (1924): 323–328.

———. "Factors Which Have to Do with the Decline of the Country Church," *American Journal of Sociology* 22 (1916): 178–179, 191–192.

———. *Hymns of Hope and Courage*, 4th Revised and Enlarged edition. Chicago, IL: Chicago Theological Seminary (1950).

———. "Inspiration in the Light of Psychopathology," *Pastoral Psychology* 11 (1960): 16.

———. *Out of the Depths: An Autobiographical Study of Mental Disorder and Religious Experience*. New York, NY: Harper and Brothers, Publishers (1960).

———. *Problems in Religion and Life: A Manual for Pastors with Outlines for the Co-operative Study of Personal Experience in Social Situations*. Nashville, TN: Abington-Cokesbury Press (1946).

———. "The Problem of Sin and Salvation in the Light of Psychopathology," *The Journal of Religion* 22 (1942): 288–301.

———. "Religion and Hard Times," *Social Action (A Magazine of Fact): Published by the Council for Social Action of the Congregational and Christian Churches* (March 15, 1930): 8–30.

———. *Religion in Crisis and Custom: A Sociological and Psychological Study*. New York, NY: Harper and Brothers, Publishers (1955).

———. "Theological Education Via the Clinic," *Religious Education* 25 (1930): 237–238.

———. *The Exploration of the Inner World: A Study of Mental Disorder and Religious Experience*. New York, NY: Willett, Clark, and Company (1936).

———. "What War Does to Religion," *Religion in Life* 14 (1945): 2.

Cabot, Richard C. "Adventures on the Borderlands of Ethics: A Plea for a Clinical Year in the Course of Theological Study," *Survey Graphic* 8 (1925): 275–276.

———. *Differential Diagnosis, Vol. I: Presented Through an Analysis of 385 Cases*. Philadelphia, PA: W. B. Saunders Company (1916).

Campbell, Joseph. *The Masks of God: Creative Mythology*. New York, NY: Penguin Compass (1968).

Campbell, Macfie. *Delusion and Belief*. Cambridge, MA: Harvard University Press (1926).

Coble, Richard. "Maneuvers in the Depths: The Politics of Identity in Anton Boisen's Pastoral Care," *Pastoral Psychology* 63 (2014): 409–410.

Coe, George A. "The Mystical as a Psychological Concept," *The Journal of Philosophy, Psychology, and Scientific Methods* 6 (1909): 197–202.

Conklin, Edmund S. "Book Review: The Exploration of the Inner World," *The Journal of Religion* 17 (1937): 296–298.

Craddock, Nick, and Michael J. Owen. "The Kraepelinian Dichotomy—Going, Going ... But Still Not Gone," *The British Journal of Psychiatry* 196 (2010): 92–95.

Crenner, Christopher. *Private Practice: In the Early Twentieth-Century Medical Office of Dr. Richard Cabot*. Baltimore, MD: The Johns Hopkins University Press (2005).

DeBono, Christopher E. *An Exploration and Adaptation of Anton T. Boisen's Notion of the Psychiatric Chaplain in Responding to Current Issues in Clinical Chaplaincy*. PhD Diss., University of Toronto (2012).

Desk Reference to the Diagnostic Criteria from DSM—5. Washington, DC: American Psychiatric Association (2013).

Dittes, James E. "Boisen as Autobiographer," in *Turning Points in Pastoral Care: The Legacy of Anton Boisen and Seward Hiltner*, edited by Leroy Aden and J. Harold Ellens. Grand Rapids, MI: Baker Book House (1990).

Dunbar, H. Flanders. *Symbolism in Medieval Thought and Its Consummation in the Divine Comedy*. New York, NY: Russell and Russell (1961).

Eastman, Fred. "Father of the Clinical Pastoral Movement," *The Chicago Theological Seminary Register* 41 (1951): 15.

Fischer, Bernard A., and William T. Carpenter. "Will the Kraepelinian Dichotomy Survive DSM-V?" *Neuropsychopharmacology* 34 (2009): 2081–2087.

Fitchett, George. "Making Our Case(es)," *Journal of Health Care Chaplaincy* 17 (2011): 3, 15–16.

Frazer, George James. *The New Golden Bough*. New York, NY: A Mentor Book (1959).

Griffith, R. Marie. "The Religious Encounters of Alfred C. Kinzie," *The Journal of American History* 95 (2008): 349–377.

Grob, Gerald N. *Mental Illness and American Society 1875–1940*. Princeton, NJ: Princeton University Press (1983).

Grotjahn, Martin. "Book Review: Recent Psychoanalytic Literature," *Psychosomatic Medicine: Experimental and Clinical Studies* 3 (1943): 309–311.

Hahn, Roger. "Laplace and the Mechanistic Universe," in *God and Nature: Historical Essays on the Encounter Between Christianity and Science*, edited by David C. Lindberg and Ronald L. Numbers. Berkeley, CA: University of California Press (1986).

Hall, Charles E. *Head and Heart: The Story of the Clinical Pastoral Education Movement*. Macon, GA: Journal of Pastoral Care Publications, Inc. (1992).

Hansen, Bert. "America's First Medical Breakthrough: How Popular Excitement about a French Rabies Cure in 1885 Raised New Expectations for Medical Progress," *American Historical Review* 103 (1998): 373–418.

Hart, Curtis W. "Notes on the Psychiatric Diagnosis of Anton Boisen," *Journal of Religion and Health* 40 (1981): 423–429.

Hiltner, Seward. "The Debt of Clinical Pastoral Education to Anton T. Boisen," *The Journal of Pastoral Care* 20 (1966): 130.

———. "Editorial: Boisen and Human Knowledge," *Pastoral Psychology* 2 (1952): 8.

———. "The Heritage of Anton Boisen," *Pastoral Psychology* 16 (1965): 6.

Hinshaw, Stephen P. *The Mark of Shame: Sigma of Mental Illness and an Agenda for Change*. New York, NY: Oxford University Press (2007).

Hoff, Paul. "The Kraepelinian Tradition," *Dialogues in Clinical Neuroscience* 17 (2015): 36.

Holifield, E. Brooks. *A History of Pastoral Care in America: From Salvation to Self-Realization*. Nashville, TN: Abingdon Press (1983).

Jakobsen, Merete Demant. *Shamanism: Traditional and Contemporary Approaches to the Mastery of Spirits and Healing*. New York, NY: Berghahn Books (1999).

James, William, *The Varieties of Religious Experience*. Cambridge, MA: Harvard University Press (1985).

Jenkins, Richard L. "Book Review: Out of the Depths," *American Journal of Orthopsychiatry* 31 (1961): 649–650.

King, Stephen D. W. *Trust the Process: A History of Clinical Pastoral Education as Theological Education*. Lanham, MD: University Press of America (2007),

Klink, Thomas W. "Anton T. Boisen: 1876–1965: A Remembrance of the Committal of His Ashes, October 6, 1965," *The Journal of Pastoral Care* 19 (1965): 230.

———. "Book Review: Out of the Depths," *Christian Advocate* (January 5, 1961).

Koenig, Harold G. *Spirituality and Health Research: Methods, Measurements, Statistics, and Resources.* West Conshocken, PA: Templeton Press (2011).

Lambert, Bruce. "A.C. McGiffert, Jr. A Seminary Leader and Educator," *The New York Times* (April 14, 1993): 100.

Larson, Edward J. *Summer for the Gods: The Scopes Trial and America's Continuing Debate over Science and Religion.* New York, NY: Basic Books (1997).

Leas, Robert D. *Anton Theophilus Boisen: His Life, Work, Impact, and Theological Legacy.* Macon, GA: Journal of Pastoral Care Publications, Inc. (2009).

Leas, Robert D. "The Biography of Anton Theophilus Boisen," *ACPE: Association for Clinical Pastoral Education, Inc.* Last accessed September 30, 2018. www.acpe.edu/pdf/History/The%20Biography%20of%20Anton%20Theophilus%20Boisen.pdf.

Lesch, John E. *The First Miracle Drugs: How Sulfa Drugs Transformed Medicine.* New York, NY: Oxford University Press (2007).

Levi-Strauss, Claude. *Structural Anthropology.* New York, NY: Basic Books (1958).

McCarthy, Katherine. "The Emmanuel Movement and Richard Peabody," *Journal of Studies on Alcohol* 45 (1984): 59–74.

North, Carol, and William M. Clements. "The Psychiatric Diagnosis of Anton Boisen: From Schizophrenia to Bipolar Affective Disorder," *The Journal of Pastoral Care* 35 (1981): 264–275.

Nouwen, Henry J. M. "Anton T. Boisen and Theology Through Living Human Documents," *Pastoral Psychology* 19 (1968): 63.

Numbers, Ronald L. "The Fall and Rise of the American Medical Profession," in *Professions in American History*, edited by Nathan O. Hatch. South Bend, IN: University of Notre Dame Press (1985).

Oates, Wayne. *The Significance of the Work of Sigmund Freud for the Christian Faith.* PhD Diss., Southern Baptist Theological Seminary—Louisville, KY (1947).

Pals, Daniel L. *Nine Theories of Religion*, 3rd edition. New York, NY: Oxford University Press (2015).

Patterson, Charles H. "Book Review: The Exploration of the Inner World," *Journal of Bible and Religion* 5 (1937): 146–147.

Powell, Robert Charles. *Anton T. Boisen (1867–1965): Breaking an Opening in the Wall Between Religion and Medicine.* Buffalo, NY: Association of Mental Health Clergy (1976).

———. "Emotionally, Soulfully, Spiritually, 'Free to Think and Act': Helen Flanders Dunbar (1902–1959)," *Journal of Religion and Health* 40 (2001): 108.

———. *Healing and Wholeness: Helen Flanders Dunbar (1902–1959) and an Extra-Medical Origin of the American Psychosomatic Movement, 1906–36.* PhD Diss., Duke University (1974).

———. "Whatever Happened to 'CPE'—Clinical Pastoral Education?" *Lecture, Ninth Plenary Meeting*, College of Pastoral Supervision and Psychotherapy (April

18, 1999), Last accessed July 26, 2019, www.pastoralreport.com/pastoralreportarticles/3778818.
Pruyser, Paul W. "Anton T. Boisen and the Psychology of Religion," *The Journal of Pastoral Care* 21 (1967): 212–213.
———. *The Minister as Diagnostician: Personal Problems in Pastoral Perspective.* Philadelphia, PA: Westminster Press (1976).
———. "Some Trends in the Study of Religion," *The Journal of Religion* 40 (1960): 113.
Putnam, Robert D. *Bowling Alone: The Collapse and Revival of American Community.* New York, NY: Simon & Shuster (2000).
Reich, Wilhelm. *Character Analysis*, 3rd edition. New York, NY: Orgone Institute Press (1949).
———. *The Function of the Orgasm: Sex-Economic Problems of Biological Energy.* New York, NY: Farrar, Strauss, and Giroux (1973).
———. *The Mass Psychology of Fascism.* New York, NY: Farrar, Strauss, and Giroux (1970).
Roberts, Jon H. "Psychoanalysis and American Christianity, 1900–1945," in *When Science and Christianity Meet*, edited by David C. Lindberg and Ronald L. Numbers. Chicago, IL: The University of Chicago Press (2003).
Salzman, Leon. "A Critique of Wilhelm Reich's Psychoanalytic Theories," *The Journal of Pastoral Care* 9 (1955): 153–161.
Sharaf, Myron. *Fury on Earth: A Biography of Wilhelm Reich.* New York, NY: St. Martin's Press/Marek (1983).
Schmaltz, Norman J. "Forest Researcher: Raphael Zon," *Journal of Forest History* 24 (1980): 38.
Simon, Jonathan, "Louis Pasteur: The Chemist in the Clinic," in *Outsider Scientists: Routes to Innovation in Biology*, edited by Oren Harman and Michael R. Dietrich. Chicago, IL: The University of Chicago Press (2013).
Snyder, Ross. "The Boisen Heritage in Theological Education," *Pastoral Psychology* 19 (1968): 12.
Statistical Manual for the Use of Institutions for the Insane. New York, NY: American Medico-Psychological Association and National Committee for Mental Hygiene (1918).
Steckel, Clyde J. "Book Review: Out of the Depths," *Journal of Bible and Religion* 9 (1961): 263–264.
Steere, David A. "Anton Boisen: Figure of the Future?" *Journal of Religion and Health* 7 (1968): 370.
Stokes, Allison. *Ministry After Freud.* New York, NY: The Pilgrim Press (1985).
Taves, Ann. *Religious Experience Reconsidered: A Building-Block Approach to the Study of Religion and Other Special Things.* Princeton, NJ: Princeton University Press (2009).
———. *Trances, Fits, and Visions: Experiencing Religion and Explaining Experience from Wesley to James.* Princeton, NJ: Princeton University Press (1999).
Thornton, Edward D. *Professional Education for Ministry: A History of Clinical Pastoral Education.* Nashville, TN: Abington Press (1970).

Turner, Christopher. *Adventures in the Orgasmatron: How the Sexual Revolution Came to America.* New York, NY: Farrar, Strauss, and Giroux (2011).

Vacek, Heather H. *Madness: American Protestant Responses to Mental Illness.* Waco, TX: Baylor University Press (2015).

Warner, John Harley. "Ideals of Science and Their Discontents in Late Nineteenth Century American Medicine," *Isis* 82 (1991): 454–479.

Worcester, Ellwood. *Life's Adventure: The Story of a Varied Career.* New York, NY: Charles Scribner's Sons (1932).

Credits

Excerpts from Ann Taves, *Religious Experience Reconsidered: A Building Block Approach to the Study of Religion and Other Special Things* (2009), republished with permission of Princeton University Press; permission conveyed through Copyright Clearance Center, Inc.

Excerpts from Ann Taves, *Trances, Fits, and Visions: Experiencing Religion and Explaining Experience from Wesley to James* (1999), republished with permission of Princeton University Press; permission conveyed through Copyright Clearance Center, Inc.

Previously unpublished material written by Henri Nouwen is located at the Henri J. M. Nouwen Archives and Research collection, University of St. Michael's College, Toronto, Ontario. This material is included here with the permission of the Henri Nouwen Legacy Trust. Visit: www.henrinouwen.org.

Excerpts from *The Works of William James—The Varieties of Religious Experience, Frederick Burkhardt*, general editor, Fredson Bowers, Textual Editor, Ignas K. Skrupskelis, associate editor, Cambridge, Mass.: Harvard University Press. © 1985 by the president and fellows of Harvard College.

Crenner, Christopher. *Private Practice: In the Early Twentieth-Century Medical Office of Dr. Richard Cabot.* pp. x, 14, 72, 74, 79–80, 80–81, 232–233. © 2005 Johns Hopkins University Press. Reprinted with permission of Johns Hopkins University Press.

Index

Association for Clinical Pastoral Education, Inc. (ACPE), 1, 2, 165; relationship with Boisen, Anton, 2

Batchelder, Alice, 15, 17–18, 20–21, 23–25, 29, 31, 48–49, 69, 70, 84, 92, 100, 103–4
Batchelder, Paul, 18, 34
Beatty, Donald, 24, 96–97, 100, 103–4, 119, 120
Beers, Clifford, 84, 87–88
Boisen, Anton Theophilus: "automatism," 70–71; critical reception, 114–19, 146–47; description of Boisen's symptoms of mental illness, 30–31; Easter Day 1898, 70; "family-of-four," 16, 24–25, 53, 68, 110; hospitalization, 1920, 26–27, 53, 83, 99–100; hospitalization, 1930, 21–23, 51, 100; hospitalization, 1935, 23, 102; individual ramifications, 67–68, 79; mental illness, 2–3, 5, 8, 12, 14, 16, 31, 56, 85, 103, 161; mysticism, 2–4, 8, 31–32, 39, 51, 53, 64, 67, 85, 161; mysticism and pragmatism, 160; on science, 68–69, 73, 78, 89, 91, 107, 114, 145–47, 163; on scientific practice of chaplaincy, 155–60; physical health, elderly years, 122; sexuality, 32, 57, 69, 80; sociological ramifications, 67, 72, 81, 83; Westboro State Hospital, 6, 12, 14, 26–28, 40, 43, 56; World War I, 74–75
Boisen, Elizabeth Louise Wylie, 22–23, 44
Boisen, Marie, 22–23, 33
Brinkman, Robert, 121, 126
Bryan, William A., 88, 95, 97
Bryan, William Jennings, 75, 82, 95
Bryan, William Lowe, 48, 54, 70, 84

Cabot, Richard, 22, 36, 86, 90, 95, 98–100, 106, 152; *Differential Diagnosis*, 154–56
Chicago Theological Seminary, 18, 20, 24, 97, 102, 113
clinical pastoral education (CPE), 95
Coe, George, 43, 45–46

Dante, *The Divine Comedy*, 25, 31–32, 47–48, 49–51, 63, 93
Darwin, Charles, 46, 78; *Origin of Species*, 46, 78
Dunbar, Helen Flanders, 17, 19, 21–23, 31, 35–37, 48–50, 69, 98, 100, 109, 120

Eastman, Fred, 15, 17, 26–27, 73, 88, 97, 99–100, 104, 106, 136
Elgin State Hospital, 1, 24, 28, 97, 102, 113, 119
Emmanuel Clinic. *See* Worcester, Ellwood

Fosdick, Harry Emerson, 82, 95
Freud, Sigmund, 12, 26, 40

Guiles, Austin Philip, 22, 36, 98, 100

Hiltner, Seward, 2–3, 30, 33–34, 68, 84, 97, 130, 160
Hinshaw, Stephen, 26
Holt, Arthur, 94

James, William, 3, 39, 43–44, 88; pragmatism, 44–45, 60, 63, 71

Kinsey, Alfred, 33–34
Kraepelin, Emil, 12–13; Kraepelinian Dichotomy, 13, 40
Kuether, Fred, 71

Levi-Strauss, Claude, 51

McGiffert, Arthur "Cush," 102
McPeek, Francis, 97, 100, 138
Medicine, Therapeutics, 8, 31, 86–87, 91
Menninger, Karl, on Boisen, Anton Theophilus, 133
Mickle, Benjamin, 57–61, 85

Nouwen, Henri, 3, 30, 48, 84, 92–93, 98, 113, 120, 122, 130

Oates, Wayne, 121, 129–33, 142, 165

Obenhaus, Victor, 1

Powell, Robert, 1, 12–13, 25–26, 49, 54, 95, 98, 121, 129
Pruyser, Paul, 3, 8, 28, 69, 116–17, 145

Reich, Wilhelm, 71, 113, 119, 121, 124–28, 138–39; Boisen, Anton Theophilus, on Reich, Wilhelm, 128, 141; Einstein, Albert, on Reich, Wilhelm, 126; Grotjahn, Martin, on Reich, Wilhelm, 124, 140; Salzman, Leon, on Reich, Wilhelm, 128, 140

Scopes Trial, 95
Statistical Manuel for the Use of Institutions for the Insane, 13
Stokes, Allison, 40
Sullivan, Charles, 1

Taves, Ann, 3–4, 39, 44
Thornton, Edward, 29, 83, 98, 121, 126

Vacek, Heather, 5–8, 67

Wendel, Lulu, 135–36
Wise, Carroll, 28–29, 34, 37, 96, 99, 105, 107
Wolfe, Theodore, 123
Worcester, Alfred, 90
Worcester, Ellwood, 14–15, 32, 39, 40–43, 62, 90; Emmanuel Clinic, 42–43, 88
Worcester State Hospital, 28, 35, 57–58, 88, 94–96

Zon, Raphael, 84, 89, 107, 148–52

About the Author

Sean J. LaBat is a clinical staff chaplain at Central Virginia Veterans Administration Medical Center in Richmond, Virginia. He is also a member of the United States Navy Reserve. His areas of research interest include spirituality experience as well as its intersections with mental illness, and the origins and development of institutional chaplaincy and its role in health care. The author is also engaged in developing evidence-based and informed modalities for spirituality care. He holds a PhD in twentieth-century American history from the University of Illinois at Chicago and an MDiv from St. Vladimir's Seminary in Yonkers, New York.

www.ingramcontent.com/pod-product-compliance
Lightning Source LLC
Chambersburg PA
CBHW050907300426
44111CB00010B/1420